Liberty's War

Liberty's War

An Engineer's Memoir
of the Merchant Marine,
1942–45

HERMAN E. MELTON

Edited by Will Melton

Naval Institute Press
Annapolis, Maryland

Naval Institute Press
291 Wood Road
Annapolis, MD 21402

© 2017 by Will Melton
All rights reserved. No part of this book may be reproduced or utilized in any form or by any means, electronic or mechanical, including photocopying and recording, or by any information storage and retrieval system, without permission in writing from the publisher.

ISBN: 978-1-59114-640-7 (paperback)
ISBN: 978-1-68247-307-8 (eBook)

Library of Congress Cataloging-in-Publication Data is available.

All illustrations by Jim Rae.
Diagrams and maps by Joshua Smith.

Book design by Horia Popa of Xtrudio, Inc.
Main text set in Adobe Caslon Pro. and chapter titles set in Clarendon.

∞ Print editions meet the requirements of ANSI/NISO z39.48-1992 (Permanence of Paper).
Printed in the United States of America.

25 24 23 22 21 20 19 18 17   9 8 7 6 5 4 3 2 1
First printing

This book is dedicated to members of my family who advised, assisted, and encouraged me in its preparation. They especially include my wife, Helen, who gave much of her time to the project, and our son Will and his wife, Eliza Childs, who helped enormously. Will's contribution included conducting most of the outside research, and Eliza spent an enormous amount of time in editing. My sons Ed and Jamie are history professors, and their suggestions added much to the quality of the final work.

Contents

	Preface	ix
	Editor's Note	xi
1	War Clouds	1
2	Plebe Year	5
3	Destination Russia: SS *Cornelius Harnett*	16
4	Convoy HX-220: First Atlantic Crossing	23
5	Convoy JW-52: The Murmansk Run	29
6	Life in the Bull's-Eye	41
7	The Treacherous Voyage of Convoy RA-53	54
8	Arctic Warriors	67
9	A Foolish Cadet Stunt	85
10	Convoy ONS-174: Homeward Bound	89
11	Kings Point Upperclassman	97
12	A Wartime Wedding at the Academy	106
13	Across the Pacific for General MacArthur	114
14	The Sinking of the *Antoine Saugrain*	127
15	Marooned on Leyte	147
16	Witness to Annihilation	172
17	Peace and Postwar Reentry	192
	Epilogue	197

Appendix 1. Men of the *Cornelius Harnett*,
    April 1943   203
Appendix 2. Captain A. Van Cromphaut's Report
    of the Attack on the *Antoine Saugrain*   205
Appendix 3. Men of the *Antoine Saugrain*,
    December 1944   208
Notes   211
Bibliography   223

Preface

Many an American boy was suddenly snatched from farm, factory, home, or classroom to serve in the armed forces in 1941–45. Most were woefully unprepared for the demands and horrors of World War II. This memoir tells the story of one such poor young man from an obscure Texas town who somehow managed to contribute to the Allies' victory over Germany and Japan.

Looking back almost ninety years to the isolation and deprivation of my childhood, I know that I am infinitely better off in every aspect of my personal life as a result of my wartime experiences. Most especially, I can point to a remarkable institution, Kings Point, which seeded in me so many of the essential elements for a successful and rewarding life. Without that wartime experience at Kings Point and at sea, I probably would not have amounted to very much professionally. I owe the Academy much of my career ambition, character development, ethical values, and intellectual curiosity. Simply put, I needed Kings Point more than it needed me.

If I have exaggerated any of the dangers I faced in combat, it is because I have never forgotten the sheer terror of it, for which I was totally unprepared. My memories of early commands of "Battle stations!" will forever be linked to shocking images of the maritime battlefield setting of Murmansk, Russia, the most depressing place I ever saw. The town's wrecked condition and my own doubts about returning home alive rekindled in me the desperation I felt at the age of ten, when my struggling family lost our father.

I embarked on this project at the request of my son Will, in the hope that all my descendants, present and future, will come to know of the son of a tenant cotton farmer who grew up in the Texas Panhandle during the Dust Bowl that contributed so much misery to America's Great Depression in the 1930s.

While I was writing this memoir, Will put me in touch with two wartime crew members he had located, Norley Hall and Joe Doriss, who contributed to this story. Both sailors remembered me and furnished accounts of wartime incidents we experienced aboard the SS *Antoine Saugrain*. Will also contacted several soldiers who were being transported on the *Saugrain* when we were attacked and forced to abandon ship on 5 December 1944. Their stories added much detail about our ship's mission as a part of Task Force 76.4.7. In addition, Will was able to tap into a growing trove of digitized primary sources, some of which answered questions I had pondered for sixty years.

If this book has a higher purpose, beyond that of a personal reminiscence, it is to recall the wartime experience of a youngster who served on four different Liberty ships. There are few surviving accounts of life aboard the Liberty ships, or about an engineer's hands-on training operating these vessels. Most of my contribution to the war effort was made aboard Liberty ships, and my travels on them reached halfway around the world. This breed of ship, 2,710 of which were built between 1941 and 1945, became the workhorse of our wartime military supply system and a critical factor in the war's favorable outcome for America and her allies. Telling this story while my wits remain is a worthy project.

Herman Melton
Atlanta, Georgia
December 2011

Editor's Note

My father's success as an amateur historian stemmed from his natural ability as a storyteller and his ironclad memory for details. When asked to tell stories of his time in World War II, however, he was usually reticent. He believed that his experiences were neither exceptional nor heroic.

As Dad neared age 90, I urged him to document more fully his memories of the war by expanding a short monograph he wrote for his grandchildren in 1993, soon after being honored at the Russian Embassy in Washington, D.C. He agreed to undertake the project if I would help him to track down historical sources and photographs to assemble a more complete story. We began with videotaped conversations about what he remembered most vividly.

In spite of the demands of caring for my mother as her health declined, he never abandoned our project. When I located five of his living shipmates and the surviving family members of several others, he tapped into their memories. The conversations with long-lost shipmates were the most rewarding part of the work for him. Thanks to his unflagging persistence, he completed the narrative before his time ran out in 2013.

Soon after our joint efforts began, a fortuitous call to Dad's alma mater, the U.S. Merchant Marine Academy, led to the American Merchant Marine Museum and Josh Smith, who directs the museum and teaches humanities courses to midshipmen. My father was proud that the Academy was interested in his story, and I am grateful for the many valuable suggestions Professor

Smith made throughout the project. It is very satisfying to have the story published to coincide with an exhibition at the American Merchant Marine Museum about Herman's time at the Academy and aboard four Liberty ships.

In editing the work, my foremost priority has been to preserve my father's original narrative and voice. As for my research contributions, he was fascinated by the many details that emerged about his convoys, their enemies, and the units his ships transported. Some of that research was completed after his death. I was careful to confirm and update all of his sources, and I hope Kings Point will make Herman's original manuscript available in the Academy's library for future scholars of World War II convoys. As a midshipman in the earliest days of the Academy and, he believed, the first appointment from the state of Kansas, his memories have particular value.

I would like to add to my father's acknowledgments several of my own. Josh Smith recruited to the project maritime historian and editor Lincoln Paine, who offered many helpful suggestions. Josh also added to our team the Scottish painter Jim Rae, whose work draws upon more than a decade of experience at sea aboard British merchant ships and the fleet of the Royal Navy. Neil Jones (USMMA'52) and Christian Ziehe were generous to the project. Last, I am especially grateful for the efforts of my wife, Eliza Childs, whose editorial experience of many years was invaluable throughout the project.

Will Melton
December 2016

Liberty's War

Chapter 1

War Clouds

In September 1941, my life took a crucial turn, thanks to my older sister Marie and her husband, Russell Brewer. They invited me to live with them in Garden City, Kansas, where Russell had found a job selling Chevrolets and Cadillacs. They offered room and board at a rock-bottom price and the chance to attend the town's college. For a jobless young man eager for an education, their offer was a lifesaver. In exchange, I provided a break from constant parenting as I became a regular babysitter for my three-year-old nephew, Gayle Brewer.

As soon as I enrolled at Garden City Community College, I joined the college's National Youth Administration program, a New Deal effort to provide jobs for thousands of needy students across the nation. Through the program I found a part-time job manning the school's athletic equipment window and sweeping the woodworking classroom after each school day. With my income, I paid Marie and Russell fifteen dollars per month for my room and board.

I was in my freshman year at the college when Japan attacked the United States naval base at Pearl Harbor on Sunday, 7 December 1941. On the morning following the attack, a somber dean cancelled classes and all students assembled in the auditorium to listen to the nationwide radio broadcast of President Franklin D. Roosevelt's response to the Japanese attack. Roosevelt called Pearl Harbor "a stab in the back," and Congress declared war on

Japan immediately. A U.S. Navy recruiting station had just opened in Garden City, and three of our classmates left the assembly to walk downtown and join the Navy. I never saw them again, but local service records show that those three boys also survived the conflict.

I registered for the draft and was ordered to report in July. Like most college boys, I started looking into the various programs that were soon established by each branch of the armed forces. Joining any of these programs seemed to be better than waiting for draft orders to enlist as an ordinary gob (sailor) or dogface (infantry private).

Prior to the outbreak of the conflict, few seamen had ever hailed from the Texas Panhandle, a place far from the coast. Nevertheless, I wrote the U.S. Naval Academy for an application and received a standard comprehensive examination for the applicant to complete and grade himself. The test results would determine whether I was qualified to become a plebe at Annapolis. My failure by a wide margin to pass the math portion of the sample exam told me enough. I assumed that West Point would be just as inaccessible for me. Becoming a pilot in the U.S. Army Air Force or the U.S. Naval Air Corps held no appeal as I had no interest in flying.

My girlfriend (who would become my wife) had an idea that forever changed my life. Helen Louise Dunn of Garden City saw a quarter-page ad in *Look* magazine asking for applicants to the new and growing U.S. Merchant Marine Academy. The ad pictured a handsome midshipman in dress blues with a sextant in his hand, gazing skyward from the bridge of a merchant ship. The text stated that the Academy was expanding to meet the needs of the nation's burgeoning merchant fleet by training officers to man the ships.

Additionally, I learned that recruits could choose a career either as a deck officer or as an engineering officer. Upon graduation, each cadet would receive a commission as an ensign in the U.S. Navy Reserve and as an ensign in the U.S. Maritime Service and could choose between the two services. So great was the nation's need for midshipmen that entrance exams and political appointments were suspended temporarily. With Helen's help, I wrote for my school transcripts and submitted my application for admittance to the U.S. Merchant Marine Cadet Corps. She and I were overjoyed when I was soon notified that my application was accepted, contingent on passing a physical examination in June at the nearest Navy physical examination center.

I have never let Helen forget my trip to Oklahoma City for the physical examination. The Academy's minimal acceptable weight for an entering cadet was 134 pounds. In the weeks leading up to the trip, I had a job with a survey party from the U.S. Army Corps of Engineers, which was building an airbase outside Garden City. Long hours in the dry Kansas heat had dropped my weight to 134 pounds exactly. Helen was very worried that I would lose another pound on the 350-mile bus ride to Oklahoma City and be disqualified for the Academy. Only five days remained until my departure and, at her insistence, I began consuming innumerable milk shakes, malted milks, and all fattening foods available. By the time I boarded the Greyhound bus, I was again tipping the scales at 137 pounds. Continuing her regimen, I drank a malted milk at every bus stop en route. As soon as I got off the bus and weighed myself I found I had actually gained weight on the trip. I drank my final malted at an ice cream parlor near the Oklahoma City naval examination center.

The newly commissioned Navy medical lieutenant in dress whites who examined me was confused by the Academy's exam form, as I was the first prospective merchant marine midshipman to be examined at the Oklahoma City center. As a result, he ordered the most rigorous exam for me, the same one that was administered to the scores of naval air cadets who were also being examined there. He did not like the looks of the pinky finger on my right hand, permanently crooked as a result of a boyhood cut on rusty barbed wire that led to blood poisoning. He gave me a waiver for the finger, but the same concern was later to delay for three months the receipt of my appointment from the maritime service.

The doctor also asked me about my high albumen level and if it was a recurring problem. If it were, he said, it could make me ineligible for the Academy. When he asked if I ate a lot of ice cream, I confessed to Helen's strategy for keeping my weight up. He warned me to lay off the shakes and ice cream or risk failing the Academy's physical exam. Helen and I later shared many laughs about her weight-maintenance strategy for me.

While I was waiting for my official appointment, delayed because of my crooked finger, my draft notice arrived. A family friend of Helen's at the Garden City draft board intervened, classifying me as 1-C (already in the service). Without her assistance, I would have lost my Kings Point opportunity.

Finally, my official appointment letters from the Academy arrived, and on 2 October 1942, I boarded an Atchison, Topeka & Santa Fe Railway passenger train to Chicago, via Kansas City. As the plains receded and the prairie advanced, the Texas Panhandle and southwest Kansas felt far, far away.

Chapter 2

Plebe Year

Although I was twenty-two years old, the train ride from Garden City, Kansas, to New York City was my first. I spent my first night on the East Coast in the old Hotel Governor Clinton before reporting the next morning to 45 Broadway for my Academy exam and induction with twenty-four other U.S. Merchant Marine Academy appointees. Other first-time experiences quickly followed. On the way to the exam I rode my first subway. The bus to the Academy passed through the Queens Midtown Tunnel, my first trip through an automobile tunnel. As Long Island Sound came into view, it was the first time I saw the ocean.

The North Shore of Long Island was just beginning its autumn display of color when the recruits of section P-214 arrived. After exiting the bus, we were escorted to Fearless Barracks, where we dropped off the civilian gear (toiletries, sweaters, socks, and the like) that we were required to bring with us. Then we were herded into an anteroom of Wiley Hall, the administration building, for orientation. An upperclassman cadet officer named Tom Horner lectured us briefly on Academy discipline and handed out a mimeographed copy of Academy rules, regulations, and schedules for muster, inspections, meals, and so on.

We next visited the supply department where we were issued basic gear, including a footlocker, underwear, dungarees, belts, chambray shirts, a mackinaw, an overseas cap, and navy oxfords. Horner told us that he would personally guide us through the next day. We were introduced to our drillmaster, Master Sergeant Tilduster of the U.S. Marine Corps (retired), with whom P-214 would spend most of the following week as a platoon.

In spite of my naiveté, when I was sworn in at the newly relocated U.S. Merchant Marine Academy on 5 October 1942, I was better prepared than most of my classmates for the spartan life of a plebe. Privation (due to poverty) was all I had ever known. On the morning after our arrival, Midshipman Horner chose a section leader for P-214 from its ranks. He inquired if anyone had prior military service. When no one responded, he asked if anyone had served in the Civilian Conservation Corps (CCC). Elwell Roberts, a plebe from Florida, held up his hand. Roberts accepted the assignment reluctantly, but in the end he proved a very competent leader.

New dormitories and classrooms were under construction around us and there was mud and trenches everywhere. Footing was so hazardous that a mountain goat would have been daunted by the terrain. Fearless Barracks was a wooden structure built to house seventy-five CCC personnel in a camp elsewhere on Long Island. Nine of these buildings had been moved here by the U.S. Maritime Service (USMS) and installed side by side on a slope southwest of Wiley Hall. They served as quarters for newly arriving recruits (plebes). We soon learned that the nine barracks — Fearless, Intrepid, Corsair, Argonaut, Bonita, Defiance, Eclipse, Greyhound, and Hornet — were named for famous naval sailing ships. Within a year this temporary housing had been replaced by the permanent limestone block dormitories that remain today.

The nucleus of the Academy had been the country home of automobile magnate Walter Chrysler and his wife, Della, on Long Island's Gold Coast. From its concrete and timber pier, Mr. Chrysler could commute to his Manhattan office aboard one of his motor yachts. The estate included twelve acres with a twenty-three-room mansion, a guesthouse, indoor and outdoor swimming pools, an eight-car garage, a large greenhouse, and the large private pier. In 1942, after the death of Mrs. Chrysler, the U.S. government bought the property, along with two adjacent estates, and established there for the first time a permanent home for its new U.S. Merchant Marine Academy. The mansion was renamed Wiley Hall.

Word got around that Mrs. Chrysler's former bathroom in the mansion was equipped with a bidet, an item of plumbing unheard of by most cadets. So vast were Mrs. Chrysler's greenhouses, which backed up to our barracks, that they served as temporary "heads" (in sea lingo) with showers for three hundred plebes. During busy times, such as the hours preceding the Saturday morning inspection and reviews, there were often waiting lines at the heads and showers.

A 5"/51 caliber stern gun was mounted at the head of the oval in front of Wiley Hall when I arrived, and it is still there today. Cadets learned its nomenclature as a part of their gunnery training. Nearby was a marble pool featuring an impressive statue of the Greek goddess Amphitrite, wife of Poseidon and queen of the sea. Members of the regiment began tossing coins into her basin for good luck before examinations. Within a year, the government would acquire additional properties in the neighborhood (one was the summer home of a wealthy movie mogul), which increased the size of the Academy considerably.

Steamboat Road, which runs through the Academy, served as a marching strip for Tilduster's training exercises. It was exquisite in its fall colors, and the views of the elegant estates that lined it were a welcome break from the rest of the plebe regimen. Tilduster marched us back and forth in cadence relentlessly. Eight hours a day for five days, he taught commands, the manual of arms, and all things basic to the making of a military unit. The drill was broken only for first-aid training and vaccinations.

Calisthenics were conducted by a genial physical education instructor. The plebes were impressed when we learned he was a famous Olympic athlete. Greg Rice, "the Little Dynamo" of Notre Dame's track-and-field team, had recently joined the physical education staff. As a long-distance runner, he had set nine world indoor track records in the two-mile and three-mile events, and he won fifty-five straight races.

Occasionally Rice led the panting pack of plebes around the parade ground at a blistering pace without being the slightest bit winded himself. I was usually one of the last to complete the lap. This was not surprising, given my pre-Academy diet. Thanks to Lieutenant (j.g.) Rice, my physical condition improved dramatically in the weeks that followed.

Classes began the second week, and I immediately saw that I would be sorely taxed to keep up in the advanced mathematics courses. Moreover, I had never been in a ship's engine room and had no knowledge of steam boilers, diesel engines, electricity, or mechanical drawing. I spent every available hour studying while the better-educated plebes lounged, engaged in bull sessions, or feasted on chow and refreshments in the canteen.

My bunkmate, Ed Ferenczy from Staten Island, took pity and provided some valuable help with my studies. Ed was brilliant, and after the war he became a chief engineer on several ships before returning to the Academy as a professor in the ship construction department. Later he served as head of that department until his retirement in the 1980s. Noting my lack of sophistication and education, Ed took me under his wing. His kindness to me began on our first night at the Academy when he volunteered to take the less-desirable upper bunk of our two-man sleeping assignments.

Fearless Barracks became more uncomfortable as the temperature dropped. I caught a bad cold during a cloudy and chilly week, and that made my life miserable. The workload increased exponentially day by day. There were no liberties to break the fast pace. Only once in our first weeks were the members of P-214 allowed to pass through Vickery Gate for contact with the outside world, a performance by the actor and comedian Bert Lahr, the Cowardly Lion in the *Wizard of Oz*, who lived nearby on Steamboat Road.

All plebes were informed of the plan for the off-campus event at our regular evening muster at 1730 hours. Kings Point's highest ranking midshipman — George Agee, a first classman and the Academy's first regimental commander — announced orders for the evening. To a green plebe from the Texas Panhandle, Agee was awesome. He was handsome, six feet, two inches tall with thick blond hair, blue eyes, and broad shoulders. Agee was from California and every inch an officer. Members of P-214 stood at parade rest as Agee issued instructions in his booming voice:

> The uniform of the day for the special program will be dress blues for all cadet-midshipmen who have been issued that uniform. These cadets will occupy the first buses to leave the Academy. Those preliminary midshipmen who have been issued dress blues will occupy the next buses. Preliminary midshipmen who have been issued khaki uniforms but not dress blues will occupy the buses next in line. Preliminary midshipmen who have been issued only dungarees will occupy the buses last in line, and my staff and I will follow in the rear. All midshipmen are expected to conduct themselves as officers and gentlemen.

This impressive performance would later become fodder for mocking by the comics in our section. As for Agee, he graduated during my sea duty, and I would go on to serve under two other regimental commanders, Jacobs and Moos, during my eight months as a second and first classman. Both were fine cadet officers, but neither was able to command the respect and admiration of the charismatic Agee. A plebe in P-214 predicted that Agee would become an admiral and perhaps superintendent of Kings Point. Although neither outcome came to pass, for hundreds of his underclassmen George Agee epitomized all the qualities of the quintessential officer.

During our outing to Bert Lahr's home, the more senior plebes of sections P-208, P-210, P-212, and so on, wore their dress blues, while the rest of us wore the only clothing we had been issued—dungarees, blue chambray shirts, olive-drab sleeveless sweaters, and navy-blue mackinaws. Still, we were delighted to be entertained by a famous movie actor.

Two weeks after this event, midshipmen of section P-214 received our khakis and dress blues, and we were allowed to wear our new uniforms at the next Saturday review. We soon had an even better opportunity to show off our new finery. Volunteers were needed to form a ninety-man Kings Point detachment for a march down Fifth Avenue in the annual Navy Day parade. The Academy command decided to fill the detachment from a list of the first ninety to volunteer from both upperclass and plebe ranks. I quickly volunteered and was accepted. This was to be my first weekend liberty away from the Academy.

I also accepted another request for a smaller detachment of sixty midshipmen to attend a prayer service for seamen to be held at New York's Cathedral of St. John the Divine on the morning of the parade. This solemn event was prompted by the heavy wartime losses among seamen aboard ships that had departed New York.

The prayer service was an impressive ceremony in a spectacular setting. As for the Fifth Avenue parade, we were excited to see Movietone News cameras focused on us as we passed in review. The icing on the cake came when we were booked into the Hotel Pennsylvania (a bargain at four dollars a night) and saw Woody Herman's band perform that evening. It was the most exciting evening of my life to that point.

We had liberty on other weekends, and every time we landed in the city we plebes from the hinterlands were overwhelmed. We gawked at the Statue of Liberty, the Empire State Building, and Grand Central Station. New York natives were inordinately friendly and kind to servicemen and that made it a good liberty town.

Among my fellow plebes of section P-214, Bob Johnson of Rolla, Missouri, was the most memorable of all. He had a tremendous wit and immediately hung nicknames on each of his classmates. He called me "Kansas" for obvious reasons, but later my nickname became "Rube," an insulting but more accurate handle for me. He gave Angelo Petrone a derogatory Italian nickname. From the start, Petrone ranked at the bottom of the class academically, and he resigned and left the Academy after four weeks for personal reasons. Johnson called Dick Gwinn from Chicago "Capone." Gwinn ran afoul of his bunkmate, Greenwald, a loner from New York whom he accused of evading his share of the cleanup of Fearless before our regular Saturday inspections. So bitter was Gwinn that he left the Academy swearing that he would rather resign than be associated with Greenwald.

Tom Neville of Ansonia, Connecticut, and I became close friends, and he invited me for a weekend visit with his family. At my request, he took me to a game at the Yale Bowl, the first major college football stadium I had ever seen. Tom became a naval officer after graduation. In the years after the war, he worked at Yale University, rising to superintendent of utilities. During our time together in P-214, Tom saw a picture of my sweetheart, Helen, hanging in my locker and made me promise that he would be best man at our wedding after graduation.

Others among the twenty-five plebes in P-214 included Warner Baylor from Springfield, Virginia, who after graduation accepted a commission in the U.S. Navy. He was wounded when his ship, the troopship USS *Susan B. Anthony*, sank after hitting a mine off the coast of Normandy the day after D-Day, but he subsequently took part in the invasions of Iwo Jima and Okinawa. He later became a radio and television news reporter in Washington, D.C., and after service in the Korean War became a speech writer for the Interstate Commerce Commission. Bob Johnson called him "Rebel" and "Red" alternately because of his Virginia connection and his carrot top. At the peak of his career, "Red" Baylor became more famous than anybody else in P-214. He also became wealthier by virtue of his early purchase of undeveloped land in tidewater Maryland, land that increased enormously in value before his retirement in his early fifties. Baylor would later serve in the sword guard for my 1943 wedding at the Academy.

Although he was "laid back" as a cadet, Steve Barlough from Detroit was to become the most successful graduate of P-214 in the maritime industry. He was also the luckiest. When cadets of

P-214 were assigned to ships bound for the war zones for our sea training, we reported to our assigned ships and then usually received a few days' leave to go home before sailing. Barlough was late returning from his leave and missed his ship. He was reprimanded before being assigned to another ship. The Liberty ship that sailed without him was loaded to the gunwales with ammunition bound for General Dwight D. Eisenhower's landings in North Africa. Just inside the Strait of Gibraltar, a torpedo from a German submarine destroyed the ship, and all hands aboard perished. The destruction was so devastating that a minute after the explosion, no debris could be seen on the surface of the sea. Several other ships in the convoy were also damaged from the blast. Steve went on to a distinguished naval career, becoming chief engineer aboard the NS *Savannah,* America's first nuclear-powered merchant vessel.

The first midshipman from P-214 to return from sea duty and assume his studies as a third classman was Jim Lombard from Elmira, New York. Bob Johnson had given Jim the nickname "Colonna" because he was a dead ringer for the famous movie comedian Jerry Colonna. Jim was a cheerful and mannerly gentleman and a favorite of all. Bill McGee had transferred to the Academy from the University of North Carolina, where he had been a lineman on the football team. I remember him as the largest physical specimen in our section.

While Dick Gwinn and Angelo Petrone were the first to leave our group, several others would choose to discontinue their studies after sea training: Johnny Boris from Pennsylvania; Donald Younkin from Somerset, Pennsylvania; Bill McGee from North Carolina; and most disappointing to me, Bob Johnson the joker from Missouri. Chuck DeJulian chose to become a "cadet special" and acquired his license later because of his ship's extended delay in returning home. Special cadets were not given regular graduating diplomas.

An important early event for P-214 came when we were marched aboard the training vessel TV *Emery Rice*. It was the first ship many of us had boarded. In the engine room we saw a steam boiler, steam engine, condenser, hot well, stern tube, bilge pump, and shaft alley for the first time. We also learned to shine brass. Deck cadets meanwhile were introduced to a chartroom and deck gear and taught how to swab decks.

As the fourth-class curriculum took shape, more equipment was issued, including drafting sets, slide rules, and several excellent textbooks. The accelerated wartime program at the Academy called for each midshipman to spend six months as a plebe (fourth classman) followed by six months at sea on a merchant ship as a third classman for hands-on training.

Midshipman Herman Melton at the U.S. Merchant Marine Academy, with the TV *Emery Rice* in the distance, 1942. *Author's collection*

On campus we were taught the principles of working with torpedoes, magnetic mines, and depth charges. The curriculum called for all plebes to receive special intensive training in 20mm antiaircraft gun nomenclature and operation. We completed this work and were also trained in the 5"/51 caliber surface gun. For me and many other plebes, the gunnery training later proved to be especially valuable during our war-zone voyages.

While at sea, each cadet was expected to complete a Sea Project. For an engine midshipman the Sea Project consisted of intensive sophomore-level algebra, trigonometry, geometry, and a smattering of calculus. The lessons were time consuming and required intensive study in steam engineering, diesel engineering, basic electricity, and ship construction. Many courses entailed drawing engine room equipment. All were in the form of lessons with a final exam.

As the plebes of fall 1942 were learning the ropes, German submarines were having a field day off the East Coast and in the Gulf of Mexico. All East Coast ports had to be closed for a few days in November. The war at sea was raging, and the new emergency cargo vessels, called Liberty ships, were coming down the ways in ever-increasing numbers, each demanding trained officers of the maritime service. These vessels were to become the sea-duty training sites for most wartime Kings Point midshipmen.

As a result of these wartime expediencies, the orderly training schedule for section P-214 was not to be. Just six weeks after our arrival at the Academy, we were told that the demands of the war required many more licensed officers to man America's merchant ships. Out of the blue, Academy headquarters issued an order canceling all further classes for several fourth-class sections, including P-214. This was shocking news for us, but many plebes were ecstatic about the cancellation of classes and the chance for action at sea. Not me; I feared that the accelerated training would lead me to fail the Academy's more difficult courses later in our studies.

Nevertheless, those with passing grades were quickly promoted to third classmen, and each midshipman was given twenty-four hours' notice to pack his gear. We were transported back to the maritime services headquarters at 45 Broadway in Manhattan for ship assignments. There we were issued orders, rail tickets, and per diems for travel to our assigned vessels. Each midshipman was handed a two-inch-thick, bound notebook titled "Sea Project," which contained the daily lessons and exercises in math, steam engineering, internal combustion engines, ship construction, electricity, and so on. While it was customary for each ship to be assigned one engine cadet for training in mechanical ship operations and one deck cadet training in ship navigation and cargo management, the desperate times called for each engine cadet of section P-214 to be assigned with as many as three deck cadets to a ship.

At the assembly point, we were introduced to our cadet shipmates and ordered to proceed together to our assignments, usually a newly launched Liberty ship. Deck cadets Irwin Erickson from Ironwood, Michigan, Joe Langer from Peru, Indiana, and Bob Ingram from Mason, Michigan, and I were ordered to proceed to Wilmington, North Carolina, where we were to report for duty to the skipper of the SS *Cornelius Harnett*, a Liberty ship recently launched at the North Carolina Shipbuilding Company yards and leased to the Black Diamond Steamship Line.

Before boarding sleeping cars for the South, we enjoyed a delicious dinner at the newly opened Howard Johnson's Restaurant on Lexington Avenue. At Grand Central Station we took the Seaboard's Orange Blossom Special to Washington, where we transferred to the Atlantic Coast Line's Palmetto Limited bound for Wilmington. Crossing North Carolina we relished the scenery and especially the sunny weather, so different from what we left behind in New York. It was the first trip to the Southeast for all of us, and we looked forward to our introduction to the great workhorse of the U.S. merchant fleet—the Liberty ship.

Chapter 3

Destination Russia: SS *Cornelius Harnett*

Perhaps for security reasons, there was little mention in the wartime American press of the launching of 2,710 Liberty ships of the EC2-S-C1 design by the U.S. Maritime Commission. More than five thousand cadet-midshipmen who trained at the U.S. Merchant Marine Academy served as deck and engine officers aboard these vessels during the war. Eighteen American shipyards in twelve states built and launched Liberty ships, and scores of other industries manufactured engines, pumps, and auxiliary equipment for them.

Liberty ships were based on a British design that was standardized so that components of each ship were interchangeable with those built by other shipyards. Each ship was 441 feet, 6 inches in length and 57 feet wide with a draft of 26 feet, 10 inches. The basic design had a deadweight tonnage of 10,474 tons and a displacement tonnage of 14,245. Five cargo holds had a capacity of 14,594 tons of stores and 2,000 tons of fuel.

Power came from a 2,500-horsepower reciprocating steam engine operating at a speed of 76 revolutions per minute with a rated speed of 11 knots, steered with a steam-operated mechanism. The engines were the product of more than a dozen American factories following standards that also enabled engine parts to be interchangeable across the entire fleet. Over a span of forty months of World War II service, I sailed in four Liberty ships, and the only difference between them that I remember was the manufacturer's nameplate on the main engine. The early Liberty ships' firepower usually included a 5"/51 caliber stern gun and a 3"/51 caliber bow gun to fight off surface vessels, and ten 20mm Swiss Oerlikon antiaircraft guns.

At that point in the war, the Wilmington, North Carolina, shipyard was launching a new ship every two weeks. The SS *Cornelius Harnett*, my first ship, had been built in three weeks, and its engine was a Hamilton, built by the General Machinery Company of Hamilton, Ohio. The ship's hull was laid in Wilmington and named for a North Carolinian hero of the American Revolution.

When we arrived in Wilmington, the four cadet-midshipmen assigned to the *Harnett* learned that the local Catholic church had installed bunks in one of its youth recreation rooms for servicemen to rent while on leave. We were directed to camp there until our shipboard berths were ready. Before our arrival, these bunks had been occupied by soldiers from the Army's antiaircraft training school at nearby Camp Davis. In a later voyage to the Philippines, I would meet soldiers from a unit trained at Camp Davis, the 237th Anti-Aircraft Artillery Searchlight Battalion. We boys in blue were a novelty for the girls from Wilmington who were accustomed to khaki-clad GIs attending the weekly dances near the harbor. The four of us decided to keep a low social profile in Wilmington, however, because we were so much in the minority and lowly third-class trainees.

The *Harnett*'s crew had been assembled and members of her U.S. Navy Armed Guard were aboard when, in my first act as engine cadet, I boarded the *Harnett* and went to the quarters of the chief engineer for instructions. Herman Mellema, a naturalized citizen from Rotterdam, the Netherlands, was a grizzled, red-haired, pipe-smoking old salt in his late fifties. He had spent his entire adult life at sea and was a graduate of his country's merchant marine academy. In our introductory conversation, he asked many questions about the Kings Point curriculum and then told me how much more was required of a Dutch cadet to complete his training. The chief promised to allow me sufficient time to complete my studies and gave me a general outline of my duties. I was to serve as a helper for the deck engineer in order to learn my way around the ship. I always believed that the chief turned me over to someone else to get me out of his hair.

The deck engineer was Andy Parks, a likable Canadian who was very considerate of my lack of experience. He was a patient teacher — especially regarding the operation and maintenance of what was called deck machinery. This training was invaluable later when the ship was in Murmansk and we had to depend on our own winches and booms to unload cargo.

We were soon introduced to the skipper and his officers. Captain Edgar W. Carver, nearly seventy years old, had recently returned from retirement on his cranberry farm in Maine to answer his country's call for experienced mariners. Having spent most of his life at sea, he was competent in all matters nautical. The captain was always a perfect gentleman with a quiet and kindly manner. The *Harnett* was his first command in several years, and he was obviously working very hard to get the ship seaworthy.

When we boarded, the *Harnett*'s crew consisted of forty-two men complemented by an armed guard crew of eleven men to serve the guns. Before sailing we would add to both crews. Liberty ships were sailed by civilian seamen who signed on for a specific voyage without the expectation of manning guns against enemy attack. Shortly before Pearl Harbor, the U.S. Navy organized an armed guard service to supply gunnery crews for American merchant vessels. Before the war was over, nearly 145,000 gunners had served in this capacity.

After ten days of final preparations, the *Harnett* was ready for sea trials. I was looking forward to participating in "bringing up steam" and was told that I could roam freely to observe all activities without assuming any responsibilities in the engine room. I had my first chance to learn the duties of the fireman and the oiler, since they had been ordered to train me. My fellow deck cadets had similar experiences topside. From my first contacts with the engine crew I was already being taught scorn for "deck apes," whose duties were "Mickey Mouse" to the "black gang" of the engine crew. The deck crew in turn looked down on us as "underground savages." After all, were they not destined to be skippers and therefore superior to chief engineers?

SS *Cornelius Harnett*, Newport News, Va., June 1945.
Library of Virginia

Each member of the ship's crew was given a battle station. In recognition of the gunnery skills I had honed as a plebe at Kings Point, I was assigned the dangerous and demanding role of loader on one of the 20mm antiaircraft guns on the port side of the boat deck. My duty placed me in a gun tub where I took down the empty magazines and handed up full ones to the gunner during an air attack.

Although extremely interesting to me, the sea trials were largely uneventful. They were conducted in the estuary of the Cape Fear River and lasted only a few hours. On 25 November, *Harnett* embarked for Norfolk without escort. The Atlantic was choppy, and on the first day out, all four Kings Point cadets were seasick. By the time we reached Lookout Bight at the southern end of

Pamlico Sound, all had recovered, and we soon became inured to the ship's rolling and bucking motion. There the *Harnett* encountered the enemy for the first time. Navy patrol planes discovered a submarine stalking the *Harnett,* and we were ordered to steam toward the safety of shallow waters to anchor for a few days. All ports on the East Coast were closed due to the submarine menace.

After the subs were driven away, the *Harnett* joined a convoy of stragglers including two Liberty ships, SS *Daniel Boone* and SS *Henry Bacon,* and merchantmen *Bosworth, Errington Court, Cockrell,* and *Annik,* escorted to Norfolk Navy Yard by a Navy patrol yacht and two 83-footer Coast Guard cutters. In Norfolk, degaussing equipment was installed on the *Harnett* to protect it from magnetic mines. This consisted of a shielded antimagnetic copper cable that completely encircled the vessel near the gunwale to prevent a magnetic contact with German mines.

There was no liberty for the crew at Norfolk, where ammunition and other combat gear were brought aboard for our voyage. After loading was complete, we proceeded to the Delaware River for the approach to the Philadelphia Navy Yard where the ship's 5"/51 caliber stern gun was to be replaced with a 5"/38 caliber unit. The 5"/51 was primarily a gun for battles with other ships, and its low elevating capacity had limited value in defending against enemy aircraft on the Arctic routes. The 5"/38 had a much higher elevating capacity to enable the gun to fire at German planes. We learned that the Liberty ships in our convoy were the first to be equipped with this newer-model stern gun, and it appeared later that German pilots were surprised when they first encountered it.

The *Harnett*'s guns were commanded by Lieutenant Richard M. Stone, the top officer of the armed guard unit aboard. He was one of the most memorable characters on the voyage. Before the war Stone had been a young tire company executive in Akron, Ohio. During the summer after Pearl Harbor, Stone answered the call to colors by entering the V-7 Navy College Training Program. V-7s were men with college degrees who were commissioned as officers after a short training course that fitted them for duty in the U.S. Navy Reserve. Officers in the regular Navy derisively called them "ninety-day wonders." Nevertheless, many performed well and served their country gallantly in its time of need.

Stone appeared to be a nervous wreck. When everything was calm and quiet at sea, the lieutenant paced the deck, unable to sleep. He was jumpy and quick to anger, and he ran his command by the book. During gunnery practice at sea, however, Stone transformed himself into a calm, collected, and efficient gunnery officer. As I was later to learn, from the captain on down, the coolest officer on the ship during combat was Lieutenant Stone. Day by day he trained his crew of eighteen (along with merchant crewmen assigned to gunnery battle stations) to a highly pitched tone, creating a nearly flawless team.

As the *Harnett* approached the Philadelphia Navy Yard, his jumpy side was revealed. Despite the obvious safety of the surroundings, he had his command on full alert with several of the armed guard manning 20mm guns. At one point inside the Navy yard, our ship was temporarily anchored while awaiting its turn to proceed. Everything was quiet and at ease around 2000 hours when a small harbor craft came putt-putting past the ship. As it approached in the darkness, Lieutenant Stone ordered his signalman on the blinker light to ask for identification. The coxswain on the small craft appeared to have no knowledge of Navy signaling or else was unaccustomed to being challenged in this manner. He simply ignored the command to identify himself, whereupon Stone sprang into action.

"Gunner number seven, train your gun on the approaching vessel and stand by for further orders," he barked to a perplexed 20mm operator. Deck cadet Joe Langer, who was on duty on the bridge next to the lieutenant, saw the developments close at hand. Fortunately, the officer on duty intervened and ordered the defenses lowered. Langer suggested later that if the harbor craft's coxswain had acted in any way suspiciously, Stone would have blown the small craft out of the water.

When we were anchored in the Philadelphia Navy Yard, once again, no liberty was granted. Only the skipper, with Stone and the radio operator, went ashore for meetings regarding convoy procedure and the new gun's installation. Then, accompanied by surface craft and a heavy aerial escort, we sailed to New York where the crew was given shore leave for several days. Just before our departure, all hands were issued heavy Arctic-weather gear. Strict secrecy was ordered against any crew member mentioning this clothing to family or friend. We were reminded of the slogan "loose lips sink ships," and a chilling reality began to sink in. The *Harnett* was destined for the Murmansk Run, the most dreaded voyage for a merchant mariner in World War II.

Chapter 4

Convoy HX-220: First Atlantic Crossing

After completing preparations for sailing, the *Harnett* moved to Caven Point, New Jersey, to load more ammunition and explosives. Caven Point sat at the end of a long causeway that juts half a mile into New York harbor from Jersey City, where the four cadets ate a final stateside dinner at a café on Journal Square. The ship moved out the next day to join a convoy headed to the British Isles. Only one of the convoy's merchantmen would accompany the *Harnett* to Murmansk, the SS *Nicholas Gilman*, another Liberty ship. Others, including two other Libertys, were loaded with supplies for Britain or for troops fighting in the North Africa campaign, which had begun just six weeks earlier.

We departed New York in a snowstorm on 21 December 1942. Convoy HX-220 consisted of thirty merchant vessels with Royal Navy ships of the Western Local Escort Force. Our commodore was a retired British admiral, Sir Arthur John Davies, aboard the steamer *Baharistan*. Three destroyers of the Royal Navy, HMS *Beverley*, *Warwick*, and *Winchelsea*, and the escort aircraft carrier HMS *Battler* were the muscle of our ocean escort at various stages of our passage.

The *Battler* had been built for the U.S. Navy but had been transferred to the Royal Navy as part of the Lend-Lease program a month before we sailed. Her decks launched Fairey Swordfish torpedo bombers, biplanes that looked straight out of World War I, but the aircraft proved to be one of the Allies' most potent weapons against U-boats. Another antisubmarine weapon with the convoy was the *Narvik*, a Norwegian whaler acquired by the British and converted to convoy defense. At any time, there were also up to six Canadian and British corvettes in the escort.

Even though many of my assignments were menial, each day was a learning experience. The seas were rough, with gale-force winds, a frightening experience for a landlubber, as were the radio reports of attacks on other convoys in the North Atlantic. Rough seas for days on end made me long for duty in the Pacific, where, according to the seasoned sailors on the *Hartnett*, the seas were calm for long periods. In one instance, big waves broke the lashings holding sixteen 55-gallon drums of lubricating oil. Some of the barrels started rolling around the forward deck, and one ruptured, making the deck slippery and very hazardous to cross. Waves blasting over the bow buckled the splinter shields on the 3"/50 caliber bow gun, and nearly a foot of water flooded the forward ammunition magazines.

Life on board a working vessel contributed much to my knowledge of the ship's mechanical equipment. I worked most closely with the deck engineer, but on many occasions I helped the maintenance crew servicing engine room equipment. I came to understand the function and operation of all equipment on board, and by the time the ship tied up in Scotland, I had become a valuable member of the crew. Freezing weather took its toll on the deck machinery, especially the winches used to unload cargo, and repairs to this equipment occupied at least half my time.

After we skirted Labrador and Newfoundland a thick fog descended on the convoy, adding the danger of collision with unseen navigation obstacles or other vessels. At several points, we lost the convoy. Once, after six or seven hours alone, we sighted the convoy directly behind the *Harnett*. Another time, close to our destination, we had to anchor until the fog cleared. Overall, it was a miserable winter voyage.

My daylight hours were occupied by duties that fell to the

lowest-ranking man on the ship. When chores were finished and there was no enemy activity, I would spend four or five hours a day studying. It seemed that either the deck cadets were brighter than me or my engineering courses were harder, because none of my three fellow cadets cracked a book during the trip to Murmansk. For me there was no time in the evening for card games or bull sessions in the wardroom and the crew's mess. Even if time had permitted, I could not afford to gamble with my fellow cadets. I had no savings or allowance from home, and as an Academy plebe, I earned only sixty-five dollars per month, with a ten-dollar monthly supplement for sea duty in a war zone.

Whenever I encountered difficult math problems in my studies, I first sought help from the three engineers on board, but they were usually no help. The chief mate, who had heard me asking questions of the engineers, offered to help since he loved math and said that he sometimes did calculus for relaxation. He encouraged me to bring any math problem to him whenever he was in his stateroom. This is how I came to know Selwyn Anderson, one of the most brilliant men I ever met.

Anderson was born and reared in rural South Dakota, the son of a first-generation Swede. His formal education consisted of eight grades in a one-room rural school in the wheat belt. Much of his practical training occurred in the blacksmith shop on his father's farm. As a teenager Anderson ran off to sea, educating himself as he sailed around the world and rose through the ranks. One of his most memorable experiences was as navigator in one of Rear Admiral Richard Byrd's ships on his second Antarctic expedition in 1934. Although a deck officer, Anderson knew as much about operating the *Harnett*'s engine room equipment as any of the engineers aboard, as he had spent years with the "black gang," as marine-engine operators are known.

Anderson, who was in his fifties when I met him, had a photographic memory and a retentive mind, and he could recall a vast reservoir of facts. He spent free time at sea reading and listening to recordings from his huge collection of classical music. He was an authority on opera, and he had visited many of the world's great art museums. Taking a special liking to me, he shared stories of his cultural and seafaring adventures. His trunks were full of books by the world's great authors. The first Renaissance man I ever knew, Anderson became my mentor during my sea training.

One incident that occurred during the dark and dangerous days of our return voyage from Murmansk revealed much about Anderson. It was a time when crewmen were cracking up under the strain of frightful weather and unrelenting contact with the enemy. One evening around 2000 hours, as Anderson helped me with a math problem, he invited me to stay longer to hear the finale of a favorite opera recording on his turntable.

Suddenly, the sound of loud voices rushed up the ladder from the crew's quarters below. One of the ship's cooks had broken down and was wielding a long kitchen knife, threatening shipmates and hurling taunts at the officers on the deck above. Anderson went to the door and called down for quiet. The crazed cook stood at the foot of the ladder leading to the officers' deck and challenged any of them to come down, cursing them by name. Anderson turned off his record player, put a pair of handcuffs in his rear pocket, and turned to me saying, "Wait here Melton, I want you to hear the rest of that music. I'll be back shortly."

Normally, I would have obeyed orders and remained above the uproar, but I sensed the potential for a serious confrontation, and I followed Anderson to the head of the ladder leading down. Upon seeing Anderson, the cook yelled: "The same goes for you, you son of a bitch! If you come down those steps, I'll cut your goddamn guts out."

"You're under arrest. Put down that knife or you'll soon be in the brig. Do you understand?"

"Why don't you try to take it from me, you son of a bitch," was the reply.

Anderson, six feet, three inches tall and 220 pounds of pure muscle, started slowly down the ladder, keeping his eyes on the cook's face. As Anderson approached, the cook raised the knife. Anderson's huge hand went out swiftly, like a cobra striking, seized the cook's wrist and slammed him against the rail. The cook's hand turned blue from the mate's iron grip and his knife tumbled to the deck. In a flash Anderson pulled the handcuffs from his hip pocket, and shackled the cook to a nearby bunk. Turning to the boatswain standing nearby, Anderson handed him the key to the handcuffs and ordered: "Leave him here and if he causes any more trouble, put him in the brig." He then climbed back up the ladder, turned to his stunned student, and said calmly, "Come with me, cadet, and we'll finish what we were doing." Back in his stateroom, he returned to the music and his critique of the opera.

Throughout our time together, Anderson showed his command of many topics during dinner conversations. In addition to his grasp of literature and music, history and international politics, he was an authority on the sinking of the *Titanic* and numerous sea battles. His defense of the British role in the present war often caused resentment and sniping behind his back on the part of our junior officers, but to me Anderson stood ten feet taller than any other member of the crew, engineers included.

Anderson also helped me to understand the stakes of our voyage. At this point in the war, the USSR had its back to the wall. Both Leningrad and Stalingrad were under siege by the advancing German army. The supply route to Murmansk was absolutely vital to Russian survival. Without Allied ships laden with products from the American industrial arsenal, the USSR might not succeed in beating back the German invasion of Russia. Josef Stalin was demanding help, and Roosevelt pressed Britain's Prime Minister Winston Churchill to protect the American merchant ships and keep the Soviet Union in the war. So desperate was the situation that, in the summer of 1942 Churchill wrote to the Admiralty that the next convoy "is justified if half [the ships] gets through. Failure on our part to make the attempt would weaken our influence with both our major allies."

During the course of the war, merchant ships carrying everything from shoes to fighter aircraft sailed on this most hazardous of all voyages for merchant seamen in World War II. Of the 800 ships that made the Murmansk Run, 97 failed to reach their destination and return. Storms, ice, mines, collisions, fires, U-boats, and the

Luftwaffe took their toll. Some 3,000 Allied seamen lost their lives in the north Russian convoys.

There are excellent records from the war that show the enormity of our support of the USSR via the Murmansk Run. Ships of the north Russian convoys carried more than 3.9 million tons of material from Allied nations to the Soviet Union. Of all American aid to the Soviets, nearly one-quarter was funneled through the narrow lanes of the Arctic convoys. Before the war was over, American shipments to the Soviet Union would total 14,795 aircraft; 7,537 tanks; 471,257 trucks, jeeps, tractors, and motorcycles; 11,155 railcars; and 1,981 locomotives. The *Harnett* carried a steam locomotive in its cargo, for use in transferring the war materiel carried by the convoys from Murmansk to the front. The need for a steam locomotive was so critical that two other ships in the convoy (one being the *Nicholas Gilman*) also carried locomotives, in the hope that at least one of them would arrive safely.

Convoys to north Russia also carried more than 345,000 tons of ammunition and TNT, and on the *Harnett* we had our share of explosives in our holds, which added tremendously to our risk. Torpedoes striking Liberty ships loaded with TNT caused mighty explosions that left little of the vessel behind, as I would come to understand during my time in the Philippines in 1944.

As the dangers loomed ever larger and more real, my studies became a refuge from fear, helping, for a few moments, to rid my mind of the risks I faced. There were quiet moments, too. Despite the bone-chilling wintry cold, my watch duty on deck was often a time of spectacular light shows by the aurora borealis, the northern lights that flashed every color of the spectrum. Other fireworks were not long in coming for the *Harnett*.

Chapter 5

Convoy JW-52: First The Murmansk Run

Convoy HX-220 arrived at Gourock, Scotland, on 11 January 1943. I was helping in the engine room when the *Harnett* docked. At the earliest opportunity, I rushed topside to view the first foreign country I had ever seen. The beauty of the countryside was evident even from a dock. I longed to go ashore, but no liberty was granted for security reasons. Only the captain, the radio operator, and the gunnery officer were allowed ashore to participate in a convoy meeting a few days after arrival. I did get to meet my first Brit, however, a naval security petty officer who came on board, and I asked him about the nature of the region and its people. In addition to answering my questions, he also provided news of the war in North Africa, where General Dwight D. Eisenhower had opened a second front against Field Marshal Erwin Rommel, the "Desert Fox."

After a few days in the Firth of Clyde, we weighed anchor and headed north for the Hebrides. On our way to join convoy JW-52, assembling at Loch Ewe, the ship steamed along the west coast of Scotland, and shipmate Andy Parks pointed out an area where the poet Robert Burns had lived. The coast there was cold, gray, and uninviting. That evening, we entered in the engine room log, "Anchored. Loch Ewe Scotland. 15 January 1943."

As with most of the Arctic convoys throughout the war, almost all the warships serving as escorts for convoy JW-52 were British. Although I remember being disappointed not to see ships of the U.S. Navy in the convoy, I was stunned by the naval might present in the escort. It included HMS *Anson*, a British battleship, which we never saw because it was far to starboard with the cruiser *Sheffield* and nine destroyers flanking both the inbound and outbound convoys, protecting us from the German battleships *Tirpitz* and *Scharnhorst*, which were stationed in the Norwegian fjords. There was also a cruiser covering force for the convoys at this time led by the heavy cruiser *Kent* with her eight-inch guns, and two light cruisers, *Bermuda* and *Glasgow*.

Commander W. H. Selby on the destroyer *Onslaught* assembled our close escort screen consisting of the destroyers *Beagle*, *Bulldog*, *Matchless*, *Musketeer*, and *Offa*, and the Polish navy's ORP *Piorun*. Our through-escort (sailing with us to north Russia) included two corvettes, *Lotus* and *Starwort*, the minesweeper *Britomart*, and two supply trawlers for supply and rescue services, *Northern Pride* and *St. Elstan*. I was summoned on deck by my cabinmates to view the *Kent* as it passed us during the assembly at Loch Ewe. It was the largest ship I had seen thus far and was commanded by Sir Bruce Fraser, who would serve after the war as First Sea Lord, commanding the entire Royal Navy.

A local escort—the destroyers *Blankney*, *Ledbury*, and *Middleton*—detached from the convoy when we reached Iceland. I did not realize at the time that the Germans were not the only navy bringing undersea boats to the contest. At least two submarines of the Royal Navy, the *Taciturn* and *Trident*, were silent hunters in the waters off Norway during our passage.

Other American merchant vessels of the convoy included the *Delsud* and *Gulfwing*, and the Liberty ship *Nicholas Gilman*, the only ship that sailed with the *Harnett* on all four convoys I was part of as a midshipman. Ships in the convoy registered to other nations included the oil tanker *Oligarch* and the merchantmen *Atlantic*, *Dan-Y-Bryn*, *El Oriente*, *Empire Baffin*, *Empire Clarion*, *Empire Portia*, *Empire Snow*, *Empire Tristam*, *Ocean Faith*, and *Temple Arch*.

Later convoys to Murmansk usually enjoyed the protection of the escort carriers whose aircraft were so effective against U-boats, such as the HMS *Battler*, which had accompanied HX-220. Although JW-52 had no aircraft escorts, Churchill was clearly determined to protect the ships' valuable war cargos. After two of the convoy's merchant ships were forced to turn back with mechanical troubles, there were as many naval escorts as merchant ships with the convoy. To me, that defensive advantage was not a comfort. Instead, it seemed an omen of dangers to come.

During my plebe year, the consensus at the Academy was that the most dangerous sea duty assigned to cadet-midshipmen was the Murmansk Run. Churchill called it "the worst journey in the world." Merchant marine veteran and author Bruce Felknor described it best:

> The defining horror of World War II for merchant seamen was and remains the Murmansk Run, a savage gauntlet into and within the Arctic Circle of German U-boats, heavy cruisers, scout planes, torpedo bombers, dive bombers and icebergs. Soviet troops desperately required munitions and all other supplies to prevent a Nazi triumph in the north. The Baltic Sea was closed. The only route lay along and around the Norwegian Coast, studded with German airfields. The port of Murmansk itself, nine hundred miles from the North Pole was under constant air attack. Winter brought night and ice-choked seas. In summer, the pack ice retreated and night never fell. Each convoy through this frigid hell was more deadly than the last.

The greatest threat to the Murmansk convoys in winter was operating in one of the world's harshest climates. Sea temperatures hovered around 28°F for weeks on end. We were told that a

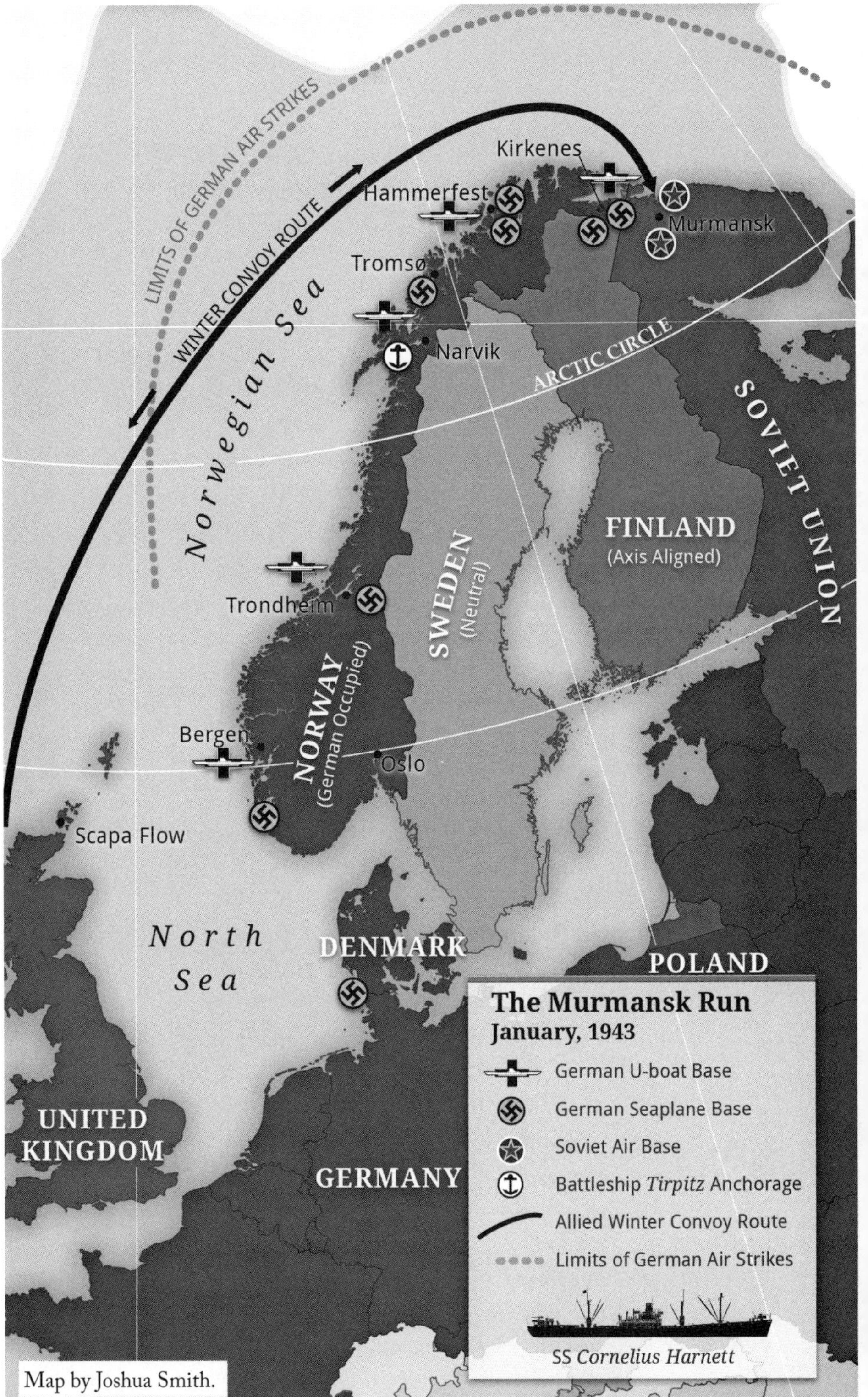
LIMITS OF GERMAN AIR STRIKES
WINTER CONVOY ROUTE
Norwegian Sea
Kirkenes
Hammerfest
Murmansk
Tromsø
Narvik
ARCTIC CIRCLE
SOVIET UNION
FINLAND
(Axis Aligned)
SWEDEN
(Neutral)
Trondheim
NORWAY
(German Occupied)
Bergen
Oslo
Scapa Flow
North Sea
DENMARK
POLAND
UNITED KINGDOM
GERMANY
The Murmansk Run
January, 1943
German U-boat Base
German Seaplane Base
Soviet Air Base
Battleship *Tirpitz* Anchorage
Allied Winter Convoy Route
Limits of German Air Strikes
SS *Cornelius Harnett*
Map by Joshua Smith.

man could survive only four minutes in water at that temperature. Worst of all were the 40-knot gales common in the region. Under these conditions the odds of surviving a sinking by bomb or torpedo were slim to none. One hazard that is usually overlooked by historians was the icing over of the vital lifeboat-launching equipment. Careful seamen made certain that these components were kept free of ice, using axes when necessary. There were tragic instances of Murmansk Run casualties that occurred when seamen failed to take this precaution.

JW-52 was one of the first convoys to make the dash for the Soviet ports after the debacle of the Murmansk-bound convoy PQ-17 in July 1942. All on board the *Harnett* knew how the British command ordered that convoy to disperse near the Arctic Circle when, with German bombers and submarines poised to strike, a false report arrived that the pocket battleship *Tirpitz* was headed for the convoy. Ultimately, two-thirds of the ships of convoy PQ-17 were destroyed. No decision made by the Admiralty during the war sparked as much controversy, and it continues to this day.

The crew of the *Harnett* had heard all about the PQ-17 disaster, thanks to our first assistant engineer, Willard L. Davis from Mountain View, Missouri. He had served on one of the convoy's merchantmen (an "old Hog Islander" he called it) that went down with loss of life. Davis was always ready to recount the horrors to anyone who would listen.

I was impressed with the seamanship of the Allied officers and men who managed to get the 43 ships of JW-52 into position without any collisions and headed them toward north Russia in remarkably short time. Because of the evasive actions that were necessary, a circuitous route of roughly 1,600 miles was navigated by JW-52 from Loch Ewe to Murmansk in eleven days.

For the first few days after our departure on 17 January 1943 there was no sign of the enemy from the air or sea, and Lieutenant Stone ordered test firing of all guns, including various fuse settings of the two large 3"/50 and 5"/38 guns that were mounted fore and aft. The *Harnett* also had eight 20mm Oerlikon cannons, and all guns were operated by Stone's Navy gunners, who bunked in the stern of the ship. At this point, Stone gave me a new general quarters assignment. My duty now was to carry ammunition magazines to the gun tub of a 20mm gun on the port side, aft of the flying bridge. He went over procedures with us again and again, honing the gun crew to a fine pitch. Meanwhile, the rest of the crew settled into a tight and guarded routine during which time I was also able to make some real progress on my Sea Project for the Academy.

As the days grew colder and stormier, the tension mounted. We could hear the escort's depth charges around us, unleashed to keep at bay an unseen wolf pack of U-boats. A periscope was sighted between the convoy columns by the *Nicholas Gilman*. Over three days, five or six floating mines were reported, some within the convoy. Six days out of Loch Ewe on Saturday, 23 January, a large Blohm + Voss BV 138 reconnaissance flying boat appeared. General quarters sounded and Stone's gunners fired two rounds of the stern gun. The plane continued to circle out of range. Hands asked one another when the first attack would come.

At 1232 hours on Sunday, 24 January, the *Harnett* was southeast of Bear Island when our questions were answered. I was in the wardroom finishing my lunch when the general quarters alarm sounded and all hell broke loose. I donned my life jacket, grabbed my helmet and emergency kit, and raced to my battle station. When I arrived at the gun tub, I got my first close-up view of the enemy. Three Heinkel He 115 torpedo bombers approached in single file from the starboard quarter at about 180 knots passing astern of the convoy. Lieutenant Stone was at his fire control station on the bridge directing his gunners.

Stone's after-action report describes how the planes came out of a snow squall that had produced a low-weather ceiling and seemed to be planning to circle the convoy. Just as the leading plane was slightly forward of the *Harnett*'s beam, it banked sharply to make a torpedo run between two escort ships, and the other two followed. According to Stone, the *Harnett* "opened up with the 5"/38 with a 6-second fuse setting with the object of keeping them well off if possible. At the same time the escorts opened with a cross fire of what looked like 20 mm" fire.

Squadron of Heinkel He 115s of Kü.Fl.Gr. 506 musters in List, Island of Sylt, Schleswig-Holstein, Germany, circa 1940. *Courtesy of Tore Eggan, Krigsbilder.net*

I remember the deafening roar of the *Harnett*'s guns as the plane was approaching, and our magazines emptied quickly. The Navy loader in my gun tub was yelling for more ammunition and I ran to the nearby magazine for more.

As Stone wrote:

> All the planes came through the escorts safely, and we opened up with the four port 20mms at a range of between 1400 and 1700 yards. At outside 1000 yards, the leading plane veered to its left and there was a definite bluish-white flame on its pontoon. Obviously, it had been hit by either salvos of the 3"/50, the 5"/38 or the 20mm. When the leading plane was broad off our port bow, the 3"/50 scored a direct hit at a one second fuse setting

Convoy course ⇧

⑥ Airplane 2 escaped, but was badly damaged

Royal Navy Destroyer

Royal Navy Destroyer

③ Airplane 1 crashed

Royal Navy Destroyer

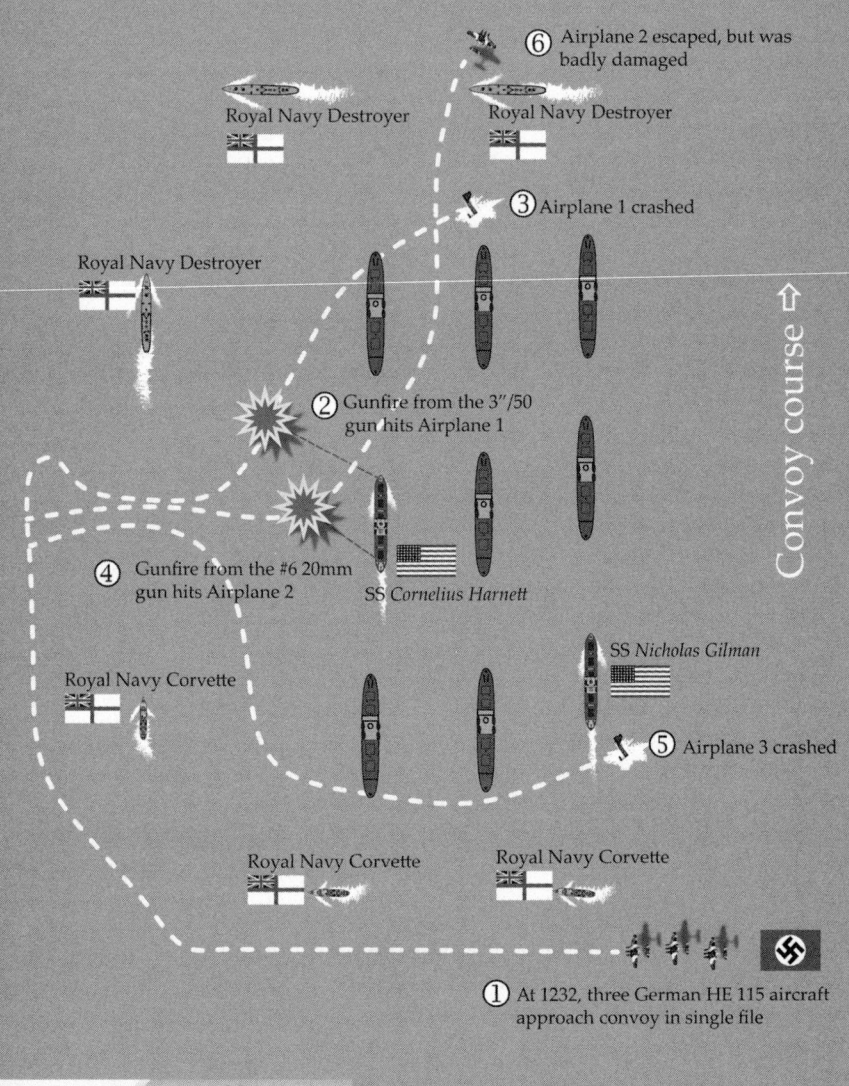

② Gunfire from the 3"/50 gun hits Airplane 1

④ Gunfire from the #6 20mm gun hits Airplane 2

SS *Cornelius Harnett*

SS *Nicholas Gilman*

Royal Navy Corvette

⑤ Airplane 3 crashed

Royal Navy Corvette

Royal Navy Corvette

① At 1232, three German HE 115 aircraft approach convoy in single file

Location of diagram

LIMITS OF GERMAN AIR STRIKES
WINTER CONVOY ROUTE
Hammerfest
Kirkenes
Murmansk
Tromsø
Narvik
ARCTIC CIRCLE

Diagram of 24 January 1943 attack based on LT Stone's sketch from Action Report by Joshua Smith.

to burst at 750 yards. Marko Jurasevich, gun captain. The plane burst into flames, passed in front of our column one leader and hit the water forward and to the left of column two. It floated down between columns one and two with only its tail showing.

The second plane came in broad on our port beam within 500 to 700 yards into a barrage of 20mm, and then banked sharply to its left when it was definitely hit on its fuselage and wings by at least 9 to 12 rounds from the No. 6 20mm on the flying bridge aft with Wilbert J. Warren GM1 firing. Just after it banked, it dropped one or two torpedoes which went ahead of our bow towards ships 11 and 21, then out ahead of the convoy and slightly to the right where two destroyers fired at it then appeared to go into a snow squall. The plane was smoking when off our port bow. The third plane veered to its right when about 1300 yards out, flew abeam of ship No. 13 and circled to the stern of the convoy where shots were heard.

Comments later in Stone's report reinforce the scuttlebutt we had heard that the *Harnett* had one of the first 5"/38s mounted on any Liberty ships. None of us midshipmen had been trained on this gun at Kings Point, where we had worked the less advanced 5"/51. It is unlikely that the Heinkel crews were expecting such a well-armed Liberty ship. The merchant ships of JW-52 mounted such a huge wall of fire I was amazed that any of the enemy planes escaped.

It was clear to me that with its large guns throwing shells 3" and 5" in diameter, the *Harnett* put up more lead in that engagement than any other merchant ship in the convoy. I am also confident that none had as cool, fearless, and competent a gunnery officer in combat as the *Harnett*. The midshipmen all later agreed that Stone was an even better officer in our eyes after his magnificent performance in our first engagement of the voyage. As for Stone, he now seemed to pace the deck less often after the crew's baptism of fire.

Sixty years later, when I first came across Lieutenant Stone's account of the action, I was startled by the credits he applied. I always believed that the gunner in charge of the 3"/50 bow gun that downed the lead plane was the wiry little gunner's mate Joe Tarczali. He was considered an old salt by the midshipmen who respected him immensely as a gunner. Stone credited the hit to gun captain Marko Jurasevich, who I do not remember at all as a member of any of the gun crews that day. I recall that the midshipmen believed that Tarczali was responsible for the hit, and we all personally congratulated him right after the action. It is presumptuous of me to question Lieutenant Stone's account of the episode, especially as I have such a high regard for him, but I will always believe that Tarczali got that Heinkel.

Another vivid exploit of Seaman Tarczali came during the most violent storm of our outbound voyage, which I mentioned in the preceding chapter. Sixteen drums of lubricating oil broke their moorings and were rolling around on the foredeck. One sprung a leak that soon made the cold deck as slippery as glass. Tarczali was trying to make his way forward in the dark to check on the condition of the bow gun when he lost his footing on the oily deck and was very nearly washed overboard.

Immediately after the attack of the Heinkel aircraft, there was much discussion between the watch and gunnery officers regarding problems encountered. Several changes in procedure were implemented to prepare for our next enemy action, and one of Stone's new orders was especially important to the midshipmen. At the height of the battle, the 20mm cartridge magazines emptied much faster than they could be refilled, and Stone's furious barrage caused several gunners to run out of ammunition at critical moments. After the attack, some of the snail-shaped magazines lay empty at the door to the small ammunition storeroom aft of the boiler stack on the boat deck. Proper refilling of the cartridge magazines was critical and had to be done with skill and care. Allowing the spring-loaded projectiles to tilt while refilling increased the rate of their jamming in the gun. The tilting problem was made worse by the grease that covered the shells and by the cotton gloves the loader had to wear in the bitter cold. And when tilting occurred, dismantling the cartridge magazine was a thirty-minute task.

Unfortunately, some of the merchant marine crew who had not been trained as loaders tried to refill magazines. They soon jammed, and the top gunner had to dismantle and refill them later. Seeing that the *Harnett*'s four midshipmen were adept at the task, Stone pulled us off the 20mms and reassigned our battle stations to filling cartridges in the ammunition room on the topside. I quickly realized that my new battle station was an even more hazardous position. It was unlikely that anyone working in that small space could survive a shell blast there.

I discovered another account of the attack in the diary of James Harcus, a Scots seaman aboard *Ocean Faith*, a British cargo ship in JW-52. The Harcus diary records ocean temperatures of 28°F, and his writing reminded me of the flurry of depth charges dropped to fend off U-boats during the evening after the bombers' attack. Harcus wrote that the bombers chose the *Ocean Faith* as their target, but all torpedoes missed. Then he claims, "We shot one down," and a few days later his diary reports that a British destroyer took credit for the second downed Heinkel.

In Murmansk, someone painted a swastika on the *Harnett*'s smokestack, celebrating our antiaircraft victory. Later, as I walked around the Murmansk docks I discovered that all the ships in our convoy had painted a swastika on their stacks to boast of shooting down one of the German planes. Exaggerations were common. To me the convincing evidence of gunner credits in the battle with the Heinkel bombers was the Silver Star that Lieutenant Stone was awarded for this action.

Weather, the persistent enemy of the *Harnett*, returned to haunt her. The convoy became so shrouded by low-hanging clouds, snow squalls, fog, and heavy seas that two days out of Murmansk, we lost contact with the convoy for twenty-four hours. As if getting lost were not scary enough, another danger created some anxious moments. The officers on the bridge discovered we had no charts for those waters. The odds against the *Harnett*'s survival increased. We all knew that being lost in those waters at that time was a formula for disaster.

Many anxious hours passed, and only the foul weather kept us from getting sunk by German aircraft or the wolf pack on the convoy's trail. So we were overjoyed on 27 January when we were found by an ally, a small Russian patrol craft, as we passed a small island group that we later determined to be Iokanka. The islands, about 175 miles beyond Kola Inlet, had become a landmark for ships lost from convoys. Kola was the opening to the fjord that leads twenty-five miles upriver to Murmansk.

The Soviet vessel led the stray Liberty back to Kola, where we embarked a tight-lipped Russian officer who qualified as a pilot for those waters. He was the first Russian most of the crew had ever seen, and he naturally became the object of much curiosity. The pilot declined to answer the crew's many questions, pleading ignorance of the language. As he guided the ship overnight into Murmansk, those not on duty got some much-needed sleep after a traumatic experience at sea.

Chapter 6

Life in the Bull's-Eye

Murmansk was obscured by cloud cover on 5 February when the *Harnett* dropped anchor in the Murmansk River between the Kola Inlet and the docks. At about 1100, Commander Sam Frankel, the U.S. Navy attaché, came aboard with the Murmansk port commissar in tow. They conferred with Captain Carver and had lunch in the wardroom where the commissar introduced himself to all of us present. The Russian was meticulously dressed and very friendly, spoke excellent English, and replied in the affirmative when I asked him if he was a member of the Communist Party.

The U.S. Navy attaché Frankel was also impressive—tall, polished, and a graduate of the Naval Academy. He had been on duty for several months in Murmansk. During lunch, the sun peeped through, and one of the *Harnett*'s deck officers asked the attaché the whereabouts of the German bombers that were supposed to be bombing the harbor around the clock. The commander leaned over the table, peered out the porthole, and answered, "If this sun keeps shining, you'll see them in less than an hour."

The words were hardly out of his mouth when a screaming Stuka dive-bomber nearly hit the ship with a powerful bomb. The *Harnett* lurched from the explosion as the general quarters alarm sent all crewmen and officers scurrying for life jackets and battle stations. That ended lunch for the officers and midshipmen. The remainder of the afternoon was spent on alert. All eyes were riveted to the sky where an awesome display of aerial

German Stukas attack convoy at Murmansk docks.
Painting by James Rae

dogfights was under way between the Russian VVS (air force) and the Stukas (Junkers Ju 87s) of the Luftwaffe. Even the least informed observer could see that the German aircraft and pilots were superior.

During our stay, nearly every Soviet fighter plane defending Murmansk and its ships seemed to be a Bell P-39 Airacobra. Although not known for the high-altitude performance that British and American fighter pilots prized most highly, the fighter was durable and well armed, with good visibility and comparatively easy handling.

The *Harnett*'s crew soon realized that whenever the weather was clear, there would be round-the-clock bombing. I was told that our ship's log recorded 153 air alerts during her twenty-eight days in Murmansk, an average of one raid every four and a half hours. Even the briefest alerts required three hours to clear. It felt as though we had a bull's-eye painted on the ship's deck.

Many of the attacks by the Germans were nuisance raids, mounted for psychological effect only. Rumor had it that the Russians sometimes sounded the alert even before the Stukas left their bases. This was possible, it was said, because sound detectors perched high on the hills above Murmansk could pick up the noise of planes warming up on the runway at Petsamo, Finland, a field in German hands about sixty miles away by air.

In early 1943, the city of Murmansk was little more than a pile of rubble except for two hotels. The more popular of the two, the Arktika Hotel, was badly damaged, and only its two lower floors remained intact. At its International Club, a lounge on the ground floor, one could get a cup of Russian tea and some American cookies. A library was adjacent to the lounge, but the only reading material found there was propaganda extolling the heroic exploits of the glorious Red

Army or the gallant Red Navy. On rare occasions when bad weather prevented air attacks, a Russian-language movie might be shown. Once I saw a memorable Soviet film on the life of Peter the Great, but I understood none of the dialogue.

Many American seamen went to the International Club in the vain hope of hearing some news of the campaign in North Africa. Each evening, the Soviet English-speaking newscaster mounted the stage in the club to read the latest news. It invariably included reports on the latest victories of Soviet forces on the Eastern Front. I was present when a truly significant victory was announced; the "glorious Red Army" had just retaken Rostov. Everyone cheered. However, I doubt that any member of the *Harnett*'s crew ever heard news of the U.S. Army in the North African campaign, then under way.

Nothing of any value could be bought in Murmansk. I managed to find six Red Army cloth shoulder patches that served very well as drinking glass coasters, and I brought them home as souvenirs. I encountered my first female barber at the hotel. This kindly woman did a respectable business cutting the hair of scores of Allied seamen and tried to make us feel welcome and appreciated. However, hygiene went the way of survival in that grim place. For months afterwards, my scalp itched painfully, and no hair tonic I tried brought relief.

Within most units, there is usually one rude and offensive member who embarrasses everyone. Years later, journalists would dub such a character "the ugly American." The *Harnett*'s ugly American was George Smelser. His rating was able seaman, and he served as the ship's shop steward for the National Maritime Union. During my brief seagoing career, I met my share of lowbrow sailors, but Smelser ranked the lowest of all. As the crew's loud mouth, his mindless chatter and opinionated arguments blasted from the crew's quarters. As shop steward he insisted on serving as spokesman for any crewman with a complaint. Most of all, Smelser loved to find an error in the payroll figures of Hardcastle, the ship's purser. We midshipmen were certain that he resented our presence and considered us to be anti-union. I stayed clear of Smelser and avoided being introduced to him throughout our voyage together.

I was in the International Club one evening when Smelser was spouting off. He was a short man with a size 50 belly that hung over his size 34 waist trousers with difficulty. That evening he was at his worst. After pointing out various Russian deficiencies to his beleaguered and captive Russian hostess, he huffed, "Answer me one thing. Us Americans risk our lives to bring you damned Russians all this war material. Then when we get here, there's nothing to do ashore. Why can't you have some beer or drinks for us and some girls to dance with? We'd ship out to Berlin if we knew we'd have a good time there!"

In spite of Smelser's protest, there was no shortage of alcohol among the merchant ship crews, as shown by the report of the gunnery officer of the Panamanian freighter *El Oriente*, one of the ships in our convoy. Her armed guard officer wrote that the ship's skipper "was continually drunk with most of the ship's officers and particularly when at anchorage.... The chief engineer has either been drunk or under the effects of alcohol ever since I joined this ship. On occasions at sea when he has been called to the engine room he has not been able to make it because of his condition."

On my last visit ashore in Murmansk on 27 February, I witnessed a Stuka's deadly attack on *El Oriente*. I was alone and had to pass through numerous gates to leave the docks. At each stood a woman sentry with a rifle and its needle-pointed bayonet, and the only English each seemed to know was the stern demand "Your pass, comrade!" After clearing the last gate and entering the town's streets, I reached a hill high above the harbor. Looking down on the docks below, I heard the frightening whine of a Stuka dive-bomber screaming down toward the pier to my left. The Stuka pulled out of its dive just as its bomb struck the stern deckhouse of the *El Oriente*, putting it out of commission and killing four men of the armed guard crew. I shivered because *El Oriente* was standing at the same dock as the *Harnett*. Somehow, the *El Oriente* was patched up in time to join our convoy, which departed three days later.

James Harcus of the *Ocean Faith* also mentioned the dive-bombing of the *El Oriente* in his diary, referring to the ship as "the *Lorentis.*"

> Sat 27th
> We have had a lovely clear day today & were settling down for a quiet afternoon when we heard a plane diving. He dropped a bomb not far from us on the starboard side & another on a ship at the wharf we left on Thursday. Some of the lads told us it was the ship that took our place, a Panamanian the Lorentis & she was lying the opposite way round from us & was hit on the stern right in the gun pit, a few number not known were killed.

Later, as the *Ocean Faith* moved to another wharf, Harcus noted that another ship, the *Empire Portia*, was being towed up the river with its no. 2 hold on fire, another Stuka victim. He also described how four German aircraft attacked Murmansk, dropping mines in the river and closing the port for shipping until minesweepers could clear the channel.

Female laborers were everywhere in Murmansk and they made up most of the stevedore crews unloading the supply ships. Their shifts were twenty-four hours on and twenty-four hours off. There was no fraternizing whatsoever, and the women responded not at all to friendly overtures. Neither did the few Russian men we encountered. Any men we saw would have been classified 4-F by an American draft board. All able-bodied men were at the battlefront.

I believe that many of the Russian workers were political prisoners, forced into slave labor and starving. One story I later heard about the unloading of the *Harnett*'s cargo involved a stevedore caught eating from a tin of canned meat that had broken open when a cargo sling failed. As the hungry worker helped himself to the spilled contents, a guard took him behind a stack of cargo and shot him on the spot. Such stories contributed immensely to the depressing atmosphere that enveloped Murmansk.

Adding to the hazardous environment was the shower of German incendiary bombs that fell on the ships and docks during each nighttime raid. These magnesium explosives were fifteen inches long and two and a half inches in diameter. A large number of them were duds, and those that ignited could be easily extinguished by dunking them in a bucket of water. Every morning after a terrifying night of bombing, Soviet children showed up on the docks carrying the unexploded bombs, which they tried to trade to sailors for cigarettes or Russian rubles. If none landed on your ship, thirty rubles could buy a souvenir that could be made into a lamp base. I had no desire to carry home one of these deadly missiles, knowing that an accident could be disastrous, and Navy bulletins warned us not to attempt to smuggle any aboard.

On the docks, long delays in unloading the merchant ships were caused largely by Soviet incompetence. The delays spelled mounting peril for the convoy crews as the incessant bombings continued. I happened to be eating lunch in the wardroom when Commander Frankel, the naval attaché, met once again with the Soviet port commissar. The exasperated Frankel was furious that a convoy of American ships (including the *Harnett*) was trapped for another week in Murmansk due to Soviet bungling. Frankel complained about the danger to American seamen while the Soviets ignored logistical suggestions from the American consulate. The commander ticked off example after example of the Soviets' intransigence and cavalier attitude. Every *Harnett* officer in the room was in hearty agreement, but the little uniformed commissar only offered more bureaucratic excuses in flawless English.

I can never forget the numbing fear that accompanied the air raids. At dockside, my battle station duties gave me no satisfaction because most of the bombers were high-altitude planes that were out of the range of the 20mm guns. We were especially helpless during nighttime air raids because blackouts prevented mustering at the guns.

During the brief hours of daylight between raids, my duties involved helping the deck engineer maintain the deck machinery, a constant task because of the extreme cold. We could never persuade the Russians operating the winches to keep a steady flow of steam filtering through their steam engines to prevent equipment freezing during long periods of idleness. We were almost constantly on deck, often in temperatures that dipped as low as −35°F, using a portable steam hose to thaw frozen equipment.

The nadir of our time at the Murmansk docks was 19 February, when wave after wave of bombers attacked. When I read James Harcus's account years later, it was like reliving a nightmare.

> He dropped bombs about fifty yards away in the water & another on the quay. We got the blast but no damage was done but the "Temple Arch" had her Radio Room smashed & most of her bridge ports. The Yank ahead had two of the crew slightly injured. The ack ack guns are sure sending up some muck and we saw the vapour trail of one bomber being turned. He dropped his bombs on a hill, a swell place for them. These raiders have dropped a great many incendiaries but they were soon put out. Two of the planes were caught in the searchlights & they sure got a peppering. They let their bombs go as soon as the light picked them up & we could see them leave the plane. The last wave was at six o'clock so after six hours of it without a break we are pretty tired. I hope he doesn't think of coming back. He started at seven o'clock in the evening, it is a beautiful night, a full moon & not so much as a cloud in sight. The huns first attacks started a large fire in the town & he dropped a stick of bombs close alongside us at the same time. The

ship heaved & shook but as they were in the water they did no damage. He then dropped a load of incendiaries at the head of the quay but they were soon put out. He continued coming in waves & still we can't see any signs of a cloud or snow shower.

In his diary entry for the following day, Harcus mentions his conversation with a Russian officer who reported that the shore batteries shot down seven planes on the nineteenth and three early in the morning of the twentieth. "We are trying to give them as good as we get," wrote Harcus.

In the darkness, the *Harnett*'s guns were silent to avoid exposing the ship's position while there were more supplies to unload. I hunkered down in the wardroom with several others while the bombers dropped their bomb loads and the shore batteries responded with an enormous barrage. That night was the most horrendous of all, and I wondered how many near misses we could endure before the real thing struck. I still have a souvenir from that raid: a piece of shrapnel from a bomb that ruptured a handrail on one of the ladders on our boat deck.

It was with much rejoicing that the weary *Harnett* crew received the orders to button up and head for home. No crew member looked back wistfully toward Murmansk as the *Harnett* pulled away from its moorings. She headed down the Murmansk River to join the large convoy RA-53 assembling at Kola Inlet. Everyone was eager to forget the previous four weeks. The convoy assembled under partly sunny skies near the mouth of the river on 28 February. Clearing skies demanded that we be alert, and the crew was ordered to general quarters after German reconnaissance planes appeared.

Shortly after noon, the Stukas arranged a farewell party for convoy RA-53, coming out of a partial cloud cover, their favorite weather. Once in range of the ships, they glided in with engines off and began their bomb run. Then, engines restarted, the wind sirens mounted on their wings screamed a sound that never failed to startle gunners on the Liberty ships. Hovering overhead were a few Russians in Airacobras. This led to one of the tragedies of the *Harnett* on the Murmansk Run.

Lieutenant Stone had the fingers of his wary gunners on their triggers. The Stuka zeroing in on the *Harnett* got a warm reception from a 20mm gun located on the starboard side just aft of midships. The Stuka pilot unloaded his bomb frighteningly close to us while under fire from that gun. The ship rocked from the explosion as the gunner continued his fire on the Stuka.

The alert Stone saw an Airacobra on the tail of the Stuka and called, "Cease fire!" I was standing inside the gun tub and despite the rattle and roar, I could hear Stone's order to cease fire. For some reason the gunner failed to heed the command and kept firing as the Airacobra came into range in hot pursuit of the Stuka. I recognized the plane as Russian but knew it was too late. Stone ran over to our gun tub, pulled off his glove, and with it slapped the gunner across the face, who then released his grip on the trigger. I heard Stone shout, "Damn it, I said, 'Cease fire!'"

Sadly, the Russian crashed with a loud explosion into the river near the left bank. All of us were stunned at the horrific turn of events. I was especially distressed because I had so much pride in my gun crew and in Stone, a fine gunnery officer. Although the German had also been hit, he miraculously escaped over the hills that rose above the river.

The convoy resumed its assembly and departed Murmansk on 1 March, and nobody was sad for the farewell. Although

Friendly fire by gunners of the *Harnett* downs Soviet aircraft.
Painting by James Rae

the Royal Navy was less visible in the remote stretches of the Kola Inlet than it had been along the River Clyde in January, our close and distant escorts were formidable. Records of the British Admiralty show that our ocean screen sailed the day after the convoy and included two heavy cruisers, HMS *Cumberland* and *Norfolk*. The senior officer for the force sailed in the light cruiser *Belfast*, which survives today as a museum ship on the Thames in London.

Our through-escort included an antiaircraft cruiser, HMS *Scylla;* four destroyers that had been battle fleet escorts for JW-52, *Eclipse, Faulknor, Inglefield,* and *Obedient;* and eight other destroyers, *Boadicea, Fury, Impulsive, Intrepid, Milne, Obdurate,* ORP *Orkan,* and *Orwell.* The destroyers were organized into two flotillas, one commanded by the captain of the *Inglefield* and the other by the captain of the *Milne.* Also with us were four corvettes — *Bergamot, Lotus, Poppy,* and *Starwort* — as well as several other Navy vessels from our outbound convoy — *Northern Pride, St. Elstan,* and RFA *Oligarch*.

As for distant cover, the battle fleet was stationed far to the southwest during our convoy and included the battleships HMS *King George V* (under the commander in chief of the Home Fleet) and *Howe,* and light cruisers *Glasgow* and *Berwick.* A screen of destroyers escorted the navy force, and four British submarines patrolled the convoy route: *Truculent, Simoon, Sportsman,* and *Sea Nymph.* Once we reached Iceland, a local escort of destroyers — HMS *Ledbury, Meynell, Pytchley,* and *Vivacious* — would accompany us to Loch Ewe.

Among the merchantmen, only one ship of outbound convoy JW-52 did not accompany the *Harnett* for the homebound voyage — *Empire Portia,* which diarist James Harcus had seen in tow after a Stuka dive-bomber set her afire.

Other merchant ships that had missed earlier homebound convoys joined our convoy for this voyage, including five Liberty ships — the *John H. B. Latrobe, J. L. M. Curry, Richard Bassett, Richard Bland,* and *Ralph Waldo Emerson* — and eight other American vessels — *Chester Valley, Executive, Gulfwing, Jefferson Myers, Oremar, Vermont, West Gotomska,* and *Yorkmar.* Also joining were three British ships, *Empire Archer* and the tankers *Empire Emerald* and *San Cipriano,* and the *Calobre* (Panama) and *Mossoviet* (Soviet Union).

War Shipping Administration records of our convoy reveal how concerned the Navy was about the effects of sea ice on our ships, noting that propeller tips had been seriously damaged on the outbound convoys. It sparked a dispute with the Soviets that Commander Sam Frankel reported by coded cable to Averell Harriman, ambassador to the Soviet Union and the envoy Roosevelt had dispatched in 1941 to negotiate the Lend-Lease deal with the Soviets. The message told that more ballast was needed on ships to ensure that their propellers would be submerged at least four feet below the surface to prevent the abrasion of floating ice.

The Soviets were adamant that they had agreed to load no more than 1,500 tons per ship. Some ship masters loaded twice that amount, and as a result there were insufficient loads to supply all ships in the convoy. Among the cargoes of the ships lucky enough to be loaded first were lumber, pulpwood, horsehair, sheep casings, furs, skins, and minerals, including magnesite, apatite, potassium chloride, and chrome ore. Unfortunately, the Liberty ships *Harnett* and *Nicholas Gilman* were among the last in line for loading.

The solution proposed by the Soviets was to load more lumber, but that would require waiting for its shipment from the Dvina River, more than 500 miles away. Unprocessed ore was the only available ballast remaining. The masters of the two new Liberty ships probably had little interest in loading such rough cargo in the holds of their newly built vessels.

Several ships in the convoy listed passengers, primarily Russian sailors dispatched to collect vessels for the Northern Fleet and Allied survivors stranded in Russian ports after their ships were sunk or destroyed. Those ships with passenger manifests included the *Empire Clarion*, the ship in which the convoy commodore, Vice Admiral Malcolm Lennon Goldsmith, had sailed to Murmansk. Perhaps to make room for passengers, Goldsmith transferred his command to the smaller *Temple Arch* for the return voyage.

Although years later I laughed when reading Harcus's comment that his ship loaded manure for ballast in Murmansk, the *Harnett*'s lack of ballast later added to our miseries in the Norwegian Sea.

Chapter 7

The Treacherous Voyage of Convoy RA-53

In our rush to escape the dangers of Murmansk, we failed to heed the Russians' reputation for ignoring cleanup regulations for ship holds. Once under way, I was ordered to help one of the engine

Convoy JW-53 arrives Kola Inlet 27 January 1943. Photo from escort destroyer HMS *Inglefield*. Four days later, the *Inglefield* would lead one of the destroyer flotillas escorting the *Harnett* and RA-53 on the outbound voyage to Scotland. *Imperial War Museum*

room wipers clean out the bilge pump suction basin (also known as the rose box) in no. 2 cargo hold. Water was building up there because the Russian laborers had failed to clean out many bushels of loose navy beans spilled in the hold. As soon as the beans got wet, they began to swell and clogged the rose box, rendering the pumps inoperative. Under light from a trouble lamp on a long extension cord, we filled a five-gallon bucket many times with the fermented and swollen beans and lifted them out of the hold by rope line. It took nearly two days to clear the jams.

Early on the fourth day out of Murmansk we began to hear the sound of depth charges resonating in the holds and engine room. They were dropped by our escorts to fight back the U-boats stalking us. As the morning progressed I went topside to join my fellow cadets for coffee, and we could see the other ships of the convoy plowing the waves. The ship was in 72°44'N, 11°27'E.

The skies were overcast and the seas were relatively calm when someone suddenly yelled, "Look! There's a couple of porpoises." I thought they were porpoises, too, until I heard the mate on duty shout, "Porpoises hell! Those are torpedoes." "Hard left!" he ordered the helmsman at the wheel.

The torpedoes were headed our way, and I felt the ship lurch to port as the weapons crossed our bow barely thirty feet ahead. The general quarters alarm drove everyone to battle stations. Then came an explosion just off our port bow as the torpedoes that had missed us slammed into the American freighter *Executive*. She was hit in no. 4 hold just forward of the superstructure on the starboard side. The blast blew off the hatch covers and booms of the hold, which rapidly flooded. Seconds after the *Executive* was hit at 0926 hours, the Liberty ship *Richard Bland* also took a torpedo. Both were victims of a single spread of three fish from *U-255*, Reinhart Reche commanding.

On board the *Executive*, the torpedo's explosion set in motion a catastrophic failure as panic engulfed the crew. Lifeboats were launched without orders and men died. I saw one starboard lifeboat just aft of the superstructure being launched and lowered haphazardly. A windlass lowering the stern end of the boat dropped its load and hung vertically as men were hurled into the icy sea. I saw one or two men in the craft crushed between the dangling boat and the ship's hull.

Then the bow end of the boat was dropped, and it left the ship with no crewmen aboard. I believe iced-up windlasses were to blame. Our own deck crews were constantly freeing the lifeboat davits and windlasses of ice. I later learned that one member of the U.S. Navy Armed Guard crew was killed along with three officers and five crewmen of the *Executive*. The ship did not appear to be sinking although it was listing, and all hands abandoned ship. An hour later, the drifting ship was scuttled by the gunfire of a British destroyer.

The torpedo hitting the *Bland* did not explode but passed through both sides of the ship leaving large holes on each side. The *Bland* started taking on water and listing to starboard. She was knocked out of line but later rejoined the convoy and gamely steamed ahead with a cracked deck and a ruptured collision bulkhead. Just as she rejoined us, a full-sized squadron of Junkers Ju 88 bombers attacked the convoy, and every ship opened fire with all guns. Bombs straddled the *Harnett* but failed to score a direct hit. The convoy's fire drove them away, and I spent several hours reloading 20mm gun magazines under threatening skies as the weather worsened.

Years later I learned that five days after this first attack, the *U-255* struck the *Bland* three more times over five hours. The *Bland* broke in two and the stern section sank. I remember that our radio operator picked up her distress call, but as we ourselves were lost, we were helpless to assist. The *Bland*'s forward section was later towed to Iceland where the ship was declared a total loss. Of the crew, some were picked up after thirteen hours in boats, but fifteen armed guards, thirteen crewmen, five officers, and the master were never seen again.

About our convoy, U-boat historian Clay Blair wrote:

> The return convoy, RA-53, comprised of thirty merchant ships that left on March

1, was also found and attacked by German aircraft and U-boats. Reche in *U-255* sank two American ships: the 7,200-ton Liberty ship *Richard Bland* and the 5,000-ton *Executive*. A fierce arctic gale dispersed the convoy and broke the American Liberty ship *J. L. M. Curry* in half. Dietrich von der Esch in *U-586* sank a straggler, the 6,100-ton American freighter *Puerto Rican*, about three hundred miles north of Iceland. One of sixty-two men on the ship, August Wallenhaupt, survived on a raft and was rescued by the British destroyer *St. Elstan,* but he lost both legs and most of seven fingers. Counting the disabled American Liberty ship *J. H. Latrobe,* which had to be towed, 26 of the 30 merchant ships in RA-53 reached British ports.

Reinhart Reche, the skipper of *U-255* was awarded the German navy's Ritterkreuz (Knight's Cross), only the second German skipper in the Arctic force to be so honored. U-boats under his command sank ten confirmed ships with a total tonnage of 53,519. Had I known that my convoy was being stalked by such a daring commander, my worries would have doubled.

The "fierce arctic gale" Blair mentions struck us several days after the attacks. It was the worst storm I ever experienced at sea, and I now believe its ferocity saved my life. Its winds grounded the bombers, and rough seas prevented the U-boats from taking full advantage of the ships that were losing contact with one another and helplessly floundering in the terrible storm. In the event of a torpedo attack, it would have been impossible to launch lifeboats under those conditions.

No one was able to sleep with the wind howling at forty knots, and the waves were high enough to send seawater down the stack. The engineers on duty were on "throttle watch." The watch engineer used the emergency lever at the throttle to shut off steam to

U-255, painted white for Arctic camouflage, returns victorious to Narvik, Norway, with four victory pennants following attacks on convoy PQ-17, July 1942. *The National Archives of Norway. Original photograph in the collection of the Riksarkivet; Reichskommissariat, Bildarchiv, U71 "Mit dem Reichskommissar nach Nordnorwegen und Finnland 10. bis 27. Juli 1942."*

the engine whenever the ship crested a giant wave. As the pitch lifted the propeller out of the water, the propeller would spin violently, shaking the whole ship. Then as the stern dipped back into the water, the propeller would bog down unless the steam was applied immediately. No headway could be made unless the man at the throttle had a skilled hand. At the height of the gale, the *Harnett* experienced a "negative slip" during one four-hour period, losing complete headway and actually slipping astern.

While in the engine room during the gale, I had to take turns at the throttle to give a brief respite to the weary engineer on duty. Thanks to Mason, the third assistant engineer who was looking over my shoulder, I learned the rhythm. Learning that skill proved to be very valuable training when I was second assistant engineer in the Pacific and my empty ship was struggling alone in a fierce storm. On that occasion, using my throttle watch technique brought back waves of fearful memories of the 1943 storm in the Arctic.

We had lost the convoy and were alone three hundred miles northeast of Iceland. Battle stations were so frequent that only necessary shipboard duties were performed. Throughout these ordeals, I neither pulled off my clothes nor shaved for six days. Any sleep was fitful with the pitching and rolling of the ship and worries about nearby German subs. The cadets stacked our Academy-issued footlockers on top of each other to provide a brace against being rolled out of our bunks

I especially recall the terrifying distress call from the *Puerto Rican*. I dashed into the radio shack as soon as word spread of her sinking. Our guess was that the *Harnett* was less than five miles away on our port quarter when the *Puerto Rican*'s message broke the convoy's order for radio silence. Lookouts on the topside saw her distress flares. I recall that the seawater temperature was close to 20°F and the air temperature was -30°F.

Our own troubles made it impossible to search for the *Puerto Rican*'s survivors. In addition to being lost and wracked by fierce winds, I learned at breakfast that the skipper had ordered the crew to fill cargo holds 4 and 5 with seawater for ballast. During the night, the engineer on duty discovered that several bolts on the stern tube gland were sheared due to the storm's stress. This was extremely dangerous and the complete failure of the gland appeared imminent. The veteran seamen of the crew told us that if it failed, the shaft alley would flood, causing the main shaft to break, and the ship to lose all forward motion. We would be helpless.

The order to flood the two holds with seawater ballast was needed to reduce the pressure on the shaft from the buffeting sea. Unfortunately, the flooding created a new crisis that frightened me even more. All Liberty ships were equipped with sweat battens, wooden two-by-sixes mounted on brackets on the inside of the bulkheads. These served as protective spacers between the cargo and the inside of the ship's hull to prevent condensate from damaging the cargo.

Normally, the sweat battens were removed before seawater was pumped in as ballast, but the ferocity of the storm and a frantically busy crew made this impossible. Deck hands reported that the battens were being ripped from their brackets by the force of the sloshing seawater as the ship rolled and pitched. The detached wood battens were smashing loudly against the wall of the shaft alley.

The cross section of a typical shaft alley resembles a Roman arch. On a Liberty ship a longitudinal wall of half-inch-thick steel ran the full length of no. 5 hold, welded to the top of the eight-foot-high shaft alley. The weight of the ballast water sloshing back and forth in the hold soon wrought havoc on the longitudinal wall. Around noon, a two-foot-long crack developed where the wall met the top of the alley, and a stream of seawater was flowing into the shaft alley at a rate of about ten gallons per minute. It was crucial that the seawater ballast be pumped out, which was usually handled by individual pumps. However, splinters from the smashed wooden battens clogged the rose boxes, causing the pumps to lose suction. The damage was so thorough that the splinters resembled shredded wheat cereal.

The seawater ballast was fast destroying the ship, and wood splinters in the pump suction prevented its removal. At about 1300 hours, the chief engineer ordered me to follow him to the shaft alley abaft the crack, ten feet away from the escape ladder that led to the main deck. The crack had increased in length by a foot or so, and the inflow was increasing. The shaft alley bilge pump ran intermittently, straining to keep ahead of the incoming water.

I helped the chief carry a manual drill with a one-inch drill bit. He said we were going to create what he called an "old man" rig by drilling holes so that the water could flow out to be pumped by the shaft alley bilge pump. We started the difficult task; within several minutes we had drilled three holes at the base of the shaft alley, and water came pouring out unimpeded. He explained that the wood splinters were floating at the top and therefore could not plug the freshly drilled holes. He said this was a desperate measure but there was no choice. As we began the fourth hole, there was a loud cracking at the break. I looked up in horror as an eighteen-inch-square hunk of metal was ripped away. A gush of water poured down and swamped us.

"Let's get out of here, cadet!" yelled the chief as he started up the escape ladder. By the time I scrambled to the ladder, I was soaked and needed no reminder to follow him. I had never before climbed that completely darkened ladder and was at least twenty feet behind him by the time he reached the top. It was a fast but lonely climb. As we emerged and started across the deck, our clothes froze instantly making it difficult to run. By the time we reached the engine room, the crew on watch had secured the shaft alley door closed. The chief ordered the door to be propped open slightly, then he flooded the bilge and the huge pumps began their task.

Meanwhile, the engine was kept running with its propeller shaft completely submerged. All available hands turned to and were either operating the pumps, changing pump filters, or hauling out splinter fragments. I cleaned filters until I was ready to drop. Several hours later, the water finally got below the rupture in the shaft alley, and we were able to pump the remaining water out and inspect the shaft. Fortunately, all bearings and lubricating equipment were intact and could be returned to normal. All that I learned about the shaft alley equipment would prove invaluable two years later in the Pacific during another encounter with the enemy.

The *Harnett* was still threatened, but we were thankful that a crisis had been averted. No U-boats had found us, and the storm seemed to be slackening. The officers concluded that the severity of the storm had kept the submarines off our trail, but we were still lost from the convoy, and the fate of the *Puerto Rican* was sobering. The *Harnett* set a course toward Iceland by dead reckoning as the dense cloud cover made it impossible to determine our exact position.

I worked in the shaft alley helping to repair damage and clean up the mess. As the sea was settling down after dinner, I collapsed on my bunk and slept for eight hours straight. It was the first time in days that I felt hopeful of cheating death on the Murmansk Run after all.

Around 1400 hours on the next day, the general quarters alarm sounded. Racing above and certain that another U-boat attack was imminent, I donned my heavy coat and life preserver and grabbed my emergency kit. Just as I reached my battle station at the topside ammunition magazine, a cheer went up on the deck and a U.S. Navy floatplane, a PBY Catalina, flew over the ship. The alarm had been sounded because a squall at first prevented the lookouts from identifying the aircraft as friend or foe.

The pilot signaled us by blinker. I remember joking happily with my fellow cadets that we were lucky Lieutenant Stone had not blown the Catalina out of the sky as soon as it broke through the clouds, but it easily could have happened. Everyone was on edge. The plane radioed a nearby Free Poland destroyer that had been ordered to find and escort us to Iceland. The friendly warship was steaming toward our position at flank speed.

All hands aboard the *Harnett* were celebrating our good luck, and the cooks prepared a better-than-usual dinner. Later, when it arrived, the destroyer gave us our position and circled for hours as we steamed along. I returned to my Sea Project after dark and worked on it for a few hours.

My studies were interrupted by the faint sound of an explosion, followed by another call to battle stations. Two of my roommates who had been sleeping scrambled to get dressed while I put on my heavy coat and life jacket. I rushed out on the port boat deck and found a mass of crewmen milling about.

Word spread that the Polish destroyer had been torpedoed ahead of us. A lookout was observing that vessel off our starboard bow when it disappeared behind a dense squall. Shortly afterward there was a blinding flash and a loud explosion. Officers on the bridge assumed that the destroyer had been sunk.

Captain Carver ordered all hands to suit up and prepare for a possible evacuation in case the *Harnett* met the same misfortune. I had already dressed and had nothing to do but pray and contemplate my fate aboard a sitting duck north of the Arctic Circle in the dead of winter. An hour passed with no further word of the Polish destroyer. After considerable prayer, a strange calm came over me as I accepted that I had very little chance of survival.

My thoughts were interrupted by a summons to the chief engineer's quarters. As I entered his stateroom, I saw him standing with a half-pint bottle of brandy in his hand.

"Cadet, I want to ask a favor of you."

"Yes, sir. What is it?"

"Members of that watch in the engine room are going through hell right now. There's a good chance that we're going to get hit any minute. They know that they won't have a chance if a fish hits the engine room. The law prevents me from giving liquor to men on watch. Will you take this bottle down there and give them a drink and come back up?"

My gut turned over as I answered, "Sure, chief." I took the bottle and headed below, as frightened as I ever remember being. As I descended the ladders to the engine room, I expected a hit any second, which would leave me trapped below the waterline where rescue is often hopeless in a torpedo attack. The three men on watch were standing together near the throttle, all eyes on me as I descended the last flight. They quickly gathered around, eager to hear the news. I forced a grin on my face.

"What's the latest?" asked Mason, third assistant engineer.

"Nothing new," I shrugged. Then as casually as I could muster, "The chief just sent me down to give you guys a drink, to cheer you up."

They took turns at the bottle and I followed suit as if I were in no hurry. "What's the latest you heard?" asked the oiler.

"Well the officers on the bridge don't see anything. The word I got is that it looks pretty good since, if we were gonna get hit, the sub would have done it before now," I lied.

I stood around for five minutes or so as if I wasn't very worried and tried to calm them by answering their questions with white lies, and all of them thanked me profusely. After passing the bottle around again, I promised that I would let them know of any new developments. I went above, returned what was left of the chief's bottle to him, passed on their hearty thanks to him, and answered his questions about their morale. Then I went to the room of Wesley Fowler, the radio technician, to hear the latest.

Nothing happened for fifteen minutes or so, and I began to hope there might be something to the lies that I told in the engine room. Then cheers rang out on deck and one of my roommates came rushing down the ladder to tell us that a lookout had just spotted the Polish destroyer; it had not been sunk after all. With good news to report I dashed back down to the engine room to report "all's well" to the watch. They fairly burst with immense relief. Another crisis had passed. Perhaps we had a chance of survival after all.

I turned in about 0230, thanked a merciful God for seeing us through, and had a good night's sleep. Later there was scuttlebutt that the Polish destroyer had located a U-boat ahead of us and dropped a depth charge at a shallow depth, exploding the U-boat just as the destroyer disappeared from our view behind a dense squall. The destroyer had since been circling us in the darkness unseen.

Our change in speed awakened me early the next morning after a night of relief and sound sleep. One of my roommates who had been on watch said that we were following the destroyer into Seydisfjordur, in eastern Iceland, where we were to drop anchor and wait until we could rejoin our convoy, which was departing soon for Scotland. At lunch I learned of another deadly threat we had nearly blundered into. While following the escort into port, the *Harnett* had no charts for the harbor and was unaware that the narrow channel threaded through mine fields designed to fend off German U-boats. The skipper, sailing blind, had strayed too far to starboard. The destroyer blinked out an emergency signal: "Danger. You are standing in a minefield. Steer to port now."

The tightness in my gut returned when I heard of this close call. I remember wondering, what is going to happen to us next? At that moment, I realized I would not feel safe again until we reached our destination on the River Clyde in Scotland.

Seydisfjordur was then a bleak-looking fishing port, but it was a welcome sight to the *Harnett*'s crew. While there, the only critical repair the engine room could do was to replace the stern tube studs. On the following morning, twenty-three ships (including a few other stragglers like the *Harnett*) assembled in convoy before departing for Scotland. Three ships remained behind in Iceland. The sea was rough all the way, and it was not a pleasant voyage. Other than the foul weather and the release of a few depth charges by our British escorts, the trip was uneventful. I was deeply grateful to see Scotland on the horizon.

No liberty was granted to convoy RA-53 in Gourock. Captain Carver and Lieutenant Stone went ashore for a daylong hearing with American, British, and Soviet officers during which the USSR protested our accidental downing of the Soviet Airacobra on our way out of Murmansk. Back on the ship, all hands were concerned about the charges against Stone. When the two men returned, we were relieved to learn that the inquiry had absolved Stone and the gun crew of all blame. Stone was later to receive the U.S. Navy Silver Star for his courageous conduct on the Murmansk Run. In a sense, the medal recognized me, too, as a member of his gunnery team. To this day I am proud to have sailed with Stone, one of the Navy's "ninety-day wonders."

While we waited to sail for America, a British petty officer came aboard. He was the first to alert me to the extent of our country's buildup in Great Britain in order to take the war to Hitler. The NCO had been an inspector all over the British Isles, and he talked about the rows of tanks, planes, artillery, landing craft, pontoons, and other materiel assembled across England for the ultimate invasion of Fortress Europe.

After weeks of danger and hardship, I felt like a combat veteran. Even more, I considered myself an "old salt," having learned the operating principles of every piece of deck and engine room equipment on the *Harnett*. I tackled my Sea Project with renewed purpose, and by the time we sailed up the River Clyde to await a convoy for the United States, I was up-to-date in my studies and proud of my progress. It was exhilarating to believe that I would make it safely back to the Academy after all.

Chapter 8

Arctic Warriors

In researching the *Cornelius Harnett*'s voyage to Murmansk, it was satisfying to resolve questions that had gone unanswered for nearly seventy years about the fighting men of five nations who participated in sea battles I survived. This chapter tells a few of those stories.

Vice Admiral Malcolm Goldsmith, British Royal Navy
Both of the *Harnett*'s Arctic convoys were commanded by the Royal Navy's sixty-year-old Vice Admiral Malcolm Goldsmith, who had been summoned from retirement to serve as a commodore of ocean convoys. His return to service was necessary because Adolf Hitler's forces had overrun much of Europe and, as 1941 dawned, Great Britain stood alone against the German juggernaut. In spite of American neutrality, in March Congress narrowly approved President Roosevelt's Lend-Lease bill and began shipping war-related materials to Great Britain. The Royal Navy alone was barely powerful enough to ensure that supply convoys crossed the Atlantic safely, and seasoned naval officers like Goldsmith would be needed.

When the Führer turned against his erstwhile ally Josef Stalin and invaded the Soviet Union that June, Winston Churchill was determined to make the Soviets a military ally against the Germans. He convinced Roosevelt to include the Soviet Union in Lend-Lease shipments of arms and other war supplies. In return,

Churchill promised escort protection for the convoys from the British Home Fleet. This was a dangerous overreach for a nation whose naval resources were already stretched to the breaking point, but British seamen rose to the challenge and wrote a new chapter in the rich history of the Royal Navy.

Dozens of Royal Navy officers served aboard the escorts that ensured the *Harnett*'s safe passage. One of them helped write the first detailed account of the Arctic convoys. Captain Ian Campbell of the HMS *Milne* led the destroyer flotilla escorting JW-52 and RA-53. He recalled that when the *Harnett*'s homebound convoy RA-53 sailed, his crew had been at sea for seventeen days with virtually no rest, and much more stormy weather and nerve-wracking attacks lay ahead before the *Milne* reached home waters.

As a young naval officer in World War I, Malcolm Goldsmith achieved distinction at the battle of Jutland where he commanded a division of destroyers; in the years between the wars he served as naval aide-de-camp to King George V. After his return from retirement, he led thirty-eight convoys in World War II and later estimated that he had conveyed 1,500 ships and "lost only 2 or 3." For his efforts, he was knighted by the king, and he was later to receive similar honors from both Sweden and Russia. The admiral, however, seemed to long for more dramatic sea battles at sea, for he said of his convoy service, "I hate my job like poison. My life is so dull."

Arctic convoy commodore Vice Admiral Sir Malcolm Lennon Goldsmith, by Walter Stoneman, March 1943. *National Portrait Gallery, London*

Airmen of Küstenfliegergruppe 1./406, German Navy

Convoy JW-52 was spotted on 23 January by a Blohm + Voss BV 138 reconnaissance plane of Küstenfliegergruppe 706. Five Heinkel He 115 crews of Küstenfliegergruppe (coastal air group) 1./406 were scrambled the next morning and dispatched to block the convoy. None of the ships were struck by the aerial torpedoes dropped by the Heinkels, but the ships' antiaircraft fire destroyed two German aircraft and ended the lives of six young naval fliers aboard the bombers.

An He 115 commanded by Oberleutnant Hans-Georg Schmidt crashed, and a sister plane under the command of Oberleutnant Arno Gratz was also shot down. Both men and their fellow crewmen were swallowed up by the Norwegian Sea. Although SOS signals were received by naval command headquarters aboard the *Grille*, in Narvik, Norway, all six men aboard the Heinkels perished in the icy Arctic waters.

Oberleutnant Arno Gratz, commander of Heinkel He 115 K6+MH, shot down by ships of convoy JW-52. *From Crewbuch X/39, courtesy of Christian Ziehel*

Oberleutnant Hans-Georg Schmidt, commander of Heinkel He 115 K6+EH, shot down by ships of convoy JW-52. *From Crewbuch X/39, courtesy of Christian Ziehel*

The aviators' squadron was based at three locations in northern Norway. The largest seaplane station in the area was on the island of Tromsø, 215 miles north of the Arctic Circle. In early 1943, two of the operational squadrons of the 406 flew from Tromsø and from Sørreisa, a smaller seaplane station 35 air miles to the southwest on the Reisafjord. A third, smaller detachment of 1./406 was based in Kirkenes, Norway, 265 miles due east of Tromsø, much closer to Murmansk and the Kola Inlet. However, the fjords in that region are often iced over in the coldest months, requiring the addition of steel skis under the floats to enable take-off and landing. Tromsø, one of Norway's earliest seaplane centers, made an appealing base because the Gulf Stream currents warm Tromsø's harbor enough to keep it ice-free year-round.

While Kü.Fl.Gr. 1./406 flew only the He 115, its sister squadron in Tromsø and Sørreisa was assigned the BV 138, a flying boat used only for reconnaissance and sea rescue. A third squadron, the 2./406, was also equipped with the BV 138, but it was based in Trondheim, 425 miles to the southwest.

One of the earliest naval squadrons of its type, Kü.Fl.Gr. 1./406 was formed in 1937 by the German navy to provide long-range reconnaissance for the defense of the fleet and its sea-lanes. In the beginning, the squadron relied on biplanes mounted on floats. Like most of the Küstenflieger units, 1./406 trained on the German island of Sylt in the North Sea south of Denmark, where there were three seaplane stations, Hörnum, List, and Rantum. The shield or emblem of 1./406 portrayed the silhouette from above of two swans, one black and one white, flying above a map of the Oder River delta, where a naval base stood along Germany's border with Poland.

The squadron flew Germany's most advanced seaplane of the war, the Heinkel He 115, which was assigned almost exclusively for use by the Küstenflieger crews. This aircraft served a multitude of roles in the war. In the early years, it was one of Germany's only effective torpedo bombers, and the pilots of 1./406 used it to help to sink several ships of the PQ-17 convoy in July 1942. The He 115 was designed to carry a crew of three: a pilot, an observer/bombardier, and a radio officer/gunner. Later models added a fourth seat for a flight engineer or additional gunner.

The Heinkel had a narrow 56-foot-long fuselage with a huge 73-foot-wide wingspan, and it mounted two nine-cylinder BMW engines, each capable of producing 960 horsepower. Although it set speed records early in its development, aircraft technology was advancing so rapidly to meet wartime needs that the Heinkel's top speed of 180 mph was eclipsed by that of the Royal Air Force's faster Hurricanes and Spitfires. Before production ended, at least 135 were built, although some writers claim that as many as 400 were manufactured.

Because of their inability to compete in the air battles against Great Britain, the Küstenflieger units flying the He 115 were concentrated on the Arctic front, beyond the range of the RAF fighters. There they gained respect and valuable experience facing the harsh winter climate of Norway to defend against Allied convoy traffic to north Russia. By 1942 the planes' floats had been reinforced with the metal skis that enabled them to operate from snow fields and frozen fjords when ice closed the waterways.

The most advanced He 115s mounted two flexible 8mm machine guns, one operated by the observer lying prone in the glass nose of the plane and the other set on a swivel at the rear of the cockpit and manned by the radioman. Two more machine guns were fixed, facing rear and attached to the back side of each engine housing. Most powerful of all, a forward-firing 20mm cannon was fixed under the nose.

As for offensive firepower, the aircraft could deliver a single torpedo, two hefty bombs, a mine dropped by parachute, or a depth charge. The versatile He 115 was also deployed for smoke-laying, scouting, weather reconnaissance, and for air-sea rescue operations. There is also some evidence that the plane was used in dropping agents behind enemy lines on espionage missions.

In the beginning of anticonvoy warfare, merchant ships were lightly armed, and the He 115s performed exceptionally well, cooperating with U-boats to make the Murmansk Run a deadly journey. In response, the Royal Navy introduced an important defensive innovation late in 1942, the escort carrier or "baby flat-top." These were merchant ships onto which short landing decks were welded. Small aircraft, such as Fairey Swordfish torpedo bombers and Martlets, the British version of the American-built F4F Wildcat fighters, flew from the carriers as part of a convoy's escort forces.

No carrier escorted JW-52, but the *Cornelius Harnett* had added to its stern a deadly new antiaircraft weapon of its own for the Murmansk Run: the naval 5"/38 caliber gun installed in Philadelphia. The He 115 pilots must have been shocked to encounter a merchant ship equipped with this firepower, especially when operated by Lieutenant Richard Stone's disciplined gunnery team. As a "dual-purpose" weapon, the 5"/38 was equally effective in defending against both surface ships and aerial attacks, for it could elevate to an angle of 85 degrees.

As a witness to the Heinkel attacks, I am confident that the *Harnett*'s gun crews downed at least one of the He 115s. A dramatic photograph captured after the war and now in U.S. Navy archives shows Schmidt's plane (K6+EH) moored in the seaplane harbor on the island of Tromsø, in the weeks or months before the attack. In the foreground is a large truck towing a BV 138, perhaps the very aircraft that spotted our convoy.

Even more poignant was the recent sale by a Norwegian military artifacts dealer of the German navy officer's jacket left behind by Oberleutnant Gratz. In researching its provenance, the collector who acquired the coat learned that Gratz and Schmidt had served together from the time of their enlistment as naval officer candidates in 1939 and through months of training in radio operations and weapons technology. Both were assigned to Kü.Fl.Gr. 1./406 and had been promoted to full lieutenant's rank just two weeks before their deaths in the attack on the *Harnett*. As naval cadet-midshipmen, their condensed military training probably had much in common with that of Kings Pointers in 1942. Their

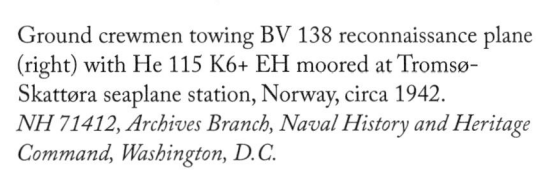

Ground crewmen towing BV 138 reconnaissance plane (right) with He 115 K6+ EH moored at Tromsø-Skattøra seaplane station, Norway, circa 1942.
NH 71412, Archives Branch, Naval History and Heritage Command, Washington, D.C.

stories are reminders that the enemy, too, were young men full of hopes and promise, but whose lives were snuffed out that day in a cold and unforgiving sea.

P-39 Airacobra Fighter Pilots, USSR

As yet no clues to the identity of the pilot killed in error by the *Harnett*'s guns have been found. It is likely that he was stationed at Vayenga, some ten miles upriver from Kola Inlet where the incident occurred. Today Vayenga is known as Severomorsk, and its airbase was built across the Murmansk River from the headquarters of Russia's Northern Fleet. In 1943, the closest German airfield was at Petsamo, Finland, about 55 miles northwest of Vayenga.

This friendly-fire accident was not unique. The senior British naval officer, north Russia, filed regular reports on all matters relating to naval affairs in the Murmansk and Arkangelsk area. In his report for the period 1 December 1942 to 20 January 1943, filed just days before the *Harnett*'s friendly-fire episode, Rear Admiral Douglas Fisher noted

> The Russians have been considerably agitated over their fighters being shot down by the close range fire of British and American merchant vessels in the Inlet.... The German level bombers come over on good flying days at a height of 14,000 feet or more, with very occasional dive bombing attacks down to 2,000 to 3,000 feet. When there is an alarm the Russian fighters take off from Vayenga (though sometimes they are already in the air) and cross the Inlet at a low height.... If this happens during an enemy attack when bombs are dropping, the merchant vessels invariably open fire on the Russian aircraft, and I have every sympathy with the ships.

This ongoing dispute explains why, as soon as we reached Iceland, the Royal Navy convened a hearing to question Lieutenant Stone on the downing of the Soviet Airacobra. For the Soviets, the pilots were national heroes, and such incidents were deeply offensive.

Soviet airmen were pleased with the performance of the American-made Bell P-39 Airacobra. It had good velocity and maneuvering abilities at low altitudes, where most of the dogfights took place over Murmansk. The plane was quick at climbing to medium altitudes, and on the ground it taxied smoothly, thanks to a single wheel under the nose instead of the tail. This setup gave the plane an upright and level stance on the ground.

The Soviets fondly called the P-39 *Kobrushka*, or "little cobra." The cockpit had a two-way radio for communication and a heater, and it was comfortably large enough for men wearing bulky winter clothing. Its thick and strong armored glass provided good protection and a 360-degree view of the sky. With the engine behind the pilot, a broken fuel or oil line sprayed to the rear and not into the pilot's face. One coveted convenience was a funnel-shaped "relief tube" for the pilot.

The Airacobra also had powerful armament, at least in its later versions. The typical P-39 Q arrived in Russia with four machine guns—two synchronized with the propeller and two mounted in the wings—and a 37mm cannon firing from the nose of the plane. The wing guns were usually removed to reduce weight, and while the cannon carried only thirty rounds, the impact of a single shell from the weapon on the engine of a German aircraft meant "one hit and it was over."

In all, more than 4,700 P-39s were sent to the Soviet Union. At least three fighter regiments flew the Airacobra aircraft in the skies above Murmansk: the 2nd Guards IAP (for Istrebitel′nyy Aviastionyy Polk, or fighter aviation regiment), 78th IAP, and the 19th Guards IAP. Units designated as "guards" had achieved especially distinguished records. The victim of friendly fire was probably from one of these units.

The men of the *Harnett* certainly wished the Soviet pilots well and regretted the pilot's death because he was trying to down one of the Luftwaffe fighter planes that made life so miserable in Murmansk for the convoys. The Soviet airmen had even more reason to want to defeat the Messerschmitt Me 109s and Focke-Wulf Fw 190s of Jagdgeschwader 5 (fighter wing). JG 5 was a large air unit with squadrons in Kirkenes, Norway, and Petsamo, Finland, and at other bases in the region, and during the war it was credited with shooting down more than 1,800 Allied (mostly Soviet) aircraft, while losing barely one-fifth as many of their own planes.

Even more frightening than the fighter planes to the men of the *Harnett* were the Ju 87 aircraft Stukas of Sturzkampfgeschwader 5 (dive-bomber wing), flying from Kirkenes. The Stuka made terrifying sounds while diving nearly straight down to release its bombs. Although the plane's slow speed and limited maneuverability rendered the Ju 87 nearly obsolete early in the war, it was dreaded by the men on the Liberty ships for its unmistakable banshee scream, produced by wind-powered sirens ("Jericho trumpets") mounted as psychological weapons on the plane's fixed landing gear.

Lieutenant Commander Stanisław Hryniewiecki, Republic of Poland Navy

The Polish destroyer whose commander tracked down the lost *Harnett* in the Norwegian Sea and led her to safety was a Scottish-built vessel, renamed ORP *Orkan* and assigned to a Polish crew that had escaped capture when the fast-moving German divisions invaded Poland on 1 September 1939. Thanks to a secret treaty with Great Britain, three Polish destroyers and their supporting vessels were welcomed in Scotland when it became clear that the Polish base on the Baltic Sea would fall to the Germans. This northern division of the Polish navy came under the operational control of the British Admiralty, and the tiny naval force was based at Greenock, on the River Clyde near Glasgow. As the war progressed and the Polish ships were damaged or destroyed, the British and Americans found better vessels for the Polish crews.

In 1940, two recently launched British destroyers were loaned to the Polish navy. Although of different designs, both were built along the River Clyde where Scotland had been building ships since the fifteenth century. The M-class *Myrmidon* became the *Orkan* ("hurricane") and the Napier-class *Nerissa* became the *Piorun* ("thunderbolt"). It was fitting that the two loaned destroyers were of Scottish origin, for Scotland hosted part of Poland's government-in-exile, which operated throughout the war under the motto "For your freedom and ours."

Today a memorial plaque at Clydebank Town Hall honors the dramatic role played by *Piorun* in March 1941 during two days of fearsome air attacks known as the Clydebank Blitz. More than one thousand civilians were killed and as many seriously wounded when bombers of the Luftwaffe tried to knock out Scotland's warship construction industry. At the time of the raid, the *Piorun* was moored in the harbor awaiting repairs, and her gun crews put up a formidable wall of iron to hold the German attackers at bay.

Two months later, *Piorun* was dispatched with the 4th Destroyer Flotilla to locate and destroy the *Bismarck*, the premier battleship of the German navy. As darkness fell, the British pursuers had lost track of the *Bismarck*. She was later spotted by the *Piorun*, which began firing at the colossal ship and, with her sister destroyers, engaged the *Bismarck* long enough for larger vessels to come up after dawn and send the *Bismarck* to the bottom.

In late 1942, the *Piorun* and *Orkan* were assigned to the waters around Iceland, where they helped to protect both the outbound and inbound Murmansk convoys in which the *Harnett* sailed. During our outbound convoy, JW-52, the *Piorun* was part of the through-escort accompanying the merchant ships at the time of the engagement with the Heinkel torpedo bombers. Meanwhile, the *Orkan* had escort duty with the Royal Navy's distant screen of battleships that guarded against the most powerful naval enemy, German battle cruisers and pocket battleships.

For our homebound convoy, RA-53, the two destroyers swapped duty, with the *Piorun* escorting the battleships and the *Orkan* herding the merchantmen from Murmansk. It was *Orkan* that appeared out of the mist after the horrific March gale to escort us to safety. The *Orkan* and Captain Campbell's HMS *Milne* had left the convoy to search for the merchantmen of RA-53 that had been separated from the convoy by the storm.

Lt. Cdr. Stanisław Hryniewiecki addressing the crew of the ORP *Orkan*. *Imperial War Museum*

The skipper of the Polish destroyer was Lieutenant Commander Stanisław Hryniewiecki, who would not live to see the end of the war. Less than five months after he rescued the *Harnett*, Hryniewiecki and the *Orkan* were part of an escort for convoy SC-143 from America to Liverpool. A Gnat homing torpedo fired by the *U-378* struck the *Orkan*, and she sank within minutes.

Among the dozen officers and 195 seamen aboard, only one officer and forty-three seamen were rescued by HMS *Musketeer*. Hryniewiecki was not among them.

Kapitänleutnant Reinhart Reche, German Navy

At the outbreak of World War II, Germany's naval surface fleet was not large enough to challenge Great Britain's dominance of the waves, yet the submarine force of the German navy soon proved to be highly effective in threatening the merchant marine lifeline of the island nation. Under the command of Admiral Karl Dönitz, Germany's U-boat squadrons developed deadly new tactics in submarine warfare. The wolf pack, U-boats organized to swarm around ship convoys in coordinated attacks, was the most dangerous of all.

Early in the war, Hitler believed that Norway would be critical as a staging ground for German forces if it proved necessary to invade Great Britain. For this reason, and to protect Germany's supply of iron ore from neutral Sweden, the Führer launched Operation Weserübung, the April 1940 invasion of Norway. By the end of summer, Norway was mostly in Hitler's grip, which enabled Germany to establish military bases there for U-boats and Luftwaffe units. Norway was key to gaining control of the North Sea and access to Baltic ports.

Kapitänleutnant Reinhart Reche, commander of *U-255*.
Courtesy of Christian Ziehel

These bases became even more useful to the Germans after the United States extended its Lend-Lease supply line to the Soviet Union. By building a string of air and naval bases along the northern coast of Norway, Hitler's forces gained access to almost the entire route of the Arctic convoys. The continuous darkness of winter in those upper latitudes provided some cover for the convoys, but the southward creep of polar ice during the coldest months forced the convoys closer to the Norwegian coast and put them well within the reach of Luftwaffe pilots and experienced U-boat crews.

Norwegian ports at Bergen, Narvik, and Trondheim became major U-boat bases, supported by fueling and refitting ports at Hammerfest and Kirkenes. Even before the U.S. entry into the war, Dönitz urged Hitler to wage open war on all shipping destined for Great Britain. Just four days after the Japanese attack on Pearl Harbor Hitler declared war on the United States, and he gave Dönitz the go-ahead to make targets of all American ships. In the winter of 1942–43, German U-boat forces in the Arctic were commanded from aboard Hitler's former state yacht, the 443-foot-long *Grille*.

The losses suffered in July 1942 by convoy PQ-17 proved the vulnerability of shipping to coordinated attacks by air and U-boat units. The U-boat that scored the most success against that doomed convoy was *U-255*, credited with four of the twenty-four vessels sunk by German naval and air forces. The stunning victories of *U-255* made national heroes of her crew and its dashing commander, Reinhart Reche, who was the first to report sighting PQ-17. After the convoy was broken up at sea by the blundering orders of Britain's First Sea Lord, Admiral Sir Dudley Pound, Reche and his fellow U-boat commanders began the brutal stalking of the unprotected Allied merchantmen. Only eleven of the convoy's thirty-five ships survived.

Kapitänleutnant Reinhart Reche began his naval career in 1934 as a training officer aboard the light cruiser *Emden* and joined the U-boat service in 1940. After two patrols aboard the *U-751*, he received his own command, *U-255*, which he skippered on her maiden patrol. The *U-255* was a Type VIIC series U-boat, among the more advanced and most popular of Germany's submarines. A total of 560 of Type VIICs went to sea, almost half of all U-boats commissioned in World War II.

When JW-52 sailed from Loch Ewe in January 1943, *U-255* was on assignment in northern waters. The war diary of the new commander of U-boats in Norway, Kapitän zur See (captain) Rudolf Peters, reveals that U-boat command struggled to locate and track the convoy. Convoy commodore Vice Admiral Goldsmith later heard from Russian sources that thirteen U-boats were circling the convoy, but other than Reinhart Reche's *U-255*, only five U-boats were dispatched by KapzS Peters. The war diaries show how aggressive an Arctic warrior Reche was during his career of 145 days at sea. He sank ten ships, an average of one boat every 14.5 days. His counterparts in other U-boats tracking our convoy averaged one boat for every 160 days at sea. There were no U-boat victories against outbound convoy JW-52, however; poor visibility and strong escort defenses stymied the pursuers. KapzS Peters complained in his war diary about the lack of German air reconnaissance and noted that the convoy hugged the northern edge of the ice limits, making it more difficult for the U-boats to intercept.

After this safe passage, as *Harnett*'s crew languished in Murmansk waiting to be unloaded, Reche and *U-255* ran up their deadly toll at sea. On 26 January, *U-255* torpedoed and sank *Krasnyj Partizan*, a Soviet merchant vessel, west of Bear Island in the Norwegian Sea. Three days later, Reche sighted another Soviet freighter, *Ufa*, and sent her to the bottom. Both had departed Kola Inlet unescorted. On 3 February, a torpedo from *U-255* opened a large hole in the hull of *Greylock*, an American merchantman traveling in convoy RA-52, which had departed Murmansk during our time there. *Greylock*'s crew abandoned ship, and British escorts sank her to prevent her salvage by the Germans.

A patrol line of just five U-boats waited in ambush for the *Harnett*'s homebound convoy, RA-53. Reche managed to slip through the escort screen to release a spread of torpedoes from his submerged boat. Barely missing the *Harnett*, one torpedo sank the *Executive*, and a second one crippled the Liberty SS *Richard Bland*. The *Bland* limped along with the convoy only to be torpedoed five days later and broken in two by *U-255*. None of the other U-boats had a successful patrol except for *U-586*, which sank SS *Puerto Rican* on 9 March just a few miles from the *Harnett*'s position.

The *Bland* was Reche's last victory at sea, for his commanders decided in May 1943 that such boldness was needed at U-boat command headquarters in Narvik, and he became chief of operations in June 1943. His new commander described Reche as a "thoughtful and quiet man," a character much at odds with the fighting spirit he displayed at sea.

Unlike many U-boat commanders, Reche survived the war. After the German surrender, he was recruited by the Allies to assist in Operation Headlight, in which 116 surviving German U-boats were taken to sea and sunk. One can only wonder what thoughts crossed Reche's mind if he happened to witness the Grinning Fox (*U-255*) sent to the bottom. In 1956 Reche joined the Bundesmarine, the navy of the Federal Republic of Germany (West Germany), and he led a U-boat training school before retiring in 1974.

Lieutenant Richard M. Stone, U.S. Navy Armed Guard
When the *Harnett* departed New York bound for Scotland and north Russia, Stone was a thirty-four-year-old native of Niagara Falls, an alumnus of Lehigh University, and one of the youngest men of his era to graduate from Harvard Business School. According to scuttlebutt on the *Harnett*, when he went to work for Firestone Tire & Rubber Company, he quickly rose to become assistant to Harvey Firestone, Jr., who took over leadership of the company during the war.

In July 1942, Stone volunteered for the U.S. Navy and was assigned to armed guard duty, earning a commission in the U.S. Navy Reserve. In the months before he was assigned to the *Harnett*, he commanded the armed guard aboard the SS *Aquarius*, a slow American freighter built in 1920. His first convoy duty took him from Halifax, Nova Scotia, to England. Thanks to the kindness of Lieutenant Stone's son, Marshall, who loaned his father's personal logs, we have a detailed account of the gunnery officer's introduction to convoy duty. The *Aquarius* departed in a thick fog with convoy SC-97 and, much to Stone's annoyance, the ship's master soon lost contact with the other ships. After being lost for two days in the fog, a convoy was sighted, but instead of SC-97, it turned out to be the faster-moving HX-204, which had departed the day after SC-97 sailed.

The *Aquarius* was invited to join the new convoy, and she successfully reached Liverpool on 6 September without encountering the enemy. Convoy SC-97 was less fortunate, losing two freighters to U-boat torpedoes, although convoy escorts sank one of the U-boats.

Stone met more bad weather on the return voyage to New York, and the master of the *Aquarius* once again allowed his ship to stray off station with only intermittent contact with her westbound convoy ON-132.

Lieutenant Richard Stone received the Silver Star for his actions aboard the *Harnett*, 1943. *Courtesy of Marshall Stone*

Once when a vessel approached the *Aquarius* at high speed, Stone could see only the upper part of the ship's superstructure, which resembled a submarine. Stone ordered his gunners to fire warning shots at the vessel, drawing an angry rebuke from the Royal Navy ship upon which Stone had fired. The convoy commodore soon relayed the message, "You fired shots at a Korvette this morning why?" Stone promptly answered, "Sighted object rel. (bearing) 210° bow on low in water could not identify fired 4 rounds relative 200° elevation 40° & craft blinked thereby identifying itself—signed LT RM Stone, USNR." There were no more messages from the commodore.

One month later, Stone must have been delighted to say farewell to the *Aquarius* and her troublesome master and to board the brand-new *Cornelius Harnett* in Wilmington. For his service on the *Harnett*'s Murmansk voyage, Richard Stone was decorated with the Silver Star, and he later received the Order of Patriotic Wars, Second Class, from the Soviet Union. After further convoy duty as an armed guard commander, he was detached from the Navy in September 1945.

After the war, Stone returned to the business world and launched an international import/export trading company, becoming one of the largest importers of specialty steel wire manufactured in Japan. He and his wife, Mary Marshall Stone, raised two sons in her hometown, Savannah, Georgia. In 1956 the whole family joined him in Europe for three months while he represented the Eisenhower administration during a three-month-long trade fair in Ghent, Belgium. Stone died in 2005 at age ninety-seven.

In 1943, Richard Stone was the *beau ideal* of a fighting sea officer to a young and impressionable cadet-midshipman.

Chapter 9

A Foolish Cadet Stunt

While we were docked at Gourock, Scotland, waiting to join a convoy headed for New York, I felt the wrath of chief mate Selwyn Anderson for the first time, thanks to some foolish conduct of mine. All crewmen were trying to rest and recover from our terrifying ordeal as we repaired damage to the ship from rough seas and bomb concussions. I also had time to polish my neglected Sea Project, knowing that the deck cadets were doing absolutely nothing on theirs. Resenting their idleness, I hatched a prank for the trio. A bulletin board mounted on the bulkhead just outside our quarters gave me an idea. I made a co-conspirator of the ship's purser, Hardcastle, who was also on his maiden voyage and unaware of the risk I asked him to take. Hardcastle typed up a letter from a draft I had spent hours composing (all names fictitious, of course):

>U.S. MERCHANT MARINE ACADEMY
>Office of the District Inspector
>4 April 1943
>Port of Gourock, Scotland
>From: Frederick L. Moore, Lt. Cmdr. USMS
>To: All USMMA Cadet-Midshipmen aboard
>   SS *Cornelius Harnett*
>Subject: Inspection of Midshipmen Sea Projects
>In compliance with Academy regulations that

require all Midshipmen Third Class on sea duty training to submit their Sea Projects for inspection by the District Inspector when in port, we will be aboard your ship at 0830 on 5 April 1943. You will be expected to have your Sea Project ready for said inspection at the appointed time. Your compliance will be expected.

Yours Sincerely,
(Duly signed)
Frederick L. Moore, Lt. Cmdr. USMS
District Inspector USMMA, Port of Gourock, Scotland

We had been told when we left the Academy for sea training that we would be subject to a Sea Project inspection at any civilized port where there was a district inspector. The purpose of the inspection was to check our progress on the Sea Project, and it was always a source of apprehension.

No one saw me mount the phony letter on the bulletin board. I soon reported to my roommates there was a letter posted and relished the terror it caused — an inspection of our Sea Projects! It took self-control not to show my glee at their frantic scrambling to show evidence of Sea Project progress when they knew it would be impossible to do so before the fictitious Commander Moore arrived the next day.

I had not foreseen how desperate my roommates would become. In my enjoyment of the success of my trick, I left the letter posted on the board instead of revealing it was only a joke. In panic, the trio went to Selwyn Anderson and asked for the afternoon off so that they could prepare for the inspection. They pleaded that enemy action had prevented them from studying, which was not a bad argument. The mate was astounded since he was unaware of any correspondence coming to the ship. He wanted to see the document.

Sitting in my room, I heard Anderson's angry voice boom, "I'm going to get to the bottom of this!" When he left his room, I rushed to the bulletin board to find that my phony letter was missing. I knew it was in Anderson's hands and would soon be headed for the skipper's attention. Realizing the bind I was in, I rushed to the mate's quarters. My fears arose when he didn't answer my knock. Trembling with fear, I trudged to the captain's cabin, knocked on the doorframe, and saw Anderson sitting in the room. I was admitted and, when asked the reason for the visit, I made a full and open confession.

My confession brought the worst tongue-lashing from Anderson that I ever received from an officer during World War II. The captain sat nodding his head as Anderson enumerated, one by one, every violation of maritime law that had occurred, plus a much longer condemnation of my immoral, insulting, and uncivilized conduct. Anderson finished the dressing-down by heaping shame on any prospective officer who slurred his shipmates in such a manner. He recommended that the captain take immediate disciplinary action and then dismissed the culprit. I returned to our cabin to face my roommates and to await the captain's sentence.

The three deck cadets soon knew the whole story and thoroughly enjoyed my misery. They began celebrating their reprieve from my imaginary inspection. It was a moral victory for them, and they crowned it with innumerable insults. They never let me forget my stupid stunt.

Soon I was summoned to chief engineer Mellema's quarters. I dreaded that I might be recommended for discharge from the Academy or lose a month's pay. After knocking and being admitted, I was surprised and a bit relieved to detect a faint grin on the chief's grizzled face. I was asked to sit down and Mellema began describing my punishment.

> Cadet, the captain has decided to leave your punishment to me, and I know exactly what to do to get rid of some of that excess energy of yours. You are to be in the boiler room at

0800 tomorrow and will be given a bundle of wiping rags, a can of kerosene, and a scrub bucket with which you will clean the piping, the bulkheads, and the deck in the fire room bilge. I want it clean enough to eat upon within four days. Any questions?

Although I would not be dismissed from the Academy, the prospect of four long days in the dirtiest place on the ship was not a comforting alternative. The fire room bilge was a cramped space where heat from the boilers above made breathing difficult. Even so, I considered myself lucky. After I had worked two and a half days in the most miserable work environment possible, fate intervened. The *Harnett* was ordered to proceed down the River Clyde to join a convoy bound for home. On the morning of the third day of my sentence the chief personally called me up from the bilge for a promise that I behave myself from then on. Aye, sir!

He explained that our sailing orders lifted my punishment, but I remained on probation. I would have celebrated, but Anderson's wrath now turned on purser Hardcastle, the innocent partner in my disaster. He, too, got a hot tongue-lashing but luckily escaped punishment. The young purser must have had a low opinion of me.

Most regrettable of all was the loss of Anderson's respect. He remained friendly and considerate, but our contacts became fewer and by the end of the voyage had stopped altogether. However, not all was lost. I grew up a bit after my self-inflicted trauma.

We all went to work on our Sea Projects, and by the end of the voyage each of my roommates' projects showed some progress. Even the chief engineer began to be interested in my project. When it was turned in two months later, I received a final grade of 92 out of a possible 100, the highest grade I ever achieved at Kings Point.

Chapter 10

Convoy ONS-174: Homeward Bound

As the New York–bound convoy departed Scotland, April had arrived, a beautiful time of year along the Firth of Clyde. Getting under way, an incident gave the crew quite a laugh (and much conversation for the next few days) related to the captain. I was on duty in the engine room trying to learn more about how to get up steam. I could hear and feel the vibration of the anchor chain winch lifting the anchor, and I saw the engine room telegraph pointer move to SLOW AHEAD as its bell banged loudly. The second assistant engineer was on duty, and I was learning what SLOW AHEAD, HALF AHEAD, FULL AHEAD, SLOW ASTERN, HALF ASTERN, and FULL ASTERN meant in terms of direction and strokes per minute of the 2,500-horsepower reciprocating engine. The second was a good instructor and he always tried to answer my questions, even the stupid ones.

Suddenly, the deck officer on duty rang STOP, then FULL ASTERN, then STOP on the manual engine room telegraph. The engineer sent me above to determine the cause. Arriving on deck, I saw a small craft headed for the *Harnett*. It came alongside and a line was passed down to it. The coxswain tied a box containing a case of Haig & Haig Pinch Scotch Whisky to the line. It was hoisted to the deck and all eyes saw it carried to the captain's cabin. Apparently, the skipper's supplier failed to deliver the order on time and then had to bring it to the ship on the run.

Steaming home, every crew member on the *Harnett* harbored some apprehension about crossing a North Atlantic infested with submarine wolf packs. While in Murmansk, "Sparks," the ship's radio operator, picked up reports of several ship sinkings along these sea-lanes. By departure time, reports of sinkings had virtually disappeared. The seas were rough, but mild compared to those we faced on the Murmansk Run. More important, there were no submarine attacks on this final leg of our voyage home.

Decades after the war I researched Great Britain's efforts to decipher the German navy's Enigma-coded messages between headquarters and its U-boat fleet. Was this responsible for the *Harnett*'s immunity from torpedo attacks on our two crossings between America and Scotland? Although Germany's top naval leaders believed the Enigma messaging system was unbreakable, they were mistaken. I will always believe that the Allies' cryptographic triumph helped to shield the *Harnett* from the growing number of U-boats in the Atlantic and the Arctic during our voyages.

As we settled down to convoy routine, I worked frantically to finish my Sea Project while my roommates did likewise. Most of my remaining work consisted of completing several sketches, a difficult task due to my lack of mechanical drawing experience. In spite of my dirty dealings with my fellow cadets over the phony Sea Project inspection, one of them, Erwin Erickson, kindly showed me some drawing tips, a subject in which he excelled.

The rough seas were tempered by the absence of enemy action on this leg of the voyage, and there were even some glimpses of sun. Having seen little of the sun for five months, I welcomed its cheering presence.

As the convoy neared New York, all officers and midshipmen on the *Harnett* were reminded by Captain Carver to dispose of any German incendiary bomb duds acquired in Murmansk. These attractive souvenirs had been showered on the Murmansk docks by German pilots hoping to set afire a ship or a stack of cargo. Given the poor quality of German armaments, the docks were littered with a host of duds after every air raid. Because they had failed to ignite, crew members assumed that these deadly weapons were harmless.

All the midshipmen were surprised when the chief engineer, of all people, became the first member of the *Harnett*'s crew to encounter the danger of the duds. He had been shown how to defuse one safely by a Russian. One night after shaving for dinner, he was confidently attempting to defuse the dud in his stateroom when its fuse ignited the device. Fortunately for him (and perhaps the ship), he had not pulled the sink drain plug after shaving. He quickly plunged the bomb into the sink water and extinguished it before any damage was done. He was left with a couple of blisters and some wounded pride.

His experience inspired most of the crew to toss their explosive loot overboard. Even so, a few crewmen insisted on holding on to their souvenirs. As soon as the ship docked in New York, the first people to come aboard were Coast Guard inspectors searching for German incendiary bomb souvenirs. Word quickly circulated that any crew member attempting to take one ashore would be arrested. At this point, the last explosive souvenirs were either tossed overboard or seized by the Coast Guard.

Entering New York harbor, I was, as usual, on duty in the engine room. The third assistant engineer gave me permission to go above for a first view of my native land in more than five months. As I emerged from below I saw the Statue of Liberty, a most beautiful sight. A few crewmen kissed the dock as soon as they were ashore, and I felt like doing so, too.

As the ship went into dry dock in Hoboken, New Jersey, everyone packed in preparation for a trip home. I was given leave and told that I was free to go. The chief engineer told me to go home and promised to telegraph me three or four days before the ship's departure for its next voyage. I gave him Helen's home address and left my excess baggage in his room.

Early the following morning we were paid off; the $1,200 I received was more money than I had ever seen before in my life. I called Helen in Kansas and my mother in Oklahoma, and both were overjoyed. I had a day for shopping before the next westbound Pennsylvania Railroad train departed. I was eager to buy my first money belt, a travel bag, a uniform dress cap, and some service ribbons. The Hudson River subway tunnel took me across to Manhattan. On the return train, I ran into a crewmate, the *Harnett*'s friendly second cook. He insisted that I have a drink with him for old time's sake before returning to the ship. Despite my misgivings, I agreed to join him at his favorite Hoboken bar. We were both in uniform and enjoyed our first drink ashore together. It being wartime, some barflies offered us another round. I declined with the excuse that I had to catch a train home. In short order, the cook had downed three rounds and was answering questions about our Murmansk experience in direct violation of the posters that warned "loose lips sink ships." By now, we were surrounded by civilians, and the cook was loving the attention lavished on him as a returning war hero. I finally managed to get away.

The next morning as I left the *Harnett* for my train, the cook appeared red-eyed and unshaven with his clothes in disarray. He had a forlorn story. Sometime after midnight he had been "rolled" in the alley behind the bar and woke up minus his wallet and his entire pay for the Murmansk Run. He asked for a couple of bucks for breakfast as the *Harnett* was no longer serving meals. Wanting to be a good shipmate, I gave him the money and learned a lesson about how loose lips could also bear a personal cost.

The next three days were spent on the train—the Pennsylvania Railroad to Chicago, then the Atchison, Topeka & Santa Fe to Kansas City and across Kansas to Garden City. It was the most crowded train I rode on during the war. I gave my seat to a soldier's wife during part of the journey to Chicago, where I had an eight-hour layover before boarding a chair car for what was usually a day's ride to Kansas City. Thanks to a delay caused by a train derailment in Iowa, it took more than twenty hours to get there. For half of the journey, I sat on my newly purchased bag in a crowded aisle after giving up my seat to an elderly woman; thereafter my cheap new bag was barely usable.

Helen met me at the depot just before midnight for a joyful reunion. She and her parents spent more than an hour asking about my experiences before I could escape for a much-needed bath and collapse in bed. The next seven days were filled with fun and parties with friends, but my unease grew as no word came from the chief engineer. I called the local Western Union office to learn that they had been trying to find me to deliver a telegram that was now three days old. In it, the chief ordered me to Bush Terminal in Brooklyn by a certain date that was now just two days away. To catch the ship I would have to fly at least part of the way. I rushed to make the night train to Kansas City and managed to board a Braniff Airways flight to Detroit, where I changed planes for LaGuardia Airport in New York. I knew it would take a miracle to arrive in time. My harrowing trip meant that I barely enjoyed my first flight on an airplane. As it was, Braniff had to bump a civilian passenger on the flight in order to provide a seat for me. I never appreciated a favor from an airline as much as I did that one. In the years to come, I flew Braniff whenever I could in gratitude.

When I arrived via taxi at Brooklyn's Bush Terminal early on the morning after my due date, I found that the *Harnett*'s departure had been delayed forty-eight hours. I had escaped what I feared would be a pier-head jump onto the ship. As I boarded, I was relieved to find all my gear right where I left it, including my Sea Project. I showered and collapsed exhausted in my bunk.

The next morning, I enjoyed a festive reunion with my fellow midshipmen at breakfast. The officers gave each of us liberty until midnight, and as we talked about our plans, a new disagreement erupted. I was the trigger of the conflict.

Our orders as midshipmen were to have our Sea Projects examined at the nearest district inspector immediately upon arrival from sea. When I announced my intentions to deliver mine that day to the district inspector at 45 Broadway, the deck cadets begged me to change my mind, saying that our six months of sea time had not quite expired, and they hoped to make another voyage before having to go back to the Academy. I said I was eager to get my license and commission so I could contribute to the war effort. More important, I wanted to get married and could not do so until I graduated. They scoffed at my suggestion that it was our patriotic duty to be commissioned for service as soon as possible.

Standing my ground, I argued that if we were torpedoed and I lost my project in the ocean, I would never recover. I reminded them that it was their own fault they were unprepared. After breakfast, I left for 45 Broadway with my project in hand in spite of several irate shipmates. I found the district inspector's office and was admitted immediately. The inspector was a lieutenant with a breast full of ribbons. As I handed him my records, he looked them over, scowled, and snapped, "You were supposed to turn these in when you arrived in port. You knew that, Melton."

I mumbled some excuse and began wondering what my punishment would be for disobeying orders.

"Are there any other midshipmen on your ship?"

"Yes sir," I said weakly.

"Write their names here and indicate which ones are deck and which ones are engine room," he barked, as he pushed a paper pad at me.

My heart sank as I printed their names and handed the pad back to him. I knew my comrades would never forgive me. He swiveled in his chair, picked up a telephone from a shelf behind him, and dialed a number. The inspector's face had the look of a mean-spirited officer who loved disciplining errant midshipmen. Soon he was speaking to an officer at the Academy. "I have four cadets for you who got in about ten days ago. They're just now reporting in, so what do I do with them?" I squirmed for several minutes as he waited for his answer. Meanwhile, he took my project, scribbled his receipt on it, and handed it back to me with my papers.

He then spoke into the phone, "Yes, sir. Will do." After he hung up, he turned to me and asked, "Can you reach your buddies right away?"

"I don't know sir, but I'll try if you want me to," I said, feeling like a rat.

"Find them and tell them to report here immediately with their papers and Sea Projects. All of you are going back to the Academy for your second-class duty. I'm giving you orders for the skipper and chief engineer of your ship for your recall to the Academy. On the double!"

I returned to the ship and packed my gear to return to the Academy, dreading the return of my shipmates from liberty. They came aboard early in the afternoon, and each one cursed me after hearing the inspector's orders and vowed to get even. We rushed by subway to 45 Broadway and our chewing out for not reporting in earlier. Fortunately, the lieutenant never examined their projects, only stamped his receipt and handed them back. That gave me a temporary reprieve from their wrath. We were told to stand by in the waiting room while our orders were prepared. When we were summoned, there was a welcome surprise from the lieutenant, "Cadets, here are your orders. The procedure is that, now that you are upperclassmen, you will receive ten days' leave before reporting back to the Academy. Good luck!"

All was forgiven as my roommates rushed to telephones to call home with the news of another leave. We returned to the *Harnett* to give Captain Carver a copy of our orders. Then we bade our shipmates farewell, loaded our gear in a taxi, and headed for our rail station destinations. Joe Langer was headed home to Peru, Indiana, so he and I caught a late train west together from Penn Station.

It had been eight months since I had last seen my family, who were living in Norman, Oklahoma. Leaving the train in Kansas, I took a Greyhound bus to Oklahoma City and then another to Norman. I spent only two days with them before I took another bus to visit Helen again in Garden City. During a three-hour layover in Oklahoma City, I bought engagement and wedding rings for her at McEntee's Diamonds, a large jewelry store downtown. They cost $600, half my pay from the Murmansk Run.

We asked Helen's parents for permission to marry immediately in secret. Her father assured us that he approved the marriage but absolutely opposed it until I graduated from the Academy.

He feared that the Academy would discover our deception and dismiss me. I have always been grateful that he did not back down. Later, I heard of several instances of upperclassman losing their appointments due to pre-graduation weddings.

Instead, we announced our engagement in the *Garden City Telegram*. We celebrated almost every night with former junior college classmates who were also on leave. Our glorious time together was marred only by a Sunday afternoon accident. We were riding in the back seat of a friend's Chevy when he crashed into a car that was braking to avoid a dog crossing the highway. My face banged against the seat in front of me, leaving a deep gash on the bridge of my nose. I failed to get the wound stitched and still carry its scar. The frequent injuries I had seen on shipboard had made me careless about my own well-being, and I wanted nothing to get in the way of my return to the Academy to get on with my studies.

Chapter 11

Kings Point Upperclassman

The most striking aspect of the Academy upon my return as an upperclassman in May 1943 was the transformation of the campus. There had been ditches and piles of construction material everywhere when I left as a plebe six months earlier. Now there was order—spanking new buildings, parade grounds, state-of-the-art laboratories, roomy classrooms, and an inviting canteen. Towering over all was Delano Hall, with a dining room that could seat several hundred midshipmen, and a massive new gymnasium and drill hall that could accommodate the entire regiment. The gym would soon be dedicated to the memory of Edwin J. O'Hara, Kings Point '43, who gave his life while on cadet sea duty.

On 27 September 1942, the Liberty ship *Stephen Hopkins* had encountered the German commerce raider *Stier* and her consort the *Tannenfels* in an area of the South Atlantic "through which no ship ever passed" about 2,200 miles east of Brazil. Because of bad weather, the ships first saw each other at a range of only two miles. Captain Paul Buck refused to stop and surrender, and in the twenty-minute battle the *Stier*, armed with six 5.9" guns, killed everyone in the *Hopkins*'s naval armed guard, who were manning one 4" gun and two 37mm antiaircraft guns. As the crew abandoned the sinking ship, Cadet-Midshipman O'Hara emerged from the engine room and made his way to the gun tub and, single-handed, loaded and fired five last shells, all of which hit one or the other of the two German ships. The *Stier* went down two hours later, the first German surface combatant sunk in World War II by any American surface ship. Buck and the eighteen-year-old O'Hara were among the forty-two of the *Hopkins*'s crew killed, and both were posthumously awarded the Merchant Marine Distinguished Service Medal. The fourteen survivors reached Brazil after thirty-one days in an open boat.

At the Academy in spring 1943 instead of mud underfoot, there were concrete sidewalks and freshly planted grass. Instead of the old drafty CCC barracks that housed all cadet-midshipmen, there were six or seven three-story dormitories built of handsome limestone blocks. I was assigned to 3319 Cleveland Hall, a room I shared with three other engine cadets, the first midshipmen to live in the new quarters. Dominating the room was a fine, large desk suitable for four cadets. Waiting on the desk for each of us was a questionnaire to be completed and turned in to Captain Giles Stedman, the Academy superintendent. The objective of the survey was to gather insight into our experiences at sea as midshipmen, third class.

Every cadet had stories to tell, some of them more harrowing than my own. Another cadet who had sailed in convoy RA-53 returned to the Academy soon after I did. Ray Holubowicz was on board the *J. L. M. Curry* when she broke up in the Norwegian Sea following the terrible gale in early March. He had entered the Academy a year ahead of me and became one of the first graduates of Kings Point. Ray's sea duty took a year to complete, coming as it did before the wartime demands for merchant marine officers accelerated the schedule for midshipmen and shortened the time required at sea.

In the May 1942 Murmansk-bound voyage of convoy PQ-16, Ray's ship, SS *Spyros* was hit by two torpedoes fired by *U-703*. The ship went down in ninety seconds and a fellow Kings Pointer, engine cadet John Brewster, perished along with the captain and ten other members of the crew, including the entire engine room watch. Ray survived because he was on deck watch at the time of the attack. Rescued and taken to Murmansk, he and the other survivors boarded the *Hybert* for the return convoy bound for Scotland, QP-13. As that convoy neared Iceland in a storm, its commodore could not locate their position, and he ordered the ships to divide into two formations. The *Hybert*'s column blundered into an Allied minefield, and she and four other ships hit mines and were sunk.

Rescued once more and returned to the United States, Ray shipped out again in the Liberty ship *J. L. M. Curry* and was horrified to learn she was destined for Murmansk. This time he was stranded for several months in Iceland as the *Curry* waited for the new winter series of Arctic convoys to begin. With Ray aboard, the *Curry* sailed to Murmansk in the first convoy that winter, JW-51A, which arrived Kola Inlet on Christmas Day 1942.

The *Curry* did not manage to unload its cargo and prepare for sailing in time to join the first return convoy of the season, RA-52, so she assembled with my convoy, RA-53, when we departed March 1. Weakened by the gale and heavy seas we faced, the *Curry* started breaking up, and her crew was ordered to abandon ship. The entire crew were safely removed before one of the convoy's warship escorts sank the *Curry* to prevent her from becoming a navigation hazard. Almost a year after his sea duty began, Ray at last returned to the Academy. He completed his studies and graduated, probably the only American midshipman to be shipwrecked three times! Ray continued in the merchant marine throughout the war and went on to a distinguished maritime career. When he retired, he was recognized as a "father of shipping containerization," the technology that transformed and modernized the industry.

At that period of the war, about a hundred cadets returned from sea every week, and the superintendent met each returning group early Monday morning in the auditorium of Bowditch Hall. When Captain Stedman arrived, we were ordered to stand at attention. Silence ruled as he made his way to the microphone at a desk in the front and then ordered us at ease and to be seated. I sat transfixed, in awe of this charismatic leader.

Giles Chester Stedman was the son of an Irish granite cutter in the famous quarries of Quincy, Massachusetts. Chet, as he was known by his buddies, longed to go to sea from his earliest boyhood. With war on the horizon in 1914, his parents finally consented to his joining the U.S. Coast Guard, and he was soon assigned to a cutter as ship's clerk. When America entered World War I, his ship and crew were transferred to the Navy and convoy escort duty. After the war, he qualified for a special officer training school and later a program for engineers at the Massachusetts Institute of Technology. Upon graduation from MIT he was commissioned in the naval reserve, earned his third mate's license, and joined the USMS. His service included three extraordinary sea rescues, and his bravery earned him the Navy Cross.

Before the war, Stedman was the first master of the United States Lines flagship, SS *America*. Cadets would later tell stories about Stedman's romances with famous and beautiful women sailing on the luxury liner. He married one of them, the wealthy widow of Colonel Jacob Schick, the inventor of the electric razor. When the United States entered the war in 1941, the government requisitioned the *America* and Stedman, after delivering his passengers to New York, sailed the liner to Hampton Roads where she began service as the troop carrier USS *West Point*. Faced with the prospect of playing second fiddle to a U.S. Navy skipper aboard the *West Point*, Stedman must have found the offer to come to Kings Point in 1942 most attractive.

When I arrived at Kings Point as a plebe, Stedman was commandant of cadets, and by the time I returned from Russia he had been promoted to superintendent. Captain Stedman was in his mid-forties, well built, dark, and handsome. His chest was lined with ribbons and his sleeves with gold. His polished demeanor and commanding personality were perfect complements to his charismatic reputation.

Stedman opened his remarks by explaining that he used the questionnaires we had completed to determine not only what we were experiencing but also what we were learning and how we were being treated. Were the ships' officers giving us enough study time, and was the Sea Project doing its job? He then said that there were a few reports that were unique. Imagine my surprise when he called for my *Harnett* roommates Erickson, Langer, and Ingram to stand first of all. I was not included; were they to be dressed down because their Sea Projects were not up to date?

"Your ship was the *Cornelius Harnett*, right?"

"Yes, sir," they answered as one voice.

"You said that you got lost from the convoy near the Kola Inlet en route to Murmansk and had no navigation charts for that area. Is that right?" Again they answered in unison, "Yes, sir."

"Did anyone say why there were no charts for that area on your ship?" he asked in disbelief. Together, all three answered, "No, sir."

"Yours are the first reports I have received of cadets crossing an area for which there were no navigation charts on board." He scanned the room, "Did anyone else here have this experience on your ship?"

No one held up a hand. Stedman thanked my *Harnett* roommates for reporting the incident, congratulated them for surviving a dangerous voyage and for carrying out their duties under so much enemy action. He had everyone's attention when he announced that he intended to look into the matter of the missing charts by contacting the *Harnett*'s owner, the Black Diamond Shipping Company.

The captain then continued to question others whose unique experiences he had noted. The highlights of my own questionnaire had been my experience with the chief engineer in the *Harnett*'s shaft alley when it collapsed during the terrible storm and our near loss of the stern tube due to rough seas. Walking out of our Bowditch Hall meeting with Captain Stedman, I remember my feelings of hurt pride. I knew that I had shared the same harrowing experiences at sea as my three shipmates aboard the *Harnett*, but I had received no acknowledgment from the superintendent. I told myself that Stedman was a deck officer, and navigation was for the "deck apes" and not for the "black gang."

My only other contact with Captain Stedman came one Saturday morning after regimental review. I was one of three cadets waiting for the Academy bus to Great Neck and its train station. As Stedman's car drove by us, he ordered his driver to pull over and offered us a ride to New York City. As I was heading only to Great Neck, for a movie, he offered to drop me off in the village. While we were in the car he asked each of us to give our names and hometowns and tell whether we were deck or engine cadets.

Other midshipmen had stories of the captain's random inspections of the dormitory floors. He paid special attention to cadets' personal hygiene, and dirty nails, rumpled clothes, or unshined shoes were certain to earn demerits. On one occasion a midshipman who was careless about his body odor was ordered to strip to his waist and then punished for a "dirty, smelly undershirt." It was many days before the offending cadet could live down the hilarious wisecracks from other cadets. I am sure that the story inspired cleaner underwear among hundreds if not thousands of midshipmen during Stedman's years at the helm of the Academy. It certainly impressed me.

After the war, and by then a rear admiral, Giles Stedman returned to civilian work with his longtime employer, U.S. Lines. Ten years later he was in charge of all the company's foreign business, traveling by sea to far-flung operations, especially on the European routes. I will always hold Stedman in awe as the most outstanding military figure I encountered person-to-person during the war. I felt privileged to serve under him.

While I was working hard in my classes during the summer of 1943, my fiancée Helen graduated from Garden City Community College. Her original plan had been to attend the University of Colorado to finish her bachelor's degree, but she persuaded her parents to let her come east for her junior year so that we could be near one another before the war took me overseas again.

I was thrilled by her idea and began researching colleges in the area. I visited Barnard, Hofstra, Hunter, and Fordham, and spent a Saturday at Adelphi looking over the campus and even met its president, Dr. Paul Dawson Eddy. Helen picked Adelphi, and we found her a boarding opportunity in the home of Professor Chester Barrows and his wife. Their daughter Louise and another boarder in their home, Ruth Sales, would later serve as bridesmaids for Helen at our wedding, and they became lifelong friends.

During my final nine months at the Academy, all members of my new section (A-254) were billeted on three floors of Cleveland Hall. I thought this was the Academy's choice location, standing close by Delano Hall's dining room. Our section leader, Earl Paullus, was a good man, and he had my sympathy on the many occasions when a cadet made his life difficult. Although the highest academic honors went to another cadet, I considered William "Black Mac" McEnroe to be our most brilliant classmate. With two years of pre-Academy studies at Rensselaer Polytechnic Institute, he could have easily won top academic honors had he worked harder. In class he often seemed to know more about the subject than the professor.

McEnroe had a tremendous wit, and with his roommates Willie Mockawetch, Bill Dignes, and Alfred New, their room was more zoo than barracks, and so it came to be called. Alfred had the style of a showman, and he was one of the more distinctive cadets I came to know at Kings Point. What set him apart was the nature of his prewar occupation as an apprentice lion tamer with the famous Clyde Beatty Circus, and he had spent many nights performing in the ring. I happened to be in the "zoo" when Mac at last managed to goad New to display his lion tamer's skills. Mac handed Alfred a stool, chief tool of the lion tamer, and convinced the short and stocky Mockawetch down on all fours to be the lion. I will never forget Willie's uncontrollable giggling as he romped around the room and lunged at the tamer. By now there was a large gallery of section mates, and we all got quite a show. I laughed more that night than any other time at the Academy.

McEnroe's mischief-making had no bounds. Several times each day our section marched by the pool with the statue of Amphitrite, Poseidon's mythological wife, posed on a clamshell. A long-standing Academy tradition about the pool dates from my era. Cadets began to bounce coins into the shell at her feet for good luck before our engineer's license exams. Before we started on one such short march, McEnroe somehow convinced Mockawetch to hand over his wallet "just until we get back to Cleveland Hall." As we passed by the pool in ranks, McEnroe and two co-conspirators grabbed Willie, threw him in the pool, and marched on in perfect cadence. Paullus, the section leader at the head of our column was completely unaware of the perfectly executed event until he heard Mockawetch giggling and sloshing as he ran, dripping wet, to catch up with the section. Back in the dormitory, Mac handed over Willie's dry wallet.

What a good sport was Mockawetch! Forty years later at an Academy reunion, when we saw one another again for the first time since graduation, the story of Amphitrite's pool brought back tears of laughter for us both. I was very close to Willie and loved visiting his room, where there was always mischief afoot. It was the most centrally located room in the section, and it became a magnet for other fun-loving cadets. The activities in the "zoo" helped to keep me sane in the face of the many pressures of those times.

Among my own roommates, I was closest to Gene Hlubick of the Bronx. I looked up to him for advice on how best to cope with the huge New York metropolitan area. Gene was cheerful and easygoing. Though hardly a scholar, he achieved great success in the marine insurance field. Right after graduation he took part in the Normandy invasion in one of the many merchant marine contributions to D-Day. His merchantman was one of dozens of "ghost ships" that were the first Allied vessels across the Channel on 5 June, D-Day minus one. Their difficult and extremely dangerous mission was to create a steel breakwater from the upper decks of heavily damaged or worn-out ships by sinking them in a line a thousand yards offshore in shallow water at the most exposed landing sites. The artificial barriers calmed the sea so that landing vessels would have an easier time once they were inside the breakwater. I can only imagine how dangerous it was to tow those battered tubs into position and then sink them with explosives amidst German artillery fire and aircraft attacks. After the war, Hlubick remained active in the naval reserve and rose to the rank of captain. Other roommates went on to interesting postwar careers. One became an engineer with General Electric and another became chief engineer aboard the USS *New Jersey*, one of the largest battleships in the fleet.

I was not allowed to sit for my final exams with my section mates because I was short of the required length of maritime service by some thirty-nine days, twenty-one of which had to be aboard ship. I served the rest of my required time aboard the Academy's training ship *William Webb*, docked adjacent to the campus. Aboard the *Webb*, I studied for exams and maintained my sleeping quarters. Otherwise, I had no duties and was not required to muster for meals, reveille, or taps.

After completing my service on the *William Webb* I came down with the flu, with a fever of 103 degrees, and was admitted to the Academy infirmary for a week's recuperation, after which I immediately tackled my final exams. Each morning I picked up my exam for the day. I was immensely relieved to be able to answer the questions without difficulty, and by mid-afternoon on Friday I was done. I am still proud of my exam grades and the inspector's red-penciled approval on my certificate of completion. With an overwhelming sense of relief I called Helen with the good news.

While I was aboard the *Webb*, my section mates graduated on 7 January 1944; my own graduation was set for 15 February. This timing upset Helen, my bride-to-be. She had arranged for our wedding to take place at the Academy on Valentine's Day, but Academy rules forbade my marriage until I graduated and became an ensign, one day later. Helen was furious and she wrote a special appeal to the administration. Her plea failed, as I knew it would. Academy rules were made to be followed.

Chapter 12

A Wartime Wedding at the Academy

Adelphi College proved to be perfect for Helen. During her nine months there she blended well into the school's social life and studied hard. Having her nearby made my final months at Kings Point the most pleasant of all. She came over to see the regimental review many Saturday mornings, after which we took the Long Island Railroad into New York for a musical, a concert, or some sightseeing. We explored New York together and that was an education in itself.

Being together on most weekends also made it possible for us to plan our wedding in the midst of wartime. With wartime travel restrictions, her parents could not travel from Kansas for the ceremony, and they were relieved that we organized it ourselves. I recruited Lieutenant Crawford, my gunnery training officer, to stand in for Helen's father and give the bride away. The bridesmaids were Helen's roommates and sorority sisters from Adelphi.

In our first days together at the Academy, I had promised Tom Neville he would be my best man. When I could not find him on campus the week before the wedding, Gene Hlubick agreed to serve in his place, if necessary. Then, ten minutes prior to the ceremony, Tom appeared, perfectly dressed and charming as ever. I had become anxious and annoyed, but it was a great relief to see him. The smiles of the bridesmaids showed that the handsome young officer would be a hit at the reception.

It was a romantic scene as the wedding party gathered for the ceremony. We had reserved the former Chrysler family chapel in Wiley Hall for the day after my graduation. I was proud that the sword guard performed flawlessly. I had trained them myself with guidance from the Academy's chief drillmaster, Horton Spurr. My classmate Willie Mockawetch, had asked me to attend to the sword guard at his wedding, which took place three weeks before ours, and Spurr trained me well.

Helen and Herman Melton sword ceremony, Kings Point, N.Y., 1944. *Author's collection*

Helen's flowers were beautiful orchids from the Mockawetch greenhouse operated by Willie's father, a florist in New Hyde Park, New York. Later, Helen's parents asked for an invoice from the florist so that they could send a check. When I called Mr. Mockawetch, he said the flowers were a gift, a thank-you for my work with Willie's sword guard. I said it had been an honor, not a duty, to train his son's sword guard. Mr. Mockawetch replied, "Just consider it a wedding present." For a new ensign with a starting salary of just $187.50 per month, it was a huge gift to us.

On this, my last day at Kings Point, Academy superintendent Giles Stedman had one final role to play. The chapel was directly beneath his office on the second deck of Wiley Hall. As the wedding party assembled in what was known as the quarterdeck, the excited bridesmaids were having a noisy good time, oblivious to the bounds of proper conduct on the quarterdeck. The chaplain, Lieutenant Commander Irving Pollard, was giving me last-minute instructions about the ceremony when Stedman's orderly appeared with the superintendent's orders to "knock off the noise and clear the quarterdeck."

Chaplain Pollard came to our rescue and said to the orderly, "Tell the superintendent that an ensign's wedding is taking place in the chapel, and I cannot control the noise. He will have to close his door if he wants silence." For me, it was a moment of panic as I expected an irate Stedman to storm out of his office and shut down the wedding. I was relieved to hear no more from the superintendent as everyone took their seats and the service began. With our wedding, my Academy career came to a joyous end.

The mother of one of the bridesmaids hosted our reception in their home nearby. In preparation for my immediate departure after the wedding, my gear was packed and waiting in my room. On the way to the reception I stopped by the barracks one last time to retrieve my bag, which sat open on my bed. On top of it I found an envelope containing a ten-dollar bill and a note from my buddy and roommate Gene Hlubick: "You never could handle money. In view of this defect, I know you will need some cash before you get home. Congratulations and good luck. Hlubick"

At our fiftieth reunion in 1994, I was privileged to see Gene and told him how much that $10.00 meant to Helen and me; when we boarded the westbound train at Pennsylvania Station after our wedding night, our only resources on hand were two chair car tickets for Kansas and $19.30, including Gene's contribution.

Our evening in the bridal suite of the Hotel Pennsylvania had been paid in advance, and when we arrived there was a bottle of champagne cooled and waiting, compliments of the hotel. This wine and the bottles served at our reception were my first taste ever of the bubbly.

We arose early the next morning to prepare for our trip to Helen's hometown, unaware of the ordeal that lay ahead. After we waited in line for three hours to board an ancient and dangerously overloaded Pennsylvania Railroad coach, Helen was told she could not board until all servicemen were aboard. When the door to the coach opened, I had to leave her on the platform while I rushed into the car with our two bags. I dropped them on two seats I was lucky to find and hurried back out to help her aboard. A big argument over the seats soon erupted. A young sailor fresh out of boot camp had pushed aside our bags while I was retrieving Helen. The brand-new Ensign Melton had to pull rank on him; the sailor moved on, but grudgingly.

Under way, our coach was more military troop transport than a passenger train, and it soon smelled like a stuffy locker room. Before long, Helen told me that she felt chilled, and I covered her with my heavy new officer's bridge coat. We both dozed off from exhaustion and stress. A short time later, I felt her forehead and was alarmed to discover she had a very high temperature. Fright turned to panic when I learned she ached all over and had a bitterly sore throat. We had no thermometer, aspirin, or other remedy at hand, and I headed through the cars to seek help. Helen begged me to keep quiet for fear that she would be kicked off the train for carrying a communicable disease.

There was a dining car on the train, but Helen was too ill to stand in line. I left her and stood in line a long time to find just two hotdogs left in the galley car. I brought them to her, but she refused the food. What followed were the most miserable twenty hours of Helen's life as we rolled across the Midwest to Chicago. There we faced a long layover, a heavily crowded station, long lines, and another scramble for seats as we boarded the Santa Fe to Kansas City. What a way to start a honeymoon!

En route to Kansas, Helen grew even worse, if such a thing were possible. During that thirty-hour leg of the trip, travelers were standing in the aisles or sitting on luggage. The train stopped on a siding somewhere for hours while crews ahead of us in Missouri untangled the collision of two freight trains.

We were both zombies by the time the train pulled into Kansas City's Union Station. The next passenger train was seven hours away. We were desperate for anything going west to Garden City, Kansas. A Santa Fe passenger agent said there was a mail train departing soon for Dodge City, but it would not go on to Garden City, and, besides, there were no passenger seats on the train. When he confirmed that the mail train had a caboose that seated four, he added that passengers could board a caboose only in railroad emergencies.

I shouted, "I have a real emergency—a desperately ill wife on my hands!" He countered that the facilities on this caboose were drafty, primitive, dirty, and unfit for the public. I assured him that we would consider them good enough for our needs.

The agent was sympathetic to my sick wife's plight but said that he would have to talk to his boss. Somehow he got an approval and told me where the mail train was loading. There was no time even for me to explain the new plan to Helen. Once on board, I realized that the agent was right; the caboose was hardly fit for human habitation. It was drafty and heated only by an ancient kerosene heater. There were no electric lights, just a little illumination from two old kerosene lamps that swung from the walls. The flat seats with straight backs were ancient, hard, dirty, and smelly. After we got under way, there were mail stops at many small towns along the route and a single surprising oasis in Newton, Kansas—a blessed USO booth on the boarding platform where I got coffee from a kind hostess before rushing back on board.

Finally, we were approaching Dodge City. I found the conductor, told him that Helen was seriously ill, and asked if there was any train that would take us to our final destination, Garden City. He told me that health regulations would not permit us to board another train without a physician's report on Helen's sickness.

At the Dodge City station there was a USO sign, and I presented my problem to a hostess. She doubted that any doctor's office would be open so late in the day, but when she saw how ill Helen was she called a doctor whom she knew. He agreed to meet us immediately at his office only two blocks away, and he was waiting when we arrived.

As Helen lay on an examining table, he opened her blouse and placed his thumb on her chest. He put a thermometer in her mouth and, seeing the results, turned to say, "Young lady, you have scarlet fever and must be quarantined immediately. With a temperature of 103 degrees, I cannot allow you to board another train and spread scarlet fever across the Southwest."

As he wrote out a prescription for Helen, he let us use his phone to call her family fifty miles away, asking them to come to rescue us. The gas tank in the Dunn family's 1938 Ford was nearly empty, and gasoline rationing was in force. We were in luck that the Dunns' next-door neighbor was a Ford dealer, and he had a new Ford with a full tank of fuel which he gladly loaned to pick up the two exhausted newlyweds. The doctor left us in his warm office to wait for Helen's parents, showing us how to lock up so that he could return home to his supper. His was the kind of small-town trust and kindness that was so common then and so rare today.

The Dunns arrived, and ninety minutes later, Helen was perking up in her own bed. Her mother immediately produced a pan full of warm soapy water and bathed her daughter. Helen's fever dropped to 101 degrees in less than two hours. She slept without stirring for hours, and by breakfast time her temperature had dropped another degree.

I, too, was caught in her quarantine. The Red Cross had to secure a leave extension for me beyond the two weeks allotted by my commissioning orders for duty in San Francisco. I notified my mother and brother in California, where they were then living, that we would be late in arriving for their first chance to meet the new bride.

Helen was carefully saving a last roll of film to record our honeymoon. On the first day of March a gentle fall of eight inches of snow blanketed southwest Kansas. I had never seen one so beautiful. While Helen was napping, I loaded her box camera and used up half of the film cartridge, not knowing that film was dreadfully scarce. Her wrath knew no bounds, and I am sure she briefly regretted marrying such a dunderhead.

By the third week in March, Dr. Minor of Garden City pronounced us both free of contagion. We bade farewell to her folks and headed west. Ahead of time, we had contacted a former social studies professor whom we both loved at Garden City Junior College. After we told him that our train would be stopping for a few minutes in La Junta, Colorado, he cancelled his scheduled class and joined us aboard the train for a marvelous reunion. We also had a thirty-minute stop in Pueblo, the next town beyond La Junta, where my uncle, Howard Melton, came aboard the train for a brief visit. In Colorado Springs we spent a night with Helen's brother and his wife before reboarding the Santa Fe for the remainder of our trip to southern California.

Once there we had a fun reunion with my family in Santa Ana, their new home. After three or four days with them, we bought tickets for San Francisco, where I checked in at the Twelfth Naval District, transferring my service from New York's Third District. With Helen in tow, I reported to the War Manpower Commission for further orders. Helen suffered a shock when the agent informed me that there was a vacancy aboard a Liberty ship that was leaving before midnight, and he asked if I could board and join the crew.

Fortunately, some of my ship's gear that had been shipped from Santa Ana (no room on our train) would not arrive until the next day. This spared us an immediate separation. The next ship departing, one week hence, was the SS *Antoine Saugrain*, and I was ordered to report at 0800 the following morning. When I did so, the engineer had no duties to assign before sailing, and Helen and I had a week's reprieve before parting. We felt blessed to have a real honeymoon in San Francisco, a city we both came to love.

Chapter 13

Across the Pacific for General MacArthur

The *Antoine Saugrain* was bound for New Guinea under charter to the Army with supplies from San Francisco for the troops and to shuttle military cargo from base to base in the western Pacific. By the summer of 1944, General Douglas MacArthur was commander in chief of the South West Pacific Area, overseeing all Allied forces within a vast area that included Australia, the Dutch East Indies, the Philippines, and much of the Solomon Islands. Beyond MacArthur's command were the powerful aircraft carrier forces and battle fleets of the U.S. Navy under Admiral Chester Nimitz, whose Pacific Ocean Area command encompassed most of the waters north of the Philippines and east to Hawaii. The two commanders in chief reported separately to the Joint Chiefs of Staff because President Roosevelt and the chiefs knew that MacArthur was incapable of sharing authority with the Navy or with any other command.

MacArthur had long ties to the Philippines. The islands had become a territory of the United States when Spain ceded the region after its defeat in the Spanish-American War. MacArthur's father had served as governor general of the islands, and Douglas himself had been stationed there several times during the 1920s. When he stepped down as chief of staff of the U.S. Army in 1935, MacArthur was appointed military advisor to Manuel Quezon, president of the Philippines, which had just become a semi-independent American commonwealth. MacArthur's mission was to build the island's military forces and defenses in the face of the rising threat from Japan.

Soon after declaring war against Britain and the United States on 8 December 1941, the Japanese invaded the Philippines; three months later MacArthur was forced to abandon his command post on Corregidor Island in Manila Bay. The ultimate surrender of the troops he left behind was a humiliation for MacArthur, and after setting up new headquarters in Brisbane, Australia, he immediately began planning his return. The Allies' recapture of the Philippines began with an island-by-island march northward, starting with Japanese-occupied New Guinea. By the time of the *Saugrain*'s voyage to New Guinea, MacArthur was probably already contemplating how, once he returned the Philippines to Allied control, he could assume supreme command for the invasion of the Japanese mainland. This daunting military objective brought dread to the hearts of most Americans, especially the men at arms in the Pacific.

In the few days before the *Saugrain*'s departure for the South Pacific, I set aside time to become acquainted with the ship and my new shipmates. Barney Hafslund, the chief engineer, was very helpful in getting me oriented. Helen and I stayed in the Manx Hotel on Powell Street in San Francisco and made the most of our remaining hours together. We did not realize it would be a year before we would see one another again. She wept uncontrollably at our parting on the morning of Good Friday 1944, as she boarded a bus for Santa Ana to spend a few more days with my family before returning to her family in Garden City, where she made arrangements to enroll in summer school at the University of Colorado at Boulder.

My new home was a stateroom on the port side of the ship's boat deck. A Liberty ship launched the previous summer from Henry Kaiser's Permanente Metals Corporation shipyard #2 in Richmond, California, the *Saugrain* had just returned from its second voyage to the South Pacific. I was relieved to be assigned to a Liberty ship, as I knew every engine room component from my time on the identical *Cornelius Harnett*.

The crew of my new watch on the *Saugrain* consisted of oiler Henry Tomlinson, a loyal and dependable Cuban-American who must have weighed 250 pounds. Although he took his job seriously, his size and strength often led him into drunken fights while in port. Norley Hall, a fireman/watertender was a fine, good-looking Mormon from Utah. Norley was the opposite of Tomlinson; he led a righteous life of abstinence from alcohol and foolish conduct, and he was always cheerful and friendly. He was also a dedicated worker who never gave me a moment's worry. As a merchant seaman, Norley had signed on to the *Saugrain* with two buddies from Utah, Glen Davidson and Phil Dunlop. Long after the war, Norley wrote a history of his service aboard the *Saugrain*, a document that was very useful to me in retelling our story.

The *Antoine Saugrain* departed via the Golden Gate on my maiden voyage as a licensed engineer. Around 2100 hours on my very first watch, it was my bad luck to have the fuel burners go out. The fireman Norley Hall yelled frantically, "My fires are out and they won't relight!" On the bridge, the third mate Mike Savnik was also standing his first watch at sea, and he clanged the telegraph bell repeatedly to find out what had happened.

I was too busy to answer right away, but I will always be indebted to my steam engineering instructors at Kings Point for training me how to confront this challenge aboard a ship under

The *Saugrain*'s Glen Davidson (left) and Norley Hall, 1943. *Courtesy of Norley Hall*

way. My lessons taught that when steaming at flank speed, engineers try to get as much speed as possible from the engine without overloading it. By opening the engine throttle and exhausting all the reserve steam from the boiler, maximum power can be generated. However, if water has contaminated the fuel, the mix under a full load can extinguish the fuel burners. The engineer then has no reserve steam to power the electric generators and the ship goes to total darkness. The only remedy is to close the throttle immediately. Kings Point had burned that warning into my brain, and I spun the 20-inch diameter throttle wheel closed without a second thought.

In addition, I had been taught to switch fuel-settling tanks in this emergency, as any water in the alternate tank would have settled to the bottom and been drained off. I took these two steps immediately before the chief engineer had time to rush to the boiler room. Although it was Norley's first engine room watch at sea, he knew how to carry out my orders, thanks to his training at the merchant marine boot camp on Catalina Island in California. The second assistant engineer, whose job it was to maintain the boilers, came down to help us to get the boilers back in service. In short order, I notified the bridge that we were under way again.

I went to my bunk that night proud of the praise from the chief engineer for my prompt response in the emergency and confident that I had passed my first test as an engineer. It was my only time at sea when we lost burner fires, a reminder of the importance of preparing even for rare contingencies. A few months later, an inspection in the Sydney, Australia, shipyard discovered a leak in a steam heating coil in a day tank. The leak had fouled the fuel.

As the voyage proceeded, Mike Savnik and I became fast friends and frequent bridge partners. He was in my graduating class at Kings Point, the only other Kings Pointer aboard. Our paths never crossed at the Academy (he was in the deck department), but I felt closer to him than to any of the engineers. Our cargo on this voyage, all kinds of gear for supporting an amphibious landing, was bound for the American base at Milne Bay on the southeast tip of New Guinea. We unloaded there and immediately boarded passengers bound for MacArthur's headquarters in Brisbane. After discharging the passengers, we were given new orders to load war cargo at Sydney.

It was beautiful steaming down the northeast coast of Australia and then inside the Great Barrier Reef. Traveling south and away from the equator, we felt the ambient cool, and by the time of our 31 May arrival at Sydney, we had all broken out our heavier jackets. I was glad that I had brought along warmer clothes, as the cooler season had arrived in the Southern Hemisphere.

Longshoremen were on strike at the Glebe Island docks, and American soldiers on leave from the fighting in New Guinea had taken their places. It took twenty-one days to load our cargo, but the crew was not complaining. Sydney is known among sailors as one of the world's great ports, and even in wartime it did not disappoint, reminding me of San Francisco. In Sydney I went on a shopping spree and found bargains among the tanned kangaroo hides and sheepskins, china, silver, and wool clothing. Sadly, none of my purchases would survive our final voyage on the *Saugrain* six months later.

During our weeks in Sydney the news of the D-Day invasion came over the ship's radio. I remember vividly how somber I became. I was off-duty at the time and felt the need to go to a church to pray. I boarded a bus immediately and headed downtown to find a Methodist church. I asked an Aussie for directions and he pointed me to a small chapel within an arcade in the center of the city. A few others were there praying, which made me feel at home. I stayed for nearly an hour and it restored me. Based on my conversations with shipmates, I believe that, other than the Mormons aboard, I was the only one of the crew who felt the urge to pray for our troops in harm's way on the other side of the world.

Instead, it was the god Bacchus that was on most men's minds. The abundance of pubs and easy access to liquor led to a rash of drunken brawls, altercations, and arrests ashore for several members of the crew. Among those taken into custody from the *Saugrain* was Henry Tomlinson, the oiler on my watch. His was the worst case of all with charges of assault, resisting arrest, and other offenses. He was released from jail only after the chief engineer agreed to the demands of local authorities that Henry be confined to ship and subjected to a strict probation. The oiler had already tested my patience in earlier scuffles with the two Chinese members of the engine crew, Fat Man (his real name, pronounced "fawt mawn") and Po Seng Ho. Knowing this, the chief sought me out to ask if I were willing to take Henry back, which I agreed to do without undue worry.

It was the cargo we loaded in Sydney that worried me very much. For the first time, the *Saugrain* was to be a munitions ship. Hour after hour, 500-pound bombs came aboard to be stored in every hold of the ship. My apprehension grew when I learned that we were to be without a warship escort to Port Moresby, New Guinea, a voyage of nearly 1,500 miles. I was little comforted by promises that Japanese submarines had been driven away from Australian waters.

An incident that occurred during the loading reminded me that bombs are mostly harmless until they are armed with fuses. My eight-hour watch in port always came in the evenings, and one night around 2000 hours I was called to repair a broken electrical cord on a trouble lamp we were using to light no. 4 hold. Only a hundred or so bombs had been loaded, which meant that it was at least thirty feet down to the stack of bombs. I pulled the lamp up by its cord to the decking and was fixing it with my back turned to the hold when I heard the clang and rattle of three bombs falling from a broken sling onto the stack of explosives far below. I had no previous experience handling bombs and suffered a moment of desperate terror followed by an immense sense of relief when quiet returned without an explosion.

During our munitions run to New Guinea, a Japanese submarine was sighted one morning several miles astern of us on the same course as the *Saugrain*. Soon, Australian aircraft were also sighted, and we credited those fliers with driving away the peril that was tracking us. I was never happier in port than when I saw the last of that cargo finally unloaded in Milne Bay on 29 June.

At this point the *Saugrain* settled into her role as a cargo workhorse for General Douglas MacArthur's island-hopping campaign against the Japanese. For weeks on end, we would load up at Milne Bay or Port Moresby, New Guinea, to join a convoy or to travel alone with war supplies to one of the Army's advanced bases. Our destinations included Oro Bay, Lae, Finschhafen, Wewak, Aitape, Hollandia (Jayapura), Wakde Island, and Biak Island, most of which had only recently been reclaimed

SS *Antoine Saugrain* Ports of Call
May–November 1944

Port	Date
Milne Bay	May 24
Langemak Bay	July 25
Hollandia	August 5
Biak	August 7
Noemfoor I.	August 23
Biak	August 24
Hollandia	August 26
Oro Bay	August 29
Milne Bay	August 31
Port Moresby	September 3
Milne Bay	September 7
Langemak Bay	September 10
Aitape	September 18
Langemak Bay	September 20
Oro Bay	September 22
Milne Bay	October 2
Wakde Island	October 9
Hollandia	October 13
Morotai	October 26
Hollandia	October 31
Biak	November 2
Langemak Bay	November 5
Humboldt Bay	November 29

from the enemy through the sacrifice of many lives, both American and Japanese. Norley Hall wrote that we sometimes had to anchor as a "floating warehouse until the situation was stable enough to allow us to unload."

I soon recognized that something similar to the massive militarization I had witnessed in Scotland in 1943 was under way in New Guinea. In Scotland, the Allies had been preparing for the landings in Normandy. In New Guinea, MacArthur was gearing up for his return to the Philippines, launching one of the largest federal engineering projects ever undertaken by America up to that time. Sprawling across 300,000 square miles of jungle on the second largest island on earth (only Greenland is larger), the U.S. Army Corps of Engineers was building thousands of miles of roads and hundreds of installations including airfields, harbors, hospitals, wharves, jetties and ports, Army camps, bridges, storage depots and oil tank farms, and staging arenas for training troops for amphibious landings and jungle combat.

In Finschhafen alone, which had been a small and remote village before the war, the Corps of Engineers hacked away dense jungle growth to construct a base capable of supporting a military city the size of New Haven, Connecticut. Army records of the period show that the Corps of Engineers had 29,000 men around Finschhafen building three large docks and wharves for Liberty ships, eight giant aircraft hangers, and a 7,000-foot-by-100-foot runway with six inches of crushed coral covered by a pierced steel surface to harden the region's muddy soil. The airdrome also had 60-foot-wide taxiways connecting to more than 137 separate hard-surfaced parking spots for fighters or medium bombers. They also built six piers for PT boat squadrons, complete with torpedo and machine shops. The fuel for these operations required storage and loading jetties for two million gallons of petroleum products and five miles of pipelines for fuel transport. The base required ten million square feet of open and warehouse storage, six hospitals with nearly 6,000 beds, 60 miles of roads, five main bridges, an electricity-generating plant to power all facilities, including 200,000 cubic feet of refrigerated storage, water tanks to store 500,000 gallons, and two full-size sawmills.

Finschhafen was just one of the stops on our supply shuttle along the northern coast of New Guinea where ten major bases were constructed. Similar extraordinary changes took place on many of the Pacific island groups captured by Allied forces. After the liberation of the Philippines, shipments through the once bustling centers on New Guinea were gradually discontinued. The base on Finschhafen was closed early in 1946 and the jungle allowed to reclaim the landscape. Few Americans realize how much the Pacific campaigns ushered in the huge expansion of the reach of the federal government ventures that concern so many Americans today.

The impact of American power was brought home to me in August when we delivered supplies to an advanced airbase at Noemfoor, a small and beautiful island in the Biak archipelago. The fighting on the island was still under way when we anchored. Although the island would soon be the site of large military installations, when we arrived there were no dock facilities. Our cargo had to be ferried to shore by lighters, small barges, and native boats, and offloading took sixteen days to complete. I was able to fight the boredom thanks to an invitation to a sightseeing tour of this idyllic island. In Hollandia we had boarded a friendly air force intelligence officer who was with the unit whose equipment we were transporting to Noemfoor. Among the scores of Army officers I met in the Pacific, he was the most memorable. The major was a lot of fun, and he truly appreciated that we included him in our meals, shipboard bridge games, and bull sessions.

During the passage, he promised me and three other officers that he would pick us up in one of his unit's LCVPs (landing craft, vehicle, personnel), plywood vessels also known as Higgins boats. A coxswain guided the vessel to a native community on the opposite side of the island. The major's description of a primitive village newly awakened from the Stone Age by the war made the excursion most appealing, in spite of the risk of an encounter with the enemy. The marvels of this trip far exceeded my greatest expectations. The major suggested that we each bring along a carton of cigarettes that we could use to barter for native mementos.

He had mounted a Browning M2 .50-caliber machine gun on the boat and we engaged in target practice along the way. As we neared the village, its protective coral reef became so dense that the coxswain had to anchor the craft and remain with it while we rowed ashore aboard one-man dinghies made from aircraft auxiliary wing tanks. The sea there had only a slow gentle swell, and I could see below to exquisitely beautiful pink coral. The sights were so stunning I forgot all about paddling to shore. Fish in a rainbow of colors darted in and out of the coral formations that were sprinkled with colorful seaweeds. It was a gigantic natural aquarium and the most beautiful portion of God's creation I ever witnessed.

We arrived as about fifty villagers of all ages were finishing their midday communal meal. They lived in sturdy reed-and-straw beach huts mounted on twelve-foot-tall stilts to shelter them from storm and tidal waters. A huge metal pot in the center of the clearing served as their kitchen. My curiosity overcame me and I walked over to examine the contents: potato-like roots mixed with seafood. Its fragrance did not inspire my appetite!

The villagers gathered around us, eager to trade. The air force major was our interpreter, communicating with the villagers through their leader. One man displayed an elaborately carved flat object that the major explained was a chastity paddle with which a man could punish an errant wife. The owner of the paddle was a sharp trader, and none of us was successful in striking a deal for this treasure. I bought a few trinkets for Helen to add to my purchases from Sydney.

Soon there arose a loud clamor among the villagers, and a runner arrived with news. A hunting party had captured a Japanese prisoner and was bringing him back to the village. The major explained that the U.S Army paid the villagers liberally for each prisoner captured, and he suggested that we cut short our visit and return to the safety of the LCVP. I readily agreed despite my disappointment in not getting to see a Japanese prisoner.

Thanks to our glowing reports, on the following day another group of our ship's officers arranged with the major to visit the native village. I did not take part, but a clumsy blunder during that trip would later bring me woe. The major was unable to come to the ship to pick up the second batch of officers, so the men asked Captain Anthony Van Cromphaut for permission to borrow one of the *Saugrain*'s two motor-equipped lifeboats. These large emergency craft hung from davits on each side of the superstructure, and I was responsible for maintaining the Continental motors on board each of them. The captain granted their request, and the officers lowered the boat to rendezvous with the LCVP at the air force dock on Noemfoor.

During the return voyage to the ship, one of the men carelessly dropped overboard—and lost—that boat's crank for its motor. When I got word of the mishap, I was furious. There were no spare cranks for these engines to be found in the South Pacific, and so every time I serviced the boat motors from then on, I had to carry our only crank between the port and starboard motorized lifeboats. This mistake greatly complicated every lifeboat drill thereafter. The skipper shrugged off the news of the loss. Being a deck man, he did not realize how serious a problem those officers had created, for a heavy open boat at sea without a crank for its motor is nearly helpless. Loyalty to my fellow officers prevented me from trying to stoke the captain's anger about the incident. Only later was I to learn how the loss of the crank would put me in the crosshairs of danger.

After seven or eight more cargo shuttles, we sailed to Morotai in the Halmahera chain—the same group of which the fabled Spice Islands are a part—which lies astride the equator. The Allied forces were in the early weeks of the battle to capture this island group as a base to support the long struggle for control of the Philippines. En route I saw my first live volcano, and while anchored off Morotai we experienced our first air raid by the Japanese. I was still suffering from nightmares about my Arctic journey, but to me this attack was little more than a nuisance compared to the horrendous German air raids I endured in Murmansk. I had already earned my Merchant Marine Combat Bar in the Atlantic Theater, but the Morotai raid qualified at least half of the *Saugrain*'s crew to add the bar to their uniforms. Norley Hall recalls that two ships were sunk off Morotai while we were anchored there.

We were in Morotai in late October when the ship's radio brought us news of the start of the Allied invasion of the Philippines with landings on the island of Leyte. We knew that our history of supporting MacArthur's most advanced positions meant that before long we were likely destined for Leyte, too. Back in Hollandia in early November 1944, we prepared for our

The *Saugrain* loading in Hollandia, New Guinea, October 1944. Photo from Herman Melton's abandon ship bag. *Author's collection*

next major voyage, but the destination was kept secret for security reasons. First, we sailed to Finschhafen, the burgeoning base on the coast some 500 miles to the southeast, to load a large gunnery unit along with their radar equipment, searchlights, and sound detectors, as well as some highly classified items. The artillerymen appeared to be a well-run unit, and their officers blended in seamlessly with ours throughout the journey.

After a slow and frustrating effort to fill our freshwater tanks, the *Saugrain* returned to Hollandia. After tying up, we learned that our delays in taking on water had forced our original convoy to sail without us. Meanwhile, we boarded three more units from the Corps of Engineers that had been waiting for us in the harbor. We were to transport 373 soldiers from the four units.

By now, conventional wisdom and the crew's scuttlebutt concluded that we were bound for Leyte. No doubt there were Japanese agents in the harbor who had access to that same grapevine. After more delays, we sailed with the next convoy, and once under way, neither crew nor passengers were surprised to learn that we were headed for Tacloban, provincial capital of Leyte. Tacloban's beaches had been the site of the Allied landings just weeks before, and MacArthur had waded ashore there to declare "I have returned!" to the people of the Philippines.

Although we heard that the fighting on Leyte was going well, the *Saugrain*'s first gunnery exercise after sailing was unsettling for me. As the ship circled a large wooden raft, our U.S. Navy Armed Guard crew struggled to hit the target. It was clear that their skills, training, and alertness were nowhere near those of Lieutenant Stone's crew on the *Harnett*, and my misgivings brought back the tightness in my gut that had plagued me in my Murmansk days. By then I had learned to trust those signals.

Chapter 14

The Sinking of the *Antoine Saugrain*

The *Saugrain*'s cargo-shuttling activities in New Guinea shifted to more dangerous duties after the first Philippine landings on 20 October 1944. Although the crew did not learn our destination until we departed Hollandia, U.S. Navy planning for Task Unit 76.4.7 began soon after the Allies successfully established a beachhead and dock facility at Tacloban.

A task unit in World War II was a naval formation created by a task force commander. In the case of Task Unit 76.4.7, the orders must have come from Rear Admiral Daniel E. Barbey, commander of both Task Force 76 and the Northern Attack Force for the Leyte campaign. Task Unit 76.4.7 was organized to reinforce the new foothold in the Philippines that the Allies had established on Leyte.

The *Saugrain*'s mission in Task Unit 76.4.7 was to transport four specialized Army units to Tacloban. The first unit to load was Battery A, 237th Anti-Aircraft Artillery Searchlight Battalion, which came on board during the side trip to Finschhafen where the artillerymen were then stationed. In Hollandia we boarded the 1619th Engineer Map Depot, the 1797th Engineer Base Foundry Detachment, and the 2773rd Engineer Base Reproduction Company. The troops were billeted in two holds on cots, as the *Saugrain* was outfitted for cargo and not as a troop transport.

Men of the 237th AAA on the deck of the *Saugrain*.
Courtesy of Thomas Holst

Some of the soldiers camped on one of the large hatches that covered the holds.

All the Army outfits were highly technical, and their trucks, generators, and other equipment crowded the deck and filled much of the remaining holds. The largest of the units was the 237th, commanded by Lieutenant Colonel William H. Hubbard. He was a young graduate of the Army's Reserve Officer Training Corps program at Virginia Tech, and he had risen quickly in the service. Hubbard was tall with a distinctive southern accent, and I saw a lot of him and his officers as they took their meals in the *Saugrain*'s officers' mess. The colonel had quarters on the boat deck's starboard side. In the evening, he played penny-ante cards with the Catholic chaplain of his unit, Captain Silvio Masante. It was fun watching the pair locked in fierce competition, and I chuckled to myself every time the colonel caught the priest cheating, which was often. Then Hubbard would threaten to quit playing because of the padre's shameless dishonesty.

We played a lot of cards on the *Saugrain*, and on one occasion I, too, was suspected of "sharp" behavior. One evening just after the evening meal and halfway to Leyte, two of the Army officers aboard asked me and Roy Christen, the ship's radio officer, to join them in a rubber of bridge. Roy and I were in top form because we played every day during the ship's months of island hopping. The cards were dealt, and Roy signaled by his bidding that he held a potential grand slam hand. We made the grand slam and on the next hand completed a little slam (winning all the tricks but one). The two Army officers got angry and abruptly left the room, charging us with foul play.

The four engineer officers of the *Saugrain*'s crew divided the watch duties in the engine room, with at least one of us below deck for each of the day's six watches. Because I spent so much of the voyage in the engine room, I am fortunate to have a copy of the wartime reminiscences written by Lee Kolankiewicz, a sergeant of the 2773rd Engineers and a fine writer. According to Kolankiewicz, our convoy steamed out of Humboldt Bay, New Guinea, on 29 November 1944, with the *Saugrain* next to last in the second column in a formation that was "six or seven ships wide and stretched several miles over the sea. The only ship behind us was one that constantly flew a red flag atop her highest mast. This was an ammunitions ship. She kept a good distance so as not to endanger anyone if she were hit."

I do not recall the *Saugrain* flying a red flag when we were a munitions ship en route to Port Moresby several months earlier, but during that voyage we were on our own without the protective luxury of a convoy. The commander of Task Unit 76.4.7 reported that we numbered thirty-seven ships in six columns, with the Liberty ship *John Burke* astern of the *Saugrain*. The *Burke* shows up as an ammunition carrier in a later chapter, which confirms that Kolankiewicz was a pretty accurate observer. Had I known that the *Saugrain* was sailing into a battle zone just ahead of an ammunition ship, my nervous gut would have bothered me throughout the voyage.

The convoy included thirteen other Liberty ships transporting troops and military cargo: *Conrad Kohrs, H. H. Raymond, James H. Breasted, James H. Lane, John Evans, John Hart, Lew Wallace, Marcus Daly, Morton M. McCarver, Peter Lassen, Richard Yates, William S. Colley,* and *William C. Ladd.* Other merchant ships included the *Anhui, Cape Gaspe,* and *Torrens.*

The Army vessels in the convoy were manned by Coast Guard personnel. Seven were FS vessels (freight ships) with hull numbers 120, 145, 158, 162, 163, 171, and 310. A steel rescue tug *LT-454* (large tug), joined the convoy; she would soon play an important role in the story of the *Saugrain*. The freighter *Mactan* had a legendary "return to the Philippines" story of her own. On 31 December 1941, she had been the last American ship to leave Manila as Japanese invaders reached the outskirts of the city. *Mactan* had been hastily painted white with large red crosses to signal her conversion into a hospital ship, and she managed to escape to Australia, transporting 224 of the most desperately wounded Allied soldiers out of harm's way. Now, three years later, *Mactan* had joined our convoy to transport the advance headquarters of MacArthur's Services of Supply (USASOS) unit, which provided the Army's logistical support for the Allies' return invasion.

Navy vessels in the convoy included the USS *Gilliam*, with Commander H. B. Olson aboard as convoy commodore; *Bootes*, an ammunition issue ship; *Porcupine*, a Liberty outfitted as an oil tanker; five LSTs (landing ship, tank) with hull numbers 460, 735, 741, 911, 1018; and *LCI 984*. The U.S. Coast Guard–manned patrol frigates USS *Belfast, Coronado, Ogden,* and *San Pedro* served as escorts, with Lieutenant Commander Harold Doebler, USCG, providing overall direction of Task Unit 76.4.7 from the bridge of his frigate, the *Glendale*.

For the soldiers we were transporting there was no privacy aboard the *Saugrain* in its unfamiliar role as a troop transport. The men took seawater showers on deck, and the latrines were boards laid along the ship's fantail, with fire hoses called into service to flush the waste. Although their officers took meals with us in the wardroom, the enlisted men had to settle for two meals a day, eating from mess kits as though they were on campaign.

Everyone on board knew that the danger increased as we drew nearer to our destination in the Philippines. Norley Hall remembers listening to the nightly broadcast of Tokyo Rose on the ship's radio. "On this night she aimed her venom at the 'unprovoked attack' on the Philippines and told of our ship and its position in the convoy. She said the entire convoy was doomed and that the Liberty ship *Antoine Saugrain* would never get its troops and radar equipment to port."

The early morning hours of 5 December 1944 brought heavy rain storms that soaked the men sleeping on deck. As the morning's tropical sun dried the mess, I reported for my morning watch in the engine room, scheduled for 0800 to 1200 hours. I had not completed my first round of equipment inspections when, at 0830, we felt a dull thud followed by the boatswaine's whistle trilling its rising note, "too-whee!" "Clang! Clang! Clang!" went the ship's bell, the call to general quarters. I sent Henry Tomlinson topside to determine the cause. He reported back right away that the port side of the convoy had come under air attack by a lone Japanese plane that appeared out of nowhere, dropped a bomb, and just as quickly vanished.

I turned back to my operations and the "all clear" soon sounded. We were distracted by some good news: the steward Bill Naismith had saved a roast beef to serve the *Saugrain*'s crew on our final day before our arrival at Tacloban. All morning I looked forward to the flavors of my first roast beef since leaving Australia five months before.

At the end of my watch I hurried above, showered, changed clothes, and dashed down to the wardroom for the feast. Joe Dorris, the good-natured and conscientious messman was all smiles as he brought me a plate of mouth-watering beef with mashed potatoes and gravy. As I picked up my knife and fork to dig in, the general quarters alarm sounded again. I never had a chance to sample even a morsel, instead rushing out of the wardroom and up to my cabin. There I put on my life jacket, slung my two-year-old abandon-ship kit over my shoulder, and headed for the passageway to the port side. My way was blocked by a swarm of crewmen and Army officers pushing through. I heard someone yell, "Torpedo! Port side!"

The drills and my Academy training took over. Moving a few steps astern down the passageway, I quickly assumed the

Second Japanese torpedo bomber attack on the *Saugrain*, 5 December 1944. Painting by James Rae

blast position I had learned at Kings Point. I faced the stern, opened my mouth, and put both hands firmly on the handrails. I got up on tiptoe and squatted until my thighs and lower legs formed a 45-degree angle, all to convert my knees into a hinge and shock absorber. Then I prayed and hoped the torpedo would miss. The blast, followed by a massive concussion, was the most violent of my life. Because I was looking astern, I could see the fantail leap at least ten feet in the air. A wave of gratitude for my training swept through my body as the handrail stabilized me and my open mouth saved me from broken eardrums as the shocking explosion burst.

I remember vividly the racing of the engine and the knocking vibration of a ship with its propeller blown away. At that instant I sensed that the *Saugrain* was dead in the water and would have to be abandoned. Starting for my battle station, I saw the chief mate darting for the bridge. He told me that the screw was gone, and my instinctive reaction was to get to my life boat. On the way there, I saw Barney, the chief engineer and his second assistant, Frank Field, closing the engine emergency shutoff valve by hand. After they closed off steam to the engine the vibration ceased, much to my relief. I was certain something would have flown apart soon otherwise.

Frank Field had relieved my watch at twelve noon and again at twelve midnight throughout the voyage to Leyte. He and Norley Hall and an oiler took over the engine room just fifteen minutes before the Japanese attack. In the confusion following the loss of our ship, we never had a chance to discuss the day's events. In the years since the torpedoing I often wondered how the watch had escaped the engine room without serious injury. Sixty-seven years later, Norley Hall's history of the events answered my questions.

As Norley Hall began his noon watch in the engine room, suddenly the bells started ringing for full steam and full ahead.

> We were trying to take evasive action....
> A second desperate call for more steam then the whole world seemed to collapse. I was working at the oil valves trying to get more pressure when the shaft alley watertight door seemed to burst and fly through the engine room. Suddenly water was gushing in ... the engine went wild with many times its normal rotation speed ... burst steam lines were hissing everywhere. I caught a quick glimpse of the engineer and oiler flying up the main ladder and heard the abandon ship whistle but there was no way to get past the engine which was spinning out of control so rapidly that it was throwing a cloud of oil and water everywhere. From the noise and sight of it I expected it to fly to pieces any second. I hit my two emergency cutoff valves for the oil and went scurrying up an escape hatch.

Norley ran to his boat station on the starboard side of the ship and found it hanging by a single davit, and "a mob of sailors were fighting each other trying to get in it." In the end, Norley would choose a long swim over the chaos of the boats.

When the general quarters alarm sounded, galleyman Roy Griffis rushed to his battle station as a loader on one of the starboard 20mm Oerlikon guns off the flying bridge. As the torpedo bomber passed over the ship, Roy yelled to the operator, "Shoot the bastard!" "I can't do that, we'll hit our own men," was the reply. From his battle station, Roy was within earshot when the captain was told, "Sir, the engine room reports 23 feet of water and rising."

Griffis believes that the unfortunate timing of the torpedo's hit was the primary cause of the flooding. The oiler on duty in the engine room later told Roy that he had entered the shaft alley to oil its gear, then passed back through the hatch into the engine room. That hatch was supposed to be closed at all times, but it was sometimes left open to pass a draft of air into the engine room in the unbearably hot conditions of the tropics. However, in light of the attack earlier that morning, the oiler knew the hatch must be shut. He turned to do so just as the torpedo struck the propeller and was hurled across the room. As water flooded into the shaft alley, there was nothing to stop its rush into the engine room and no way to close the hatch.

Roy Griffis also remembers that when the first torpedo struck, one of the deck officers panicked and encouraged the crew to abandon ship, an order only the skipper could give. This mistake led some men to throw life buoys overboard, planning to climb the rails to jump in after them. When they were then ordered back from the gunwales, the buoys were left far behind in the ship's wake, ensuring that the men's life vests would be their only survival gear.

Arriving at my own boat, I witnessed the order to get away from the gunwales. It was one of the most dramatic incidents of my war experience. The captain rushed to the port side of the bridge with a pistol tucked in his

Saugrain crewmen Joe Dorris (left) and Roy Griffis (3rd from left), on leave from Catalina Island training school, 1943. *Courtesy of Victoria Dorris*

belt and a megaphone in his hand. Hundreds of panicking soldiers lined the ship's port gunwale preparing to jump overboard and abandon ship. A few were actually perched on top of the rail. I recognized immediately the danger of the moment. The skipper put the megaphone to his mouth and spoke in a booming voice that I had never heard from him before: "Attention all hands! This is the captain speaking. I'm ordering everybody to get away from the gunwale right now. I mean immediately! Get away from that gunwale! This ship is not sinking yet. Nobody leaves this ship until I say so, and I'll shoot the first son of a bitch that tries to jump. That's an order!"

The captain got results immediately; soldiers left the gunwale in droves. The proof of the skipper's wisdom was not long in coming. Another Japanese plane immediately appeared on the port side of the *Saugrain*. It was a single-engine bomber with a long canopy and a gunner in the rear. He dropped a torpedo and, as he came over the deck, I could have hit him with a piece of coal if I'd had one in my hand. I don't know how our gunners could have missed him; maybe they were too scared to fire straight. The pilot then crossed the convoy at mast height in the face of ear-splitting but unsuccessful firing from our guns. As he escaped our ship's gunfire I heard once again, "Torpedo! Port side!"

I grabbed hold of the gunwale of my soon-to-be-launched lifeboat and quickly crouched in blast position. The second torpedo struck no. 2 cargo hold on the port side with another loud explosion and its powerful shock wave. Had the captain allowed men to jump into the water before the blast, many would doubtless have been killed from the underwater concussion of the second torpedo's detonation. Other soldiers would have died from being struck by the heavy rafts, which had to be launched whether or not there were men in the water below. Many men owed their lives to the captain's wise and forceful command of the situation. I regret that in his report (reprinted in the appendix), Captain Van Cromphaut failed to mention how, between the two torpedo strikes, he drove men at gunpoint from the side of the ship.

THE SINKING OF THE *ANTOINE SAUGRAIN*

A very few minutes after the second torpedo struck, he gave the "Abandon ship!" order. I had been well trained to recognize this signal from the ship's whistle: six short blasts and one long blast. Third mate Mike Savnik ordered our lifeboat lowered, and, by procedure, I climbed aboard as it was being lowered so that I could start the engine as soon as it hit the water. The engine responded at the first crank and was soon purring. Crewmen assigned to our boat were climbing down the rope ladders in good order, and Mike was directing the operation coolly when a crewman from the matching power lifeboat from the starboard side handed down to Mike a small rope line. We had rehearsed this procedure in lifeboat drills ever since the men of the starboard lifeboat lost their engine crank off Noemfoor Island. I cursed them under my breath but tied our precious crank to the lowered line, realizing that we could never get it back. It meant that we had to keep the motor running at all costs.

The *Saugrain* lists to starboard as men take to the boats and rafts. *Courtesy of Thomas Holst*

Mike ordered me to the stern to man the portable rudder, while he, as commander of the boat, would man the engine throttle. I realized immediately this was a mistake. He knew nothing about the gasoline-powered engine, and there were others on board who could man a rudder. Still, who was I to dispute the commander of my lifeboat?

The water was thick with swimmers, and we helped soldier after soldier aboard until the sea lapped the gunwales and swamping seemed imminent. I remember pulling aboard an artilleryman I knew. He had his M-1 rifle strapped to his back, and as I lifted him aboard, its barrel struck me in the mouth and nearly broke several front teeth. The water from his clothes drenched all the papers and contents in my abandon-ship kit. I am ashamed to admit that I regretted pulling him out of the water.

At last, we could take no more men aboard. It was distressing to refuse help to men floundering in the water, but we had no choice. Mike directed me to steer toward an escort vessel we spotted that was standing by a half mile away to pick up survivors. We had traveled 50 yards or so toward that vessel when we heard a loud hail from the *Saugrain*'s boat deck. Waving frantically to us was our first assistant engineer, the Russian Vasily Falin. I knew that he was assigned to our boat, and I shouted to Mike that we had to go back and retrieve him.

Our lifeboat's engine controls could shift from full ahead to full astern only by pausing the gear shift in neutral for a few seconds to avoid overloading the engine. Mike was unaware of this crucial detail, and he yanked the lever full astern, killing the engine. With no power and no crank to restart the engine, our only choice was to break out the oars and row back to the ship. Simply getting to the oars was difficult with so many men aboard. We finally managed to dig out the oars and shipped them in their locks, but having to return to a ship under attack upset everyone aboard.

We rescued Vasily, but when I learned why he was late reporting to the lifeboat station, I wanted to push him overboard. Without notifying anyone, he had run back to his stateroom to retrieve a favorite wrench to add to his abandon-ship kit. When he retraced his steps to the boat deck, he found that he had been left behind. Never in my entire tour of duty at sea was I so disgusted by a shipmate who should have known better. We had lost more than fifteen minutes to Vasily's folly, and I was growing anxious. If the Japanese pilots returned to strafe us, we faced disaster.

Fortunately, the escort vessel had sent small power launches out to rescue swimmers and to tow any rafts or lifeboats to safety. We continued our slow row across the water until one of the rescue teams hooked on to us and towed our boat to the mother ship, which turned out to be the frigate *Coronado*. In clambering aboard, I scraped my right knee severely and needed wound care from the medics aboard. Even so, I knew how lucky I was to escape the day's calamities with just a minor injury.

One of the crew members who ended up in the ocean, Norley Hall, stripped off his shirt and shoes and swam as quickly as he could away from the *Saugrain*. He vividly remembers swimming past a case of cigarettes with a wharf rat sitting on top. Hall was eventually plucked from the sea by the tug *LT-454*, which was assisting the *Coronado* and *San Pablo* in the rescue effort.

In a 25 January 2011 telephone conversation with the author, Joe Dorris, childhood buddy of Roy Griffis from the galley crew, also recalled choosing to swim for safety. Assigned to the same lifeboat as Norley Hall, Joe had released one of the davits for lowering the boat only to have the release on the other end bungled by clumsy soldiers who didn't know how to work it. In the muddle that ensued, Joe's hand was injured. The boat was finally lowered with Joe aboard, but soldiers began jumping into the boat from the deck. Worried that he would be seriously injured by one of the leapers, Joe decided he would be safer in the water, and he leaped overboard. He was not a great swimmer and had no life jacket, but he swam away from the ship as fast as he could and stayed afloat until he was picked up by *LT-454* two hours later. When that tug reached capacity, she transferred Joe Dorris, Norley Hall, and the other seamen and soldiers picked up from the *Saugrain* to the *Coronado*.

The crewmen and soldiers who ended up in the sea had plenty to worry about besides the sinking ship's downward suction pulling them under. Sharks, strafing by enemy aircraft, and getting left behind as the convoy sailed ahead were on many minds. A soldier of the 2773rd Engineers, Leonard "Lenny" Scinto had been assigned to an abandon-ship station on the port side. As the *Saugrain* listed heavily to starboard, the port side was lifted higher, and it was a long drop from the deck to the sea, perhaps forty feet. He watched a buddy cut loose one of the huge rafts on deck, and it splashed into the sea far below. Wearing a life jacket, and with his helmet fastened under his chin, Lenny jumped. He plunged deep below the surface and then "popped up like a cork." Except for his trousers, all his clothes and his helmet were gone, and he never saw the life raft again, either. His heart sank as he watched the convoy disappearing, "just pinpoints on the horizon." Lenny floated and swam for four hours before being picked up.

Coast Guardsmen assist in the rescue of the *Saugrain*'s crew.
Courtesy of Thomas Holst

By the time I hobbled onto the *Coronado*, the deck was crowded with men from the *Saugrain*, and we were interfering with the ability of crew members to carry out their duties. The *Coronado* and the Army tug *LT-454* had been ordered to remain with the *Saugrain* until a decision could be made about her fate. The Japanese had their own ideas about what to do with the *Saugrain*, and several of their bombers soon appeared on our starboard side. It was frightening because the smoke from our guns obscured the attackers. Everyone from the *Saugrain* lay down on deck, but I ducked behind a ventilator and then stuck my head out to view the action. Unlike the ineffective firing from our guns in the earlier attack, the *Coronado*'s crew sent up an awesome wall of fire from the starboard guns. Then the ship lurched as its captain pivoted 180 degrees to deliver a murderous barrage from the port guns. After losing a couple of planes, the Japanese turned away in the face of such a heavy cannonade. I had never been aboard a ship that delivered such withering fire. After an hour, the "all clear" sounded; there was no more enemy action that night.

Miraculously, the crew of the *Coronado* managed to feed all the rescued men aboard as well as its own crew, and I ate a generous helping of potato stew at a table in the officers' mess. While eating, we were welcomed aboard by the skipper, Lieutenant Commander Ned Strow, who briefed us on the situation. He reported that the *Saugrain* was down severely at the bow and listing badly to starboard, but he guessed that she could make it to Tacloban.

We later learned that there were no casualties among those aboard the *Saugrain*, but other ships had not fared so well in the attack, including the *Coronado*. When the first torpedo bomber attacked the *Saugrain*, the *Coronado*'s port guns opened fire 3,000 yards astern of us. As the plane crossed above our ship, a cease-fire was ordered on the *Coronado*, but it was too late to prevent the friendly-fire death of Lieutenant (j.g.) Godfrey Constable of Gig Harbor, Washington. Constable stepped into the line of fire of the ship's starboard bow gun, and his head was blown from his body. By the time I was plucked from the sea by the *Coronado*, Lieutenant Constable's remains were in the sickbay where those of us needing first aid saw his shrouded body. Four other crewmen were injured in the incident. The commander's after-action report stated that steel fragments from the bursting shell caused their injuries, but Dorris recalled that *Coronado* crewmen told him and Griffis that the men were struck by bone fragments from the lieutenant's body.

The attack I witnessed from the deck of the *Coronado* occurred three hours after the *Saugrain* was torpedoed, and some seven Japanese aircraft were involved. After being driven away from the *Saugrain*, the attackers flew on to the convoy where one of them managed to drop a bomb. It missed its target, the Liberty ship *Marcus Daly*, which had been in column next to the *Saugrain*. The aircraft and a sister plane then formed to launch suicide dives upon the *Marcus Daly* and *Mactan*, the floating headquarters of General MacArthur's Services of Supply unit. The first kamikaze plane exploded on the bow of *Marcus Daly*, made a hole "large enough to drive a train through" and started a raging fire. The plane aiming at the *Mactan* was hit by ship's gunfire, overshot its target, and exploded when it hit the sea. Aboard the *Marcus Daly*, the master reported twenty-two killed, fifty missing, and thirty wounded. The blaze was finally brought under control around midnight, and the ship limped into Leyte the next day. The final tally of fatalities numbered sixty-five. Five days later the *Daly* was attacked again by a kamikaze pilot with further loss of life.

The Liberty ship *John Evans* was also a target of the kamikaze attack. Diving through heavy gunfire, the Japanese pilot managed only to graze the stack and topmast, crashing into the sea next to the *Evans*. There were no fatalities on board, but bomb fragments wounded four Americans. The Navy's 1946 history of its armed guard units called the air-naval action on 5 December 1944 "one of the fiercest and most destructive air attacks of the entire campaign for Leyte." The enemy suffered even more, however, and by the end of December the Japanese had gambled most of their airpower resources and lost.

With the coming of darkness, I was bone-weary from the exhausting day. After I was issued a blanket I stretched out on the *Coronado*'s deck and was soon asleep. Our convoy had long since continued on for Tacloban, but the *Coronado* circled the towed *Saugrain* all night. The next day, 6 December, dawned bright and clear, and I arose at sunup. I could see the *Saugrain* being towed from the stern by *LT-454*. A boarding party that included Captain Van Cromphaut, the *Saugrain*'s armed guard commander, the tug's skipper, and officers and men from the *San Pedro* had determined that the Liberty could not be sailed to port. The boarders rescued some logs and other papers and a large shipment of mail bound for American troops on Leyte, always considered precious cargo.

The tug had towed the *Saugrain* all night, crossing about half the distance to Tacloban, and we had cleared Dinagat Island near where Surigao Strait meets Leyte Gulf. This was the site of the last battleship-versus-battleship naval action in history just two months before. Six battleships of the U.S. Seventh Fleet, flanked by eight cruisers, set a trap for the Southern Force of the Imperial Japanese Navy in what some consider the decisive action of the battle of Leyte Gulf.

I was happy that we were under way and had no interest in lingering in these historic sea-lanes. My hope was to reach Tacloban before the Japanese struck again; there had been enough action for a while. The enemy saw to it that we had no breathing spell. At 0741 *Coronado* went into battle alert when its radar picked up the blips of two approaching bombers. It was soon obvious that their target was the *Saugrain*. One plane was shot down or turned back as the other veered toward the *Saugrain*. As soon as the bomber was in range, the *Coronado* opened fire with a deafening roar and blinding smoke. The plane suffered several hits by our guns but continued to descend in its murderous assault. It was obvious that it was a kamikaze attack directed at the *Saugrain*. Clearly that ship was more than unlucky; she had been singled out as a vital target.

What followed was the most classically beautiful wartime scene of my career at sea. The second plane was within a quarter mile of the *Saugrain* when, out of the blue, four U.S. Lightnings (P-38 fighters) swooped down on the torpedo bomber. Using the propaganda lingo of that day, the men of the 7th Fighter Squadron "sent the pilot to meet his honorable ancestors" in a crash one hundred yards or so from the *Saugrain*. Everybody cheered as the Lightning pilots executed their victory rolls. By then I was fascinated by the P-38, and several times during our island hopping, I had seen them perform the victory roll (announcing a "kill") as they came in to land.

Soon thereafter we reached an area in Leyte Gulf where there was adequate air cover. *Coronado* was relieved as escort to the *Saugrain* by the destroyer USS *Halford*, and we proceeded at flank speed to San Pedro Bay at Tacloban. Having grown accustomed to a maximum speed of ten knots on Liberty ships, it felt as though we were flying across the water. Our fast sailing to a safe harbor was a very pleasant feeling.

It was late afternoon before a score or more of us were transferred to an Army LCI (landing craft, infantry), which landed us just off White Beach. I remember the sense of treading a historic path in the footsteps of MacArthur at the very site where he first waded ashore. Surrounded by the sounds of aircraft landing and taking off from the nearby base, we waited for a truck to take us inland to a site designated as a casualty camp. I sat down to rest, but within minutes sirens were sounding and the whole beach shook from bombs and other explosions at the airbase. We were in an air raid! Everyone flattened face down on the beach. The staccato of machine-gun fire signaled a Japanese infantry attack that unfolded over the next hour or so before all was quiet again. The next day we learned it was a sneak attack on the airbase. A captured American plane loaded with suicide soldiers made a surprise landing, the first Japanese action at Tacloban in several weeks. The attackers blew up a few planes on the field and did considerable damage before all were killed. I remember wondering why enemy action seemed to erupt everywhere I went. Once again I felt lucky to be alive.

After dark, Army trucks arrived to load us for a long bumpy ride out into the country. Lining the ditches on both sides of the dirt road for miles were drums of aviation fuel, widely scattered to limit destruction from strafing. It was an unpleasant ride that ended at a darkened and abandoned Catholic church where I sprawled on a pew for rest. I soon realized I was too hungry and thirsty to sleep. A few hours later, an Army dump truck backed up to one of the blown-out front windows to dump several ten-pound cans of Spam, each equipped with key-type openers. One fellow survivor had a knife and a flashlight, and we all shared a can. I ate my fill, but the salt in the canned meat only worsened my thirst.

The remainder of the night was marked by increasing thirst and more bomb explosions from the direction of the airport. Even though I was exhausted, swarms of insects, no bedding, and my growing thirst made it a sleepless night, the most miserable I remember from the war. At dawn, more thirsty than at any other time in my life, I saw a soldier drinking water from a can. He directed me to a well site where a three-foot-high post stood with a filthy rope line attached to an empty coffee can. I dropped it down into an eight-inch-wide hole in the ground until I heard it hit the water. I pulled it up and drank my fill. After eighteen hours without a sip of water, it was truly refreshing, and I then washed my face with what was left in the can. Back at camp after the sun rose, I looked out across the field to the well site and saw water buffalo grazing nearby. I decided to drink no more from there! Later in Tacloban, I saw signs warning Americans servicemen not to drink local water without boiling it first in order to sterilize amoebic dysentery and other dangerous microbes. Throughout the action on Leyte, our troops were plagued by ingesting parasitic flatworms (schistosomes) and giant round worms from water on the island. I was anxious for several days, but my luck held. It is astonishing that the casualty camp had no potable water and no warnings about the only water source on site.

One disappointment in completing this account is the failure to identify the Japanese airmen who torpedoed the *Saugrain*. Various reports claim the attackers flew the Nakajima Ki-43 "Oscar" single-engine fighter or the Yokosuka P1Y (twin-engine bomber). The most convincing evidence, however, points to a Nakajima torpedo bomber, either the B5N "Kate" or its replacement the B6N "Jill". Both were naval aircraft, the branch responsible for most Japanese aerial torpedo strikes, and both were single-engine bombers with a crew of three flying beneath a long cockpit canopy.

These planes were designed to launch from aircraft carriers. They had led the successful attack on Pearl Harbor, and they were a formidable threat to our fleets in the Pacific until late in the war. In the weeks before the arrival of the *Saugrain*'s convoy, however, the remaining Japanese carrier fleet had been destroyed in the battle of Leyte Gulf (23–26 October), and any surviving torpedo bombers in the Philippines were forced to fly from airfields on the islands. What little information can be learned from postwar interrogations of Japanese commanders suggests that the torpedo bombers that escaped destruction were based on the islands of Cebu and Mindanao.

Many historians believe that the fight for Leyte was a crucial turning point in the Pacific war, and the Allies steadily gained the upper hand in the skies over the islands. The Japanese army and navy aircraft in the Philippines were destroyed at a shocking pace, and no replacements arrived. The resulting chaos for the enemy ensured that few of their air battle records survived. Virtually no accounts from 1944 of Japanese torpedo bomber units exist in translation today. If the publication of this account results in the discovery of their stories, it will add a valuable chapter to the English-language history of the war.

Chapter 15

Marooned on Leyte

The next day, after a long wait, we were taken on another bumpy ride back to Tacloban where we boarded the Liberty ship *Gus W. Darnell*, which had been much damaged by an aerial torpedo and now served as a supply depot and temporary crew quarters. Once on board we had a joyous reunion with shipmates who had been rescued by the USS *San Pedro*. The USMS official in charge of the agency's port affairs briefed us and said there would be a meeting of the entire crew on the *Darnell* after all had been fed. We were quite hungry, and the K-rations were most welcome.

At the meeting we learned the fate of the *Saugrain*. News of the loss of the ship less than an hour from the entrance to Leyte Gulf came as a rude shock. We were stranded far from home with only our survival kits and the clothes on our backs, and our days as a united crew were coming to an end. But the meeting had an additional purpose: it was a call for volunteers to sign on as crew for the *Augustus Thomas*, a badly damaged Liberty ship at anchor in the harbor. It was hardly an appealing option, for we would have to restore the Liberty to service before we could sail her home to America.

Named for a noted American playwright and scriptwriter from St. Louis, the *Augustus Thomas* had been built and launched in September 1943 at the same Richmond, California, shipyard as the *Saugrain*. In her first year at sea the *Thomas* undertook a role similar to that of the *Saugrain*, shipping war supplies throughout the Southwest Pacific. Most recently the *Thomas* had arrived on 22 October from New Guinea with 3,000 tons of ammunition and 1,000 barrels of high-octane gasoline to support the first Army units landed on Leyte. After two days at anchor in San Pedro Harbor, she was the target of what some consider to have been the first successful Japanese suicide air attack of the Philippines campaign.

At 0840 on 24 October the Japanese pilot of a Mitsubishi G4M "Betty" bomber, with one of his plane's engines aflame from the gunfire of Allied ships in the harbor, aimed his aircraft at the *Thomas* and the USS *Sonoma* ATO-12, an Army tug, ocean, taking on water from the Liberty ship. The plane crash-dived into the stack of the tug setting her deck on fire, then burst into the hull of the *Thomas*, ripping open a ten-by-twelve-foot hole in her engine room. The skipper of the *Sonoma* coolly pulled her away from the Liberty ship, averting a disastrous explosion in the ammunition-loaded holds of the *Thomas*. Many men on board the two American ships were burned, and several were blown into the ocean unconscious. Miraculously there were no fatalities other than the seven members of the Japanese bomber crew.

The *Thomas* remained afloat after the attack, and the *Sonoma*, which was steadily taking on seawater, was towed toward shore where her hull settled eighteen feet below the surface of the bay with only her mangled stack and upper superstructure above water. In his report for November 1944, Admiral Nimitz included a report on the threat of suicide air attacks. The *Sonoma* and *Augustus Thomas* are among the first four incidents mentioned. Just four days before, the increasingly desperate enemy had decided to stake its remaining airpower on turning back the Allies in the Philippines. As part of this initiative Admiral Takijiro Onishi, commander of Japanese naval air forces in the Philippines, announced to his airmen the establishment of "special attack" (kamikaze) units.

In the attack on the *Thomas* there was little damage to the superstructure and deck equipment, but with the engine room blasted and filled with twenty feet of water, the ship would need major repairs to its power train. An underwater welding crew was already working to repair the hull, a job expected to take several more weeks. Once that was completed, our work could begin, adding six more weeks to the job. The USMS representative appealed to our patriotic instincts. The *Thomas* would be badly needed for the forthcoming invasion of Japan, he said, and those who restored her to service would then sail the vessel to San Francisco for a complete refitting, where the volunteers would be honored with medals and recognition from a grateful maritime service and from the steamship company that operated the ship. Moreover, each of us would receive double pay until we disembarked in California.

A worrisome hitch was that there would be no U.S. Navy Armed Guard crew on board for the voyage, but the man from USMS assured us that there were few enemy threats between the Philippines and San Francisco. Those men of the *Saugrain* who did not wish to volunteer were to be repatriated to America whenever space opened aboard other homeward-bound Liberty ships.

Most of the crew turned down the offer on the spot. Although some would be stranded in Leyte for weeks awaiting transport home, we never saw them again. I decided to think it over, attracted by a patriotic urge and the promise of recognition. Also, I knew there would be little threat of enemy action during the repairs, which appealed to me in light of the nervous state I was in after our sinking. I agreed to go aboard the *Thomas* to examine the dead vessel while I considered my options.

After a night on the *Darnell* I joined twenty officers and men aboard an LCI that transported us out the mile or so to where the *Thomas* was anchored. As we climbed aboard, I was amazed at the excellent condition of every part of the vessel except for the damaged hull and flooded engine room. The staterooms were shipshape and furnished with bedding and towels, and the galley was clean and fully equipped. The fuel tanks were relatively full as were the freshwater tanks. But only the main deck's plumbing could be used because the flooded generators meant there was no electricity to power the freshwater pumps to operate the heads on the lower decks.

There was much conversation and soul-searching among the visiting crewmen. Some fifteen of us agreed to stay overnight on the vessel for further consideration. Without power we would have to dine on Army rations by flashlight, but we were assured that food supplies and a five-kilowatt portable generator to run the ship's lights, plumbing, and galley service would soon arrive.

At the urging of the *Saugrain*'s chief engineer, I agreed to help restore this much-needed ship. He assured me that if the work became too onerous or dangerous, he would arrange my transport home. As for the others, after a trial of three days aboard the *Thomas*, only eight volunteers remained. The volunteers became a tightly knit team, and almost seventy years later I still have many memories of some of the more colorful characters. Like seamen marooned on a deserted island, we came to know one another far better than we had during our previous months at sea.

The *Saugrain*'s master, Anthony Van Cromphaut, was among the first to volunteer. He was in his sixties and a native of the Seattle area. Descended from a long line of European seafarers, he had spent his entire life at sea. Six feet, three inches tall and well built, he loved poetry. His favorite verse was "The Yarn of the Nancy Belle" by W. S. Gilbert of the Gilbert and Sullivan operetta duo. It was a long musical tale about the crew of a ship that ran aground and perished off an island in the South Seas, a very fitting story considering our own predicament. In the story, only ten men survived the wreck. They stayed alive by cannibalizing their shipmates, each drawing lots, one by one, until only the narrator, soon rescued by a passing ship, was left. I can still remember some verses the captain recited from the boat deck of the *Thomas* after a couple of drinks:

> *'Twas in the good ship* Nancy Bell
>   *That we sailed to the Indian Sea*
> *And there on a reef we come to grief*
>   *Which has often occurred to me.*

And pretty nigh all o' the crew was drowned
  (There was seventy-seven o' soul);
But only ten of the Nancy's men
  Said "Here!" to the muster roll.

There was me, and the cook, and the captain bold,
  And the mate of the Nancy brig,
And the bos'un tight, and a midshipmite,
  And the crew of the captain's gig.

These lines are fixed in my memory because the drinking went on right outside my stateroom. The happy-hour festivities usually degenerated into maudlin drunken bouts (the skipper was a regular), which often kept me from sleep. The skipper's loud reciting of his favorite lines was hammered into my skull. Yet I had come to respect Captain Van Cromphaut after witnessing his cool command during the crisis aboard the *Saugrain*. He was not one to compliment a subordinate for doing his duty, but if you did your job well, he would treat you with dignity and few cross words. Indeed, when we parted in California some months later, he said, "Mr. Melton. I'd be happy to have you in my crew anytime." That was good enough for me.

As our repair efforts got under way, I was once again working under the *Saugrain*'s chief engineer, Barney Hafslund. His excitement about the salvage operation had turned the tide in my decision to volunteer. Barney started his years at sea as a Navy man, rose through the enlisted ranks, and then joined the merchant marine and earned his chief's license. Hafslund was the only bearded engineer I sailed with during the war, and it gave him the look of the old salt that he truly was. As a Navy petty officer he had once helped to train a young midshipman who, years later, would become one of the great heroes of the Pacific war, Admiral William "Bull" Halsey.

During the salvage process Barney gave me a temporary promotion to second assistant engineer, the job I held for the rest of our service together. He delegated to me at age twenty-three much more authority than I probably deserved, and he always showed me the respect of a colleague. Our superb working relationship greatly accelerated the overhaul of the two Liberty ships we tackled in the Philippines. When we said farewell back in California, he handed me a glowing recommendation he had written for me that I still have among my war souvenirs.

My favorite among the volunteers from the *Saugrain* was second mate Robert Stone (no relation to the *Harnett*'s armed guard commander). A competent officer and navigator, he, too, received a temporary promotion to chief mate. His wry sense of humor kept me laughing. Who else but Stone would travel with a monkey in tow? He bought the animal when it was a few weeks old from a native in New Guinea during one of the *Saugrain*'s side trips. The monkey became attached to Stone, slept in his stateroom, and was often seen clinging to Robert's waist while the mate made his rounds. Crewmen loved to pretend to attack Stone, which always prompted an angry scolding from the loyal monkey.

We all took a liking to the monkey and teased him without mercy. As he matured, he became more bold and inclined to mischief. He would grab a crewman's cap or handkerchief, run out on deck, and scamper up the mainmast to perch and chatter as if he were laughing. Then he would climb down, leave the stolen clothing on the deck, and run back up the mast.

The boatswain from the *Saugrain*, Daniel O'Neil, was the most radical person I ever met. O'Neil was in his forties and had spent much of his life at sea. An Irishman, he was an active and unrepentant member of the outlawed Irish Republican Army and fierce in his hatred for the English. He ranted endlessly in his brogue about the "limeys" and loved to boast about his prewar guerrilla activities against the British. He had many stories to tell about how he came to hate Great Britain.

Daniel's drive to become a better IRA guerilla nearly cost him his life during the sinking of the *Saugrain*. When a crewman yelled "Torpedo portside!" everyone not on gun duty scurried for cover. All, that is, except for O'Neil, who ran toward the action, watching the torpedo's progress with great curiosity. Thinking it would miss us, he leaned over the gunwale at the fantail to determine, as it passed, whether a Japanese torpedo had one or two propellers. The "tin fish" struck the ship's propeller just beneath him and exploded. O'Neil was blown off his feet and several feet inboard, lost consciousness for several minutes, and had to be helped to his lifeboat station on the boat deck. Although his ears afterwards rang for as long as we sailed together, he never seemed to regret his foolishness on the fantail of the *Saugrain*.

Paul Jackson, the *Saugrain*'s purser, was another capable shipmate. Jackson was well read and educated, but he was unpopular among the crew because of his radical political views and agnostic religious beliefs. He was a card-carrying member of the Socialist Party and an admirer of Norman Thomas, the pacifist and six-time Socialist Party candidate for president of the United States. Most men on the *Saugrain* were uneducated, and for them there was little difference between a socialist and a communist.

Because the purser had a wife and family in Utah, his shameless womanizing did nothing to improve his standing among the men. During the repairs, he immediately got involved with a young Filipino girl and spent as much time ashore as possible. Jackson reported that he hoped to buy a few hectares of land where he could build a simple hut and establish a common-law marriage with his new lover. Paul confided in me that he was also trying to meet friendly local leftists who might connect him to a flourishing socialist colony in China's Sinkiang (Xinjiang) province. When he finally bought a small tract of land on Leyte, it became a trysting site for him and his girlfriend.

After our return to the United States, Paul quickly took up with a secretary in the office of the United Fruit Company (the ship's owners), and he divorced his American wife in order to marry her. When I asked him about the Filipino woman waiting back in Tacloban, he was evasive. Paul and I exchanged addresses when we parted. The next note I received from him, a year or so later, was a second divorce announcement. I was hardly surprised.

As our work went on, the captain became acquainted with some prominent citizens of Tacloban. The provincial treasurer invited us to his home for a party where we met other townsfolk and were introduced to *tuba*, the Philippine national drink. *Tuba* is distilled by passing the vapor from fermented coconut mash through tubes of green bamboo, condensing it into a brick-red liquor. We were all sadly disappointed by the product; one sip sent me to the back of the crowd where I could spit out the vile-tasting drink. The party also featured music (better described as noise) from a discordant band accompanying a beautiful and talented Filipino dancer who seemed to be well connected among the island's elite.

It was my first social event since leaving the United States, but I was glad to board the craft that took us back to the ship. When the captain later invited his new friends aboard the *Thomas* to reciprocate their hospitality, our party was even more boring, for it was a dry event. Liquor (other than *tuba*) was exceedingly hard to come by in Tacloban.

When the *Saugrain* went down, I lost all my uniforms and other clothing, my dopp kit, personal letters and belongings, souvenirs I had collected in the Pacific, and the gifts I bought in Sydney for Helen and my mother. A boarding party led by Captain Van Cromphaut after we abandoned ship rescued some of the *Saugrain*'s records, but the records of other units aboard were lost. The Army is known for its compulsive record keeping (in duplicate), however, and its archives revealed some of the stories of these Army units to add to the history of the *Saugrain*'s final voyage.

237th Anti-Aircraft Artillery Searchlight Battalion, Battery A
The guns, searchlights, generators, tools, and top-secret radar equipment of the 237th were lost when the *Saugrain* plunged to the sea bottom. I was told by officers aboard the *Saugrain* that we were carrying highly sophisticated radar controlled by a "computer," a new word for me at the time. Several commanders of the escort ships of Task Unit 76.4.7 mentioned in their action reports the special efforts made to save the *Saugrain* because of "valuable radar equipment" aboard. If the *Saugrain* was indeed the primary target of the convoy for the Japanese bombers, this equipment and the gunners who manned it would have more

than justified the enemy's persistence in finishing off the ship after she was first crippled.

With nearly three hundred soldiers on the *Saugrain*, the 237th was the largest unit aboard, nearly five times the number of the ship's crew. Nevertheless, when Michele Smith, a daughter of Sergeant Efrain Ramirez of the 237th, launched an online search for other veterans of the unit in 2003, she located only one, Sam Wilks. Michele's father, a native of New York City, told her that he had been trained on Signal Corps Radar 268 equipment. The SCR 268 used a long-wave signal to lock onto a night bomber and direct powerful searchlights to illuminate the attacker so that the gunners of the battery could see and fire on the target. This technology was developed in England well before the war, and by the time of MacArthur's invasion of the Philippines, it was already outdated.

A radical advancement in radar technology replaced the SCR 268's long wave. Also invented in England, SCR 584 technology emitted a shorter "microwave" to produce a more rapid and accurate return signal from a target. Radar engineers in the "Rad Lab" at MIT wired the SCR 584 to a new American analog computer, the M-9 gun director from Bell Laboratories, to calculate azimuth and range in order to control the traverse and elevation of an artillery gun barrel as it tracked a fast-moving aircraft using the rapidly developing technology of gun-laying, or automated aiming. Equally groundbreaking technology was the proximity fuse, developed at Johns Hopkins University during the war, which could detonate a

Sgt. Efrain Ramirez of the 237th AAA.
Courtesy of Michele Ramirez Smith

shell when it passed close to a target, whether or not the explosive actually struck the object.

This triad of innovations—microwave radar, gun-aiming by computer, and proximity fuses—were first successfully combined to block the V-1 rockets launched across the English Channel by Nazi Germany. An estimated 85 percent of the V-1s were destroyed. The SCR 584 system first appeared with frontline Allied troops during the Anzio landings on the Italian coast in January 1944. The invasion of the Philippines was probably the first successful application of SCR 584 with antiaircraft artillery in the Pacific. Whereas the receiver of SCR 268 was attached to a huge rectangular grill operated by two men seated on its control deck, the SCR 584's receiver used a much more compact circular device, the precursor of today's satellite dish. The SCR 584 system was so advanced that it was still in use nearly thirty years later during the Vietnam War.

Most unit training records of the 237th that survive refer to the SCR 268, but an intriguing drawing, a "Searchlight Defence Plan for Tacloban, Leyte," also survives. Dated 15 November 1944 (two weeks before the *Saugrain* departed Hollandia), the plan shows four proposed command stations for Battery A's use in protecting the Tacloban airstrip. These command stations appear to control four installed "584 gun radar" points and several "proposed radar" sites in the plan. SCR 268 is nowhere mentioned on the drawing. Clearly there were plans to deploy the 237th with the newer technology. The stories of hush-hush radar equipment among shipmates on the *Saugrain*'s crew suggest that the ship's holds probably contained at least one of the advanced SCR 584 radar systems. My shipboard friend who commanded the 237th, Bill Hubbard, never shared with me details about his gunners' technology, and it is likely that he was instructed to keep those secret.

If the training records of the 237th make only cursory mention of SCR 584 radar, how could the unit be expected to move into fortifications around Tacloban airstrip that depended on the newer technology? The answer may lie in a brief notation in a 12 October 1944 troop movement inventory of units due to embark from Finschhafen, New Guinea. Listed is the twenty-man "Radar Det[achment] SCR 584," under the command of the Army Air Force and not part of any artillery unit. Did this small specialized unit board the *Saugrain* in Finschhafen along with Battery A in order to train and work with the 237th to fill some of the "proposed radar" positions on the Searchlight Defence Plan? Until a cargo manifest is found for the *Saugrain*'s final voyage, the specific radar equipment in the flooded holds of the *Saugrain* on the bottom of Leyte Gulf will remain unknown.

In May 1943, the artillerymen had originated as a detachment of the 197th Coast Artillery Regiment (New Hampshire National Guard), which had arrived in Australia two months earlier. The third battalion of the 197th was redesignated as the 237th Anti-Aircraft Artillery Searchlight Battalion, comprising a headquarters battery and three combat batteries (A, B, and C) that were assigned to three separate coastal locations around Townsville, Queensland.

After September 1943, Battery B operated autonomously, and the batallion's remaining units (combat batteries A and C and the headquarters battery) moved to strengthen the antiaircraft defenses surrounding Finschhafen. There they trained and operated until Battery C was shipped to Leyte for the first wave of MacArthur's invasion, and the *Saugrain* picked up the rest of the battalion in Finschhafen as we loaded for Leyte.

Arriving in Hollandia, the commander of the 237th, Lieutenant Colonel Hubbard, ordered the unpacking of twelve of the battery's .50-caliber machine guns to supplement the firepower of the *Saugrain*. The armed guard commander on board, Lieutenant Dean Matthews, countermanded that order, and the machine guns were repacked and stowed. It is interesting to consider whether this additional armament could have helped to drive off the attack of the torpedo planes on 5 December.

Certainly the men of the 237th were expecting much more exciting action when they arrived on Leyte, but after the sinking of their guns and radar, they, too, were marooned. A small number of the troops were transferred to other batteries, but most spent the rest of the war in boring tasks such as guarding the docks of Tacloban and prisoner-of-war stockades. Replacement equipment was promised, but as 1945 advanced and Japanese air forces in the Philippines steadily declined, the 237th found itself fighting tropical disease and parasites rather than Axis enemies. As Sam Wilks remarked, after the sinking of the *Saugrain*, his unit "never actively or aggressively regained our usual duties."

Of the hundreds of artillerymen aboard the *Saugrain* with me en route to the Philippines, I have details about only two. Efrain "Ram" Ramirez was born in San Juan and grew up in a tightly knit Puerto Rican–American family in New York. After the war, he returned home and began a thirty-year-long career with the U.S. Postal Service. Efrain married Anita Piotti, the daughter of family friends, and together they raised a son and two daughters. Retiring to Florida, he died two weeks shy of his ninetieth birthday in 2009. I never again saw his commander, my friend Bill Hubbard, who retired as a full colonel in the regular Army in 1970 after serving in Korea, France, and Germany. In his final assignment, he was chief of staff of the Test and Evaluation Command at Aberdeen Proving Ground in Maryland, where much artillery technology is developed. During his military career, he was awarded the Legion of Merit with oak leaf cluster and, for returning to the *Saugrain* after it was abandoned, the Bronze Star.

1797th Engineer Base Foundry Detachment

Little has been written about the roles of the many engineer maintenance units operating with the Services of Supply in the South West Pacific Area, and the 1797th Engineers and its seventeen soldiers is no exception. During our passage, I had no idea they were even aboard the ship. The Army's foundry units fabricated replacement parts for heavy equipment and marine machinery and built customized tools and jigs for the engineering and construction battalions working on military installations, all of which was needed throughout the rest of the war in the Pacific. This unit was called on for casting molten bronze, iron, and steel, especially when the Army could not wait for a spare parts shipment from the United States. Replacement equipment must have been provided, for the unit was later commended for its service in the Philippines. The 1797th was reactivated in 1965 for service in the Vietnam War as the 579th Engineer Detachment.

1619th Engineer Map Depot Detachment
MacArthur's plans for fighting on Leyte called for map depot detachments to provide timely intelligence to small-unit commanders and all supporting forces. As the island hopping in the Pacific accelerated, depots and their staffs were established at strategic points in the war zone to receive bulk shipments of maps from Australia and America and to store, index, and distribute such critical campaign supplies. Sub-depots were likewise established closer to the front to meet the needs of assault commanders.

The life-or-death responsibilities of these map units led to tremendous pressures on them to perform, and the fluid battlefield conditions in the Philippines demanded frequent updates and unreasonable requests. Often, the units had less than a week to identify and transport the map grids that would be needed on the front lines.

Loaded onto the *Saugrain* were the men of the 1619th Engineer Map Depot Detachment. This squad-sized unit of some twenty men was activated in Brisbane in May 1944 and then moved to Hollandia. There they found other map units already on site, working day and night to supply combat troops fighting on New Guinea and other Army units training for the Leyte landings. The 1619th Engineers were ordered to work alongside the 1615th Engineers to design and establish a base map operation on Leyte.

The *Saugrain* transported the men of the 1619th Engineers and their depot equipment as well as an estimated fifty tons of map stocks organized by the unit for the Luzon operation, which was scheduled for 20 December. These actions were to be followed by landings on Iwo Jima by Admiral Nimitz's forces. The sinking of the *Saugrain* and the loss of these map materials less than two weeks before the date set for the Luzon landings may have been a factor in the decision to delay the landings until 9 January. This decision forced a delay also in the launch of Nimitz's landings on Iwo Jima. What is known is that the Corps of Engineers staff at headquarters in Hollandia had to shift into high gear to reassemble the lost map stocks and ship them without delay to Leyte.

It was more than a coincidence that 1619th Engineer Map Depot was transported with the 2773rd Engineers, as the two units would eventually co-locate in Tolosa, on Leyte about fifteen miles south of Tacloban airstrip. Their adjacent location facilitated the express printing of map detail enlargements and other special needs to accommodate the changing situation on the ground for the troops.

After MacArthur's Sixth Army landed on Luzon, the fighting there increasingly drew the attention and resources of all at MacArthur's headquarters. As the fighting on Luzon and the battle for the capital city of Manila advanced in the spring of 1945, it was necessary for the two map depots to transfer their facilities to that island. There they joined two other map supply units, the 1618th Engineers from Hollandia and the 1604th Engineers from Brisbane, to meet the relentless map demands of the fighting troops and to prepare for the invasion of the Japanese mainland, China, and Korea.

The Japanese surrender meant these invasions were unnecessary, but by October 1945, the 1619th had moved its operations to Tokyo for its critical role of indexing and preserving maps acquired in Japan for the occupation and administration of the conquered foe. By the end of 1945, the four map depots had handled, in that year alone, more than 55 million maps weighing a total of 2,500 tons.

2773rd Engineer Base Reproduction Company
The *Saugrain* was carrying only twenty-eight men from the 2773rd, but their additions to this story are numerous. They formed a volunteer advance echelon for their company, escorting supplies and equipment and preparing for the rest of the unit soon to follow.

Accompanying the men on the voyage was the 2773rd's mascot, a Boston terrier named Miss Ha'Penny, who is portrayed in the unit's emblem. When the attack came, she apparently found refuge deep in the ship and could not be found. Miss Ha'Penny went down with the *Saugrain*.

The company began service as the 1500th Engineer Reproduction Platoon and was expanded into a company shortly before the voyage to Leyte. When replacement equipment and the rest of the company arrived in January, they established a printing plant in Tolosa adjacent to the 1619th's map depot with printing presses in two vans parked on site. There was also a cartographic unit in the Philippines, the 648th Engineers, which drew detailed maps that the printers could reproduce in large quantities. The 2773rd printed Philippine editions of *Time* magazine and the military newspaper *Stars and Stripes,* as well as a myriad of communication jobs for MacArthur and his senior staff. The unit's history was recounted in *Brisbanilla Odyssey,* published and printed on the unit's equipment. The 2773rd produced at least one other similar publication, the wartime history of the Army's 32nd Infantry Division. Less than two months after landing on Leyte, the company was on the move again, headed for Luzon on *LST 1017*.

One of the first veterans to contribute stories about the *Saugrain*'s voyage for this book was Tom Holst, whom I spoke with by telephone on 14 March 2010. Tom grew up in Omaha; after high school, he went to work for the Union Pacific Railroad as a photostat and blueprint operator. On 7 December 1941, Tom was emerging from a movie matinee when he learned about the attack on Pearl Harbor. He soon enlisted in the Nebraska State Guard and, based on his railroad company skills, he was transferred to the U.S. Army Signal Corps's night school to learn Army communications.

Called to active duty early in 1943, Tom entered basic training at Ft. Leavenworth, Kansas, and was posted to a troopship in San Francisco. After a weeks-long passage to New Guinea, he transferred to a ship bound for Brisbane, Australia, where he began work with the Corps of Engineers in black-and-white photographic print reproduction, lithography, and other press duties using the company's offset, letterpress, and photostatic printing equipment. Tom learned quickly that maps and other intelligence products were desperately needed in the South West Pacific Area (SWPA). Operational maps for commanders, terrain studies and target maps for the infantry, geodetic maps for the Navy, and air photos for pre-invasion plans became his regular duties in May 1944 when Tom's unit became the 1500th Engineer Reproduction Platoon.

When Tom's unit was notified of deployment to the Philippines, the group was expanded to become the 2773rd Engineer Base Reproduction Company. Once embarked on *Antoine Saugrain*, Holst remembers:

> Our unit was camped on deck with cots under tarps strung about to block the sun and rain. Being on deck, I spotted the Japanese plane as soon as the alarm sounded. It was a single engine job, and I got an unforgettable view of its pilot grinning at us through his goggles. His cockpit cover was open to enjoy the view and fresh air. I'm sure he was the squadron leader, and he headed straight for the *Saugrain* as if we were the prime target of the attack. I will always believe that the Japanese had a spy in Hollandia who knew what valuable cargo our ship was carrying, an advanced radar system, an antiaircraft battalion, and a Corps of Engineers unit on its way to supply maps and other intelligence reports to General MacArthur's headquarters for South West Pacific Area. After the first torpedo hit, I scrambled under one of the trucks on deck because I feared we would be strafed, so I never saw the second torpedo bomber.

Several of the photographs in this book from the *Saugrain*'s final voyage and sinking were scanned from Tom's collection. These images were taken by Tom and other photographers of the 2773rd, including George Wessels, and James Foster.

Pressman Tom Holst (left) and photographer George Wessels of the 2773rd Engineers, 1944. *Courtesy of Thomas Holst*

Sergeant James "Shorty" Foster had grown up on the South Side of Chicago, part of a closely knit Irish-Catholic family. Drafted into the Army at age twenty-four, he worked as a draftsman but soon developed special skills in photography and lithography. James joined the 2773rd in June 1943 and served with the unit for the remainder of the war. Foster enjoyed the freewheeling intelligence work of the 2773rd, and he volunteered with Kolankiewicz and Holst in the unit's forward echelon of twenty-eight men on board the *Saugrain*. Their mission was to transport supplies and equipment to establish a new base adjacent to the 1619th Map Depot in Tolosa.

When working in the base plant, Lee Kolankiewicz served as a stripper in the preparation of maps. In a message to the daughter of his comrade Lenny Scinto, he explained his work:

When a job first arrived at our company, it was logged in, and then sent through the lithographic process. The first stop for a document was the Camera Section. The copy camera was a huge piece of equipment kept in a separate room, and it had a target surface of four feet square. A negative was made and sent to the Layout Section. Layout would make corrections to the negative and prepare it geometrically and layout-wise for the making of a zinc plate in the Plate Section. The zinc plate, with the impression of the document etched on its surface would then be sent to Lenny Scinto and his friends in the Press Section. The presses would produce the required number of copies which were delivered back to Engineer Intelligence SWPA for distribution.

We did other jobs of course that were produced in quite large quantities, thousands. Terrain studies, aerial photographs, topographic maps, studies of many different types were all part of what we had to do.

Lee's more exciting work, for which he and James Foster volunteered, was to serve with MacArthur's intelligence team in small groups of four to six men, traveling to forward areas, island by island, as the invasion advanced. Their task was to photograph and survey towns and buildings in the Army's path, and to gather information from local people. Their photos were analyzed for potential threats, and their draft maps were used to assess possible landing and invasion zones. The work of the different teams was highly classified and dangerous, and the men were never told what other groups were doing. One group photographed a liberated POW camp in northern Luzon. Sometimes one group would be sent to spy on another. In September 1945, MacArthur awarded the 2773rd a Meritorious Unit Citation. Before disbanding, the company served in Korea as part of MacArthur's army of occupation.

The advance team of the 2773rd was, according to Kolankiewicz:

> attached to MacArthur's headquarters in Engineer Intelligence, South West Pacific Area. Working for the general were his G-2 (Intelligence) and G-3 (Planning) Sections. These two groups were responsible for reporting on enemy troop dispositions, strengths and locations. G-3 section would then proceed with the planning involved in operations against the enemy. The top commanders in the SWPA had to be kept advised of all this intelligence, and it was our company's job to reproduce the documents that G-2 and G-3 produced. This would be about 75 copies that were then distributed to the generals and field commanders who were involved so that they could then properly plan for the contemplated actions necessary. Documents coming from G-2 could have as high a security classification as SECRET. Documents coming from G-3 were usually classified TOP SECRET because they contained the dates that invasion plans were to be executed.

It is remarkable that so many veterans of the 2773rd emerged in the research for this book. Their accounts make clear that the marooning of their company was brief, and within a month it had resumed its core mission. The men of the 2773rd would serve in the Philippines until victory in the Pacific was assured. Their memories of this period added tremendously to this story, and it is unfortunate that more living members of the other units on board could not be found during the research for this chapter.

After the war, the men of the 2773rd took different paths to career and family. Lee Kolankiewicz went to college and earned a commission in the Army engineers. He was recalled to active duty in the Korean War. Discharged a captain, he worked as an engineer in the program to build America's nuclear submarine fleet and, with his wife, Arlene, raised a family of five children. He still has homes in Pennsylvania and Florida. Tom Holst married Margaret, had children, and settled in Iowa where he was employed by Pocahontas County building bridges and roads. Later he worked in the grain storage business. Tom died in 2014.

James Foster used the GI Bill to earn a degree and continued as a draftsman until he purchased a ServiceMaster franchise in

Lee Kolankiewicz (left) and comrade James "Shorty" Foster of the 2773rd Engineers, Philippines, 1945. *Courtesy of Patrick Tobias*

Illinois, which he operated until his death in 1991. He and his wife, Betty, were blessed with four children. Leonard Scinto returned to the printing business, first in sales and later as an owner and operator of a printing firm in Elk Grove, Illinois. He married Carmel and they raised four children before her death. He was also married for ten years to Carol, and she survived him after his death in 2009.

The 49th Fighter Group

Another Army unit on Leyte was critical to the *Saugrain*'s story. The publication in 1996 of the history of the 49th Fighter Group of the Fifth Army Air Force revealed the names of the P-38 Lightning pilots who fought off the first kamikaze attack on the crippled *Saugrain* and our rescue vessels. Thanks to them, I escaped being shipwrecked twice in one day when our rescue ship was attacked. Fighter pilots flew without a crew aboard, manning not only the plane's controls but also its guns, a tremendously demanding feat. Their roles were to guard our bombers from enemy fighters and to attack the enemy's bombers.

The 49th was the most celebrated and successful fighter unit in the Pacific, and one of its pilots was the top American fighter ace of World War II. Major Richard Bong shot down forty enemy aircraft during the war, twenty-one of them as a member of the 49th Fighter Group. The unit arrived in New Guinea in October 1942 with the Fifth Air Force. Over the next two years, it took part in many of the brutal air battles that took place over the vast island while flying Curtiss P-40 Warhawks, Republic P-47 Thunderbolts, and the Lockheed P-38 Lightnings with their distinctive planform of nacelle and twin booms. The Japanese air forces were steadily repulsed. By May 1944 the 49th was flying out of Finschhafen and Hollandia in New Guinea while preparing for the upcoming air support of the Philippine landings and the battles that followed. A convoy carrying some of the first invasion troops delivered the pilots and aircraft of the 49th Fighter Group to

Leyte where, after a seesaw battle, the Allies wrested command of the airfield at Tacloban that the 49th would soon call home.

On 5 December, as Task Unit 76.4.7 neared Leyte, a separate convoy embarked carrying troops and equipment for General MacArthur's first landings on the west coast of Leyte. Our troubles with Japanese dive-bombers that afternoon were likely due in part to the diversion of so much Allied airpower to defend the other convoy. The Allies' surprise attacks that are today known as the battle of Ormoc Bay unfolded over the next several days.

Fortunately, not all Allied airpower was diverted west. When dawn broke on 6 December, the morning after the rescue of the men of the *Saugrain*, P-38 Lightning pilots of the Screamin' Demons (7th Squadron of the 49th Fighter Group) were already on patrol. As a member of the unit wrote about their defense of the *Saugrain* in the history of the 49th, "Capt. John Haher with wingmen Second Lt. Bill Thompson, element leader Lt. Jim Jarrell and wingman Second Lt. Ollie Atchison were at 6,000 feet above a support convoy in the eastern waters of Surigao Strait off Dinagat Island" when they spotted a Japanese Mitsubishi Ki-46 "Dinah" aircraft. Like the Lightnings of the Screamin' Demons, the Ki-46 was a remarkable airplane. It became one of the fastest in Japan's air arsenal when it was fitted with a pair of fuel-injected 1,500-horsepower engines and a streamlined nose and canopy. That version, which also saw duty as a heavy fighter plane, could reach speeds of 390 mph and climb to 26,000 feet. Until 1944, the Dinah was used primarily in reconnaissance, but

Fifth Air Force pilots (7th Squadron of the 49th Fighter Group) defeat Japanese attackers determined to sink the crippled *Saugrain*.
Painting by James Rae

by the end of the war it was also used as a heavy fighter and a kamikaze weapon.

The attack of the Ki-46 described by the Lightning pilots matches what everyone on the *Coronado*'s deck witnessed:

> All four Demons dropped their tanks and advanced their throttles up for the expected routine high altitude pursuit of the twin-engine speedster, but that morning, the Japanese Naval Air Force crew intended to have a close look at the American vessels. As Haher's flight turned in behind the Dinah, it suddenly nosed down and headed straight for the convoy ships. Haher pressed after the spy plane at 400 mph, and after a full minute of pursuit down to a thousand feet above the sea, he had only closed to maximum firing range. He fired all the way down to point blank, but despite numerous hits, the victim remained airborne. The captain fired off his last tracers at the sturdy Mitsubishi, then wheeled aside to let elements Jarrell and Atchison have their shots. After Atchison fired and overran the rugged target, Jarrell finally hit the left engine which began to emit smoke. Before Thompson could fire, the wounded Dinah slowly dropped off on its right wing until the wingtip snagged a wave and it tumbled into a spectacular explosion.

Having the rare experience of witnessing at close range such dramatic aerial combat, it is no wonder I was forever enamored with the P-38 Lightning. I was not alone, for Harley Earl, one of the most famous automobile designers of the postwar era, was so inspired by the Lightning that he credited the aircraft as the inspiration for his bold tailfin-design cars, including the 1948 Cadillac and the first Corvette models.

The men on the *Coronado* that morning had reason to be grateful for the sharpshooting of Lieutenant Jarrell and the timely and aggressive flying of his 7th Fighter Squadron comrades. Their success, along with that of the other squadrons of the 49th Fighter Group made the 49th the top unit in the Pacific Theater, recording 668 enemy aircraft destroyed in the air.

Chapter 16

Witness to Annihilation

For the refugees from the *Saugrain*, restoring the *Augustus Thomas* to service was taking more time than expected. The ship was anchored in San Pedro Bay where underwater welding on her hull was going slowly. Nothing else could be done to the engine room until the hull was sealed and all the water pumped out. We had boarded the ship on 7 December and when the holiday season arrived, we still had no electrical power on board. The U.S. Army furnished us a complete Christmas dinner of turkey, dressing, gravy, brussels sprouts, cranberry sauce, and mince pie, but it was the bleakest Yule I ever experienced.

By this time the shortage of liquor in the war zone had shut down the heavy drinking bouts of the repair crew. Some foul-tasting medical alcohol was acquired from shore by the captain, but even the hard-core drinkers had to dilute it heavily with grapefruit juice to get it down. This "Kickapoo joy juice," named after the hillbilly's cocktail in the Li'l Abner cartoons, prompted a party outside my stateroom on Christmas Eve. The festivities soon descended into a mournful affair.

I longed to sing the traditional carols with others, but no one showed any interest. With my flashlight I retreated to the bow of the darkened vessel where I sat and recited what I remembered of the second chapter of the Gospel of St. Luke. The Bible I had dutifully packed for the voyage, like all my belongings from the *Saugrain*, was at the bottom of the sea. Singing aloud to myself those carols I knew by heart, I thought of my wife and my family back home and cursed myself for turning down a chance to be shipped home in time for Christmas.

We resumed our work on the *Thomas* on the day after Christmas. Without electricity we had no ship's radio and so were unaware of the recent landings on the Philippine island of Mindoro to our northwest. General McArthur had ordered the invasion so that airstrips could be built on the island much closer to his prime objective, Luzon, and its principal city of Manila. The Mindoro operation led to some of the most deadly attacks faced by the merchant marine in the Pacific Theater of the war, and we were soon to get an unpleasant personal introduction to casualties of the invasion.

On the day after New Year's in 1945, I was awakened before dawn by the sound of a ship tying up alongside the *Thomas*. Sitting up in my bunk and peering out of the porthole, I saw a spotlight from a live vessel in control of a derelict Liberty ship that had been horribly mangled and burned. Soon the wreck's stench overwhelmed the air of the *Thomas*.

Dressing quickly I went on deck with flashlight in hand where I could see more details of the carnage, but the unbearable smell forced me to retreat forward where I could hear men talking. Bob Stone, the recently promoted first mate, was assisting the tie-up with the help of two Filipinos who were working with us on the *Thomas*. Bob told me that the Liberty ship had been the victim of a kamikaze attack during the invasion of Mindoro, a place unknown to either of us. The Navy vessel towing the derelict had been ordered to tie it up to our ship. I was outraged and wondered if I was to be stuck forever in the war zone repairing Liberty ships blasted by kamikaze pilots.

The arrival of the SS *William Sharon* sparked both curiosity and confusion for all hands of our skeleton crew. The stench made sleep impossible, so everyone retreated to the starboard side and gathered around the captain. He reported that someone from the maritime service would arrive after daylight with a cleanup crew. On the ship were dead bodies from the ship's crew and the

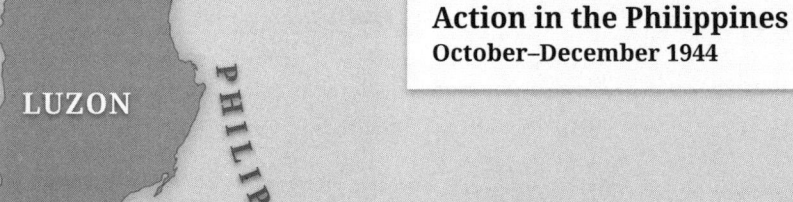

Action in the Philippines
October–December 1944

24 October 1944: As the Army tug *Sonoma* takes on water from SS *Augustus Thomas* a Japanese bomber crash-dives into the two vessels, sinking the tug in a suicide attack.

6 December 1944: After nearly 24 hours under tow, the *Saugrain* is the target again for Japanese bombers which sink the *Saugrain* in 40 fathoms of water

28 December 1944: A kamikaze dive-bomber crashes onto the deck of SS *William Sharon*, killing eleven crewmen. An ammunition ship near the *Sharon* is also struck and disintegrates, killing all aboard and further damaging the *Sharon*.

5 December 1944: In convoy from New Guinea to Leyte, SS *Antoine Saugrain* is attacked by Japanese torpedo bombers and crippled. The ship's crew abandons ship, rescued by U.S. Navy patrol frigates. Ocean tug *LT-454* attempts to tow the *Saugrain* to Tacloban.

Map by Joshua Smith

Japanese kamikaze plane, which had to be removed before anything else could be accomplished. Also, he warned us, explosives were stored below along with several tons of rotting beef. The foul meat had to be cleared from iceboxes in the refrigeration compartment that had stopped working when the ship's power was snuffed out.

The same USMS official who had put us aboard the *Augustus Thomas* arrived later that morning. He brought along soldiers from Graves Registration Services, whose duty it was to remove the bodies and see to their proper burial. Another crew of Filipino workers carried out the rotted beef, and the attending Army tug pumped in seawater to hose everything down. Gradually the stench abated somewhat. We helped with the work, and I came across a hand-sized piece of the suicide plane's fuselage and part of a crystal bombsight lying among the debris on the starboard side. Both would become lifetime souvenirs of the Pacific war.

While he was on board, the administrator conferred with the captain and the chief engineer about transferring our whole volunteer crew to the *Sharon*. It appeared that the *Sharon* would require less work than the *Thomas* to become seaworthy enough to sail her to a shipyard in America for major repairs. This plan would mean a loss of comfort for the crew, as all officer quarters were destroyed when the *Sharon* was hit. We examined the part of the engine room that was above the nine feet of water present, inspected other vital equipment, and toured the crew quarters where we would be housed.

The new proposal, which included the same conditions as those we assumed with the *Thomas*, aroused both hopes and doubts for me. Overriding all concerns was the huge hole slashed into the engine room hull of the *Thomas* by the kamikaze plane. The underwater welders might never be able to close that breach. Which ship would get us home faster and alive? We faced a critical decision that involved many factors, and I immediately set out to determine the extent of the *Sharon*'s mechanical damage.

Once on board I noted that the exhaust stack would have to be cut away completely and replaced from the boat deck up, a huge task. I made my way to the fiddley deck for a bird's-eye view of the flooded engine room. From the beam of my flashlight, I saw that the three idle steam-powered generators appeared to be perfectly normal, dry and undamaged. Knowing that a functioning electrical system would soon be possible was an essential advantage. I descended the ladder to the electrical switchboard on the platform level with the generators. All of its equipment looked completely dry and sound. Most of the main engine stood above water and appeared to be undamaged. In fact, only the main and crank bearings were submerged.

Although I would be involved in all equipment repairs, as the newly promoted second assistant engineer my primary responsibility would be the operation of the boilers and their blowers and fuel pumps. I knew that my most critical task would be to rebuild the brickwork in the boiler boxes damaged by the burning Japanese plane. It promised to be a staggering task and one I had never performed on a ship. There was no instruction in the Kings Point curriculum for this repair.

Despite our many reservations, by the time the administrator returned on the following day, each of us had decided to sign on for transfer to the *Sharon*. As the only engineer other than the aging chief, I insisted that the portable generator we had been promised be delivered without delay, and the USMS officer agreed. We transferred our few personal belongings to the *Sharon* and said good-bye to the *Thomas* and nearly a month of wasted efforts.

The next morning I went right to work to adapt the *Sharon*'s electrical wiring to the portable gasoline-powered generator that we would soon receive. All hands looked forward to having lights and fans for our quarters and power for the galley appliances. While awaiting the generator I blocked off all electrical circuits to the destroyed upper decks by cutting and then taping the wiring leading to each. Doing this would enable me to run wires from the generator to any critical switchboards that remained.

Dining on cold rations, the repair crew speculated about what the *Sharon* had been through over the past week. It would be years before I would discover details about how her stack and superstructure had been so burned and mangled. Her voyage from Leyte to Mindoro turned out to be one of the most horrific Pacific convoys of the war.

The SS *William Sharon* was launched in San Francisco in October 1943 and was soon in the South West Pacific, plying many of the same routes as the *Saugrain*. On 27 December she departed Leyte with the third resupply convoy for the Mindoro invasion, which had begun two weeks earlier. MacArthur's choice of Mindoro as the next invasion site after Leyte had surprised the Japanese commanders, and the Allies found the island only lightly defended. After gaining the upper hand within forty-eight hours, the Allies' engineer battalions began building an airbase at San Jose on the southern tip of Mindoro. It would be used to launch bombers and fighters to support the landings on Luzon planned for January.

The Mindoro resupply convoy, designated L-3 U Plus 15, assembled off Leyte in three divisions arrayed in five columns across. Twenty-six LSTs were in the lead division carrying all kinds of equipment and personnel to support, man, and fortify the new Mindoro airstrips, including pilots and ground crews of the 49th Fighter Group. We had loudly cheered men of this unit when their P-38 Lightnings drove off the Japanese aircraft attacking the *Coronado* three weeks before. The airmen of the 49th were eager to trade the mud, mosquitoes, and malaria of Tacloban airdrome for the drier landing strip of Hill Airfield, which had been completed in just eight days at San Jose.

Division 2 of the convoy transported cargo and supplies, much of it highly combustible fuel and munitions. There were six Army freight and supply ships and five Liberty ships, including one outfitted as a tanker (SS *Porcupine*) by the Navy to carry aviation gasoline. The *Lewis L. Dyche* and the *John Burke* were loaded to the gunwales with ammunition, bombs, and fuses. The *William Sharon* carried trucks, pontoons, 3,000 tons of ammunition, 3,000 cases of beer, and 1,000 tons of beef and other rations. The *Sharon* was also towing an LCM (landing craft, mechanical).

The convoy's third division was transporting a large diversionary unit, Task Force 77.11, MacArthur's top-secret deception strategy for his planned knockout blow in the Philippines. The mission of TF 77.11 was to simulate an amphibious invasion of the southern coast of Luzon in order to mask MacArthur's real objective, large troop landings in Lingayen Gulf, northwest of Manila. There were two Japanese divisions near the south coast, and MacArthur wanted them held in place to prevent their reinforcement of the Lingayen Gulf defenses.

Among the resources of Diversionary Task Force 77.11 were twenty-nine PT boats. These patrol torpedo boats were speedy, well-armed plywood vessels driven by powerful diesel engines, and they would serve during the convoy's passage to attack any ships or aircraft that slipped through the Navy's powerful screen of nine destroyers circling the slow-moving ships. Two seaplane tenders steamed astern of the convoy on each side, operating radar and sonar systems for security.

Central to the diversionary plan was a flotilla of twenty-three LCI(L)s (landing craft infantry, large) "loaded to capacity with ordnance, supplies and equipment of Beach Jumper Units; spare ammunition, smoke, dry stores, avgas and base equipment and 176 personnel for PTs; plus 965 troops of 21st Infantry Regiment, 24th U.S. Army Division." The commander of Diversionary Task Force 77.11 was Captain George Mentz. With a flotilla of large landing craft, a battalion of infantry troops, three squadrons of PT boats, and 160 commandos, Captain Mentz had a formidable deception force and a wealth of tricks up his sleeve.

In contrast to the formidable escort of destroyers, there was surprisingly little air cover for the convoy. The commander of one of the seaplane tenders called the convoy "a running battle all the way, and we paid heavily in men, ships, and supplies to get it through." Neither the *Sharon* nor the *Burke* would "get through" the Japanese kamikaze air attack. At 0310 hours of 28 December, and again five hours later, Japanese spotter planes were sighted above the convoy, beyond the range of the largest guns of the escorts. By 1020 hours that morning, Division 2 of the convoy was under attack by six enemy Aichi D3A "Val" dive-bombers. The first attacker burst into flame from ships' fire; he tried to dive into one of the ships but, missing his target, crashed into the sea. Close behind, a second plane exploded amidships on the *John Burke,* igniting a dangerous fire. Within minutes a third aircraft crashed on the deck of the *Sharon,* followed within seconds by the colossal explosion of the burning *Burke* as its raging fire reached the ammunition in the holds.

From two miles astern, the commanding officer of the seaplane tender USS *Half Moon* witnessed the annihilation of the *John Burke* and later wrote, "Only those who have seen an ammunition ship go up can understand what that explosion was like. It defies description in mere words. The sea seemed to boil out from below while the heavy clouds above split to make room for the blast. Then the smoke blotted out everything, even the sky."

The *Burke* vanished with all hands. More than a mile from the site, Lieutenant George Johnson, the medical officer of the destroyer *Bush,* happened to be filming the attack, and his brief 16mm clip has been digitized and posted on the Internet. It is one of the most astonishing war scenes ever filmed. The film clip opens as the second kamikaze plane ignites just before exploding on the deck of the *William Sharon.* Then Lieutenant Johnson quickly swings the camera left to capture the *Burke*'s stunning blast, and its shockwave rushes past the camera and instantly parts the clouds above. In addition to extinguishing the lives of the sixty-eight men aboard the *Burke,* the blast sank a nearby freight and supply ship and opened the seams of one of the PT boats some distance away. Debris from the massive explosion killed three soldiers and a sailor on nearby ships and wounded twenty-three others. Among those killed on the *Burke* was merchant marine cadet-midshipman Donald J. Kannitzer.

Kamikaze aircraft were circling overhead, a huge column of smoke from the *Burke*'s explosion blanketed the center of the convoy, and a dangerous fire was raging on the deck of the *Sharon.* Six members of the *Sharon*'s crew and five gunners from the ship's armed guard had perished in the action. Moving to the rescue without hesitation at 1043 hours was the destroyer *Wilson*. For the *Wilson*'s sailors, who had just watched as a large Liberty ship next to the *Sharon* seemed to vaporize in an instant, it must have been terrifying to plunge into harm's way.

The *Wilson* had first to deal with the obstruction caused by the LCM the *Sharon* was towing. The skeleton crew of the smaller vessel had been either stunned or blown into the water in the massive explosion. Although the *Sharon* was dead in the water, the LCM's engines were stuck "all ahead full." The vessel was cut loose, and she took off like a wild colt. The *Wilson* fired a shell into her hull, but when last seen, the LCM was sailing unmanned northward with her engines turning over full speed. After several false starts due to "flash red" warnings of air attacks, the *Wilson*'s first responders were soon aboard the *Sharon*. The *Wilson*'s sailors were fighting fires, tending to wounded men, and evacuating crew members who had been dazed by the phenomenal blast on the sea's surface and by its seismic echo under water, a concussion that rocked the deck beneath them like an earthquake.

At 1430, after nearly four hours of anxious duty, the *Wilson* reported all fires on board the *Sharon* extinguished. One of the derelict's anchors was veered out to slow her drifting, and the *Wilson* resumed her course to catch up with the convoy. A few planes of combat air patrol had appeared overhead after the morning attack was over, but it wasn't until 1220 that there was reasonable air coverage, almost twenty-four hours after the convoy had got under way.

Early in the evening, four Allied ships buried the dead at sea. The day's attacks were not over, however. One observer described the Japanese kamikaze strategy throughout the three days of attacks: "Normally they circled about at great range, apparently selecting targets, then dove to the attack at angles varying from ten degrees to an almost vertical dive. Most of the attacking planes came in with the intent of crashing their targets and most were successful. These invariably burst into flame just prior to the crash, and it is believed by this command that these flames are self-inflicted by the plane to add to its destructive capacity."

For the next two days, flights of Japanese aircraft, three or four airplanes at a time, attacked ships in the convoy and the ships' gunners were usually able to drive them away with the help of air cover that belatedly arrived in the form of twenty-eight P-38 Lightnings and four Vought F4U Corsairs. However, one Japanese aerial torpedo found its mark, striking *LST 750* and setting off a tremendous explosion. Within thirty minutes it was clear that the ship was finished, and after her survivors were rescued, the destroyer *Edwards* was ordered to sink the LST by gunfire.

On 30 December the convoy reached its destination, Mindoro's Mangarin Bay, and the LCI(L)s disembarked their troops and found anchorage. But thanks to the persistence of the kamikaze, the ships' harrowing ordeal was not yet over. At 1550 hours, four kamikazes returned and three of the planes selected targets. One picked the destroyer *Gansevoort*, patrolling outside Mangarin Bay, and dived into her amidships, setting her afire. The second dived onto the Liberty fuel tanker *Porcupine*, which began burning furiously. Fires on the *Gansevoort* were brought under control an hour later, and she was beached. The *Porcupine* was less fortunate and the red-hot ship had to be abandoned, burning to its waterline in a pool of its own oil.

The third pilot, carrying a 500-pound bomb, bounced off the sea into the gunwale of the *Orestes*, the PT boat tender and flagship of Captain Mentz, who commanded Task Force 77.11. The bomb burst through the deck and exploded, and the plane set the *Orestes* afire. Her fire-fighting water mains were severed and all power was lost. Captain Mentz was on the bridge and he was blown into the sea, breaking both of his arms. His chief staff officer was killed as was the commander of one of the beach jumper units. The waters around the ship were soon filled with swimming men blown overboard or jumping into the sea to escape the flames. In all, forty-five men aboard were killed or declared missing in action with another eighty-five wounded. Commander Vernon Jannotta of Flotilla 24 brought his LCI(L) alongside to fight the fire and tend to the dead and wounded. Fortunately, the 60,000-gallon gasoline tank aboard the *Orestes* never ignited, and the fires were eventually extinguished. The *Orestes* was beached and later salvaged.

Convoy L-3 U Plus 15 had suffered forty-one air attacks. Over three days of combat, many air-to-air dogfights, and more than 250,000 rounds of ships' gunfire, at least twenty-five Japanese aircraft had been downed. The kamikaze attacks on the convoy anchored in and around Mangarin Bay were to continue for five days after the ships arrived. The final kamikaze attacks, on 4 January 1945, doomed the convoy's other ammunition ship, the *Lewis L. Dyche*, which had not yet been unloaded. The Liberty ship exploded with much the same destructive force as the *John Burke*, killing all seventy-seven hands aboard, including the third assistant engineer, Kings Point graduate Peter Chung Yin Chue of Berkeley, California.

This time there was no cameraman nearby, but the devastation was equally shocking. In addition to vaporizing anyone aboard, the blast lifted out of the water two PT boats that were two miles away, and unexploded shells from the *Dyche* landed in a gun tub of *LCI(L) 621*, killing a sailor and wounding four.

By the time the convoy had finally disbanded, hundreds of sailors had been killed or wounded, and eleven ships sunk or heavily damaged, including two merchant ships, a tanker, three LSTs, two destroyers, one tender, and at least two LCMs. The tactical toll upon the Allied forces was equally great, creating a critical condition in the supply situation at Mindoro. Shortages forced the 49th Fighter Group and its bomber comrades to ration gasoline and ammunition for weeks, and the ambitious diversion plans of Task Force 77.11 were derailed. Its commander, Captain Mentz, was severely wounded and evacuated, turning over the task force to Commander Jannotta. MacArthur's massive deception gambit had to be delayed, which meant that the impact of the scheme was blunted. In spite of these setbacks, success crowned the Allied invasion at Lingayen Gulf on 9 January, and Manila was liberated two months later.

As for the *William Sharon*, crippled and abandoned in the Mindanao Sea when the convoy moved on, she drifted some twenty-five miles from her last reported position before USS *Grapple* reached her on 29 December. The *Grapple* was a new kind of combat salvage vessel, and her crew put out the remaining fires that had smoldered for nearly eighteen hours. Escorted by the destroyers *Converse* and *Stanley*, *Grapple* towed the *Sharon* to San Pedro Bay, relinquishing her control to the commander of the *Gus W. Darnell*, the supply ship on which we rested after landing on Leyte. That officer arranged for the *Sharon*, reeking from four days adrift in the equatorial sun, to be tied up to the nearby *Augustus Thomas*.

In early January 1945, after her mauling in the kamikaze attack, it would be easy to think the *William Sharon* was destined either for the sea bottom or the scrapyard. Her ragged exterior matched the character of her disreputable namesake, William Sharon (1821–85), a U.S. senator who could put to shame some of today's worst political scoundrels.

The *William Sharon* was battered and hardly a pretty ship as we set about making her seaworthy again. When the generator arrived, my preparations paid off, however, and we had lights before nightfall. I insisted on being its sole operator and set up a schedule that restricted its use to meal times and a few hours each evening. These strict measures enabled us to conserve gasoline so that we had sufficient power until the ship's regular generators were operating several weeks later. For the first time, I began to feel optimistic about our prospects for getting home in 1945.

Our next urgent task was to pump seawater out of the engine room so that repairs there could begin. We used an acetylene torch to cut a large hole in the after bulkhead of the engine room at the tween deck level. Through it we lowered a gasoline-powered water pump with a long hose, enabling us to pump water overboard. After two days of torch work and pump action, we began the lengthy job of cleaning up from the blasts. I spent many hours overhauling the boilers and fire boxes. The chief engineer looked to me to decide when we could bring up steam pressure, and I took very seriously how much everyone was depending on me.

It boosted our morale when the maritime service sent over new crew members: two cooks, a licensed second mate, and a first assistant engineer. The mate, Mike Santiago, had been born in Central America, and he was very proud of his body's wild array of tattoos, the most elaborate I had ever seen. Santiago served on my watch, and we quickly became friends. The new first assistant engineer was from Florida, and he was friendly, good-natured, and more experienced than I. It was reassuring to have another engineer's judgment, and I came to rely on him to solve engine room problems that lay beyond my youthful experience.

The Filipinos in the crew spoke little English, but they were industrious, conscientious, and eager to learn. Their native dialect was a mystery to the rest of us, but thanks to more than four centuries of Spanish colonial rule, all of the Filipinos knew some Spanish. I was the only man from the *Saugrain* who spoke any Spanish, and my two years of basic study in my Texas grammar school was a valuable asset. Knowing the numbers and pronunciation of the alphabet helped immensely in teaching the Filipinos the nomenclature of the engine room.

Some of their names were soon Anglicized. Crispola Baconawa became "Crispy Bacon," and Feliciano Amboyamo became "Felix." Together we developed functional communications, and soon I was spending half of my time training Filipinos to become oilers, firemen, water tenders, and wipers. I came to love and trust them, and I will always be grateful for the respect and loyalty they showed me. Their motivation to sign on for the voyage to the United States was a burning desire to acquire a commercial fishing net, a highly coveted possession in Leyte.

Restoring the *Sharon* to a condition we could trust for a Pacific crossing was an enormous undertaking, and over the coming weeks I worked harder than at any other time in my life. Although all the licensed officers were earning double pay as a bonus for volunteering, the extra money was scarce compensation for the grueling work required of us.

During our fourth day on the *Sharon*, six soldiers of the 96th Infantry Division came aboard and moved into the stern quarters that were usually occupied by armed guard gunners. Their orders were to prevent the looting of the large supply of beer stored in no. 5 cargo hold. Two months before, these same soldiers had helped to wrest the Leyte beaches from the Japanese. They were fun-loving boys who mostly hailed from Pennsylvania, and I loved hearing their stories of the Leyte campaign. Fortunately, they had determined that sharing a few beers with us during meals and the evening's happy hour was fully justified by their orders.

It was nearly a month before the Army removed the beer, and during that time one of the soldiers on guard fell victim to a humorous but fearful episode. After drinking too much beer one evening, he staggered to his room to sleep it off. Realizing that he was going to be sick, he poked his head and shoulders out the porthole above his bunk to vomit. When he tried to wriggle back into his cabin, he became hopelessly stuck. Hearing his plea for help, we tried greasing him with soap and then lard from the kitchen, all to no avail. As he started to panic from the strain, we erected a temporary support for his head and shoulders, and this gave him some relief. All night and into the morning, his buddies worked in vain to extract him. By 1500 hours the following afternoon, an Army welder and his helper returned to the *Sharon* with a large pile of asbestos blankets. They covered the exhausted soldier's body with the blankets and used asbestos shields to protect him from molten metal and to diminish the heat from the cutting torch. It took two hours to cut a large steel ring around the unlucky fellow, which was then removed with his body. The ring was then split to free him from his self-imposed prison.

Once the stores of beer were removed and the guard of soldiers departed, we encouraged the Filipinos to move into the armed guard quarters above the fantail area, and we plunged ahead with our work. The Army welders focused on the biggest single job facing us: fabricating a temporary stack to carry away the engine exhausts. When that job was completed we were able to get up steam and bring back to full function all the engine-related equipment. Doing this involved servicing and testing steam relief valves and numerous other repairs and overhauling. We took extreme care to bring up steam pressure slowly. I was relieved and breathed a prayer of thanksgiving when, after many hours, we had the engine at maximum operating pressure. This convinced us that the engine room equipment was capable of making it to San Francisco and that all that lay between us and our departure was a test run in the bay.

We soon discovered otherwise. Once the ship was in motion, it became clear that the monumental concussion from the explosion of the SS *John Burke* had buckled the structure of the ship enough to crack, all the way across, five of the nine twelve-inch-diameter shaft bearing caps. After the chief engineer discovered the problem, he conferred with the officers aboard to seek our opinions. The news was extremely unsettling to me, and I could envision how, without solid supports, the shaft would flex, fatigue, and fail. If that occurred during a storm, we would be unable to propel the ship and could easily be swamped and lost with all hands. Had I known of this damage from the beginning, I probably would have joined the men from the *Saugrain* who opted for the first berth back to the United States.

The chief argued that we had to make a scheduled stop for supplies at Hollandia, New Guinea, before turning for home. This first leg of the journey would give us ample opportunity to observe the shaft in operation. If necessary, we could lay over there while awaiting replacement parts shipped from the States. We had worked so hard and made so much progress, I could not bring myself to walk away at that late date. It was a worrisome decision, but we all agreed to the chief's plan.

By the middle of February 1945, the maritime service in Tacloban completed the staffing of the ship's licensed officers. Among the new additions was a third assistant engineer, Harlan Johnson of Kansas, who had just been released from the hospital after an illness. I was delighted to have him aboard to reduce further the load I had carried for three months. Everyone was relieved by the addition of a licensed radio operator who managed to get his systems operating. This ensured our communications for emergencies and enabled us to receive radio news of the war, which we had missed throughout the repairs. By then, all the reports from the war in Europe were good.

Each of the engineers, now four in number, stepped up the training of the Filipino crewmen who would serve as wipers and oilers on each watch of the voyage home. The *Sharon* would travel without escort, but we were assured that the Japanese air force and submarines had been driven out of the seas we were to cross. By the time *William Sharon* steamed out of Surigao Strait heading for New Guinea, I was thin from overwork and strain and eager to get home. I was deeply grateful that we encountered no enemy action on the voyage; I had been through enough war and was ready for any form of soft shore duty. Throughout the voyage I kept a vigilant eye on the ship's shaft, but we noted no excess noise, flexing, or overheating. In Hollandia all four engineers concurred that, barring a typhoon, we could make it home.

The delays in Hollandia for refueling and further refitting of the *Sharon* seemed interminable, but we finally weighed anchor on 17 March and headed east by northeast, stopping only at Manus in the Admiralty Islands. During the long voyage home we followed intently the news accounts of the military collapse of Germany and the unexpected death of President Roosevelt on 14 April.

After so many uneventful days at sea I felt certain that danger was finally behind us when, two hundred miles west of the Farallon Islands (themselves only twenty-seven miles from San Francisco), we were blasted by the worst gale I ever experienced in the Pacific. It was a grim reminder of the deadly storm that two years earlier struck the *Cornelius Harnett* on the Murmansk Run. The chief placed the engineers on throttle watch. My experience on the voyage to Russia served me well as I worked the delicate throttle techniques I had learned in the earlier storm. Most worrisome to me was the terrific flexing of the shaft with its damaged bearings as we battled the gale's rough seas. I stood three exhausting throttle watches before the winds laid down.

Two days later as I was beginning my watch the chief came down to the engine room to report that the Golden Gate Bridge was in view. I longed to take the men of my watch up for our first view of America in twenty months. Duty kept us below, and my watch brought the faithful old warhorse to the shipyard dock in Richmond, California. I will never forget the feeling when the order "FINISHED WITH ENGINES" rang up on the engine room telegraph.

After we secured the main engine and the boilers, a shipyard crew relieved and congratulated us. I rushed up on deck for the longed-for view of my native land and said a prayer of thanksgiving. All hands were free to go, knowing that our payoff in cash would take place at 1000 hours the following morning in the United Fruit Company offices at the foot of Market Street in San Francisco. I went to my room and changed into freshly washed Army fatigues, the only clothes I had worn since all my belongings went down with the *Saugrain*.

Going ashore, I noticed several cocktail bars immediately outside the harbor gates. But what interested me was the milk and ice cream bar next to them. I walked up and promptly ordered two pints of fresh cold milk, which I relished as I slowly finished them off. It was my first fresh milk in eight months.

I called Helen's home, and her mother promised to have her waiting by the phone after she returned from work at 5:00 p.m. When I reached her, we talked for at least an hour. Helen was immensely relieved, and she agreed to take a train west to join me without delay. Next I called my mother and could sense her relief, too. I promised to visit her before leaving California. My dinner in a nice restaurant included a huge lettuce and tomato salad, two fried pork chops with French fries, a glass of California Rhine wine, and a slice of my favorite, coconut pie. After ending this memorable evening with my first movie in several months (*Here Come the Waves,* a Bing Crosby musical), I returned to my bunk a happy man.

After living for so many months with constant stress and pressure, it was hard to adjust to the casual outlook on the war back in America. With the victory in Europe behind us, people had a sense of "mission accomplished." I was not yet aware that the press was bringing good news about the war to every American household every day, and the attitude of people at home bothered me, knowing that men were still dying in the Pacific. But it did not take long to remember that I was home and nothing else mattered.

Memories of the next day still make me smile. I wore my best clothes — clean Army fatigues — and noticed how many people stared at me on the bus ride from Richmond to San Francisco. We were paid in cash (maritime union regulations). I was so worried about walking around with $3,902 in cash on my person that I asked the paymaster for the location of the nearest bank, and I ran the two blocks to a Bank of America branch to open my first bank account, depositing in it the largest sum of money I had ever held. Then I found a uniform shop to refit for my reunion with Helen.

When she arrived in Oakland we had a glorious celebration complete with drinks at the posh Hotel Sir Francis Drake and, after dinner, an iced bottle of champagne in our room at the Hotel Manx. When I reported back to the *Sharon* the next day I learned

Celebrating my return, drinks with Helen in the Persian Room of the Hotel Sir Francis Drake, San Francisco, May 1945. *Author's collection*

that I was the only engineer from the ship still in the area; the other three had headed home to their families. The shipyard was badly in need of a veteran of the voyage to guide the repair crews. The superintendent urged me to stay on as an advisor, promising that it would be easy to find an apartment for Helen and me. I had him over a barrel, I thought, but all he could offer was an ensign's pay of $187 per month.

I was waiting for an opening in upgrade school anyway, so I accepted the shipyard's offer, and Helen and I lived for two months in a Richmond apartment. It was one of many that had been hastily built to house shipyard workers who had flooded into California from states still mired in the Great Depression like Arkansas, Oklahoma, and Texas. She and I still laugh about how the mattress in our very first apartment was stuffed with corn shucks.

In spite of my modest wages, the shipyard managers treated me royally, and Helen and I enjoyed evening country music performances by "Okies" and "Arkies" on the sidewalks of Richmond. We took several delightful trips to San Francisco, and the opening of the new United Nations coincided with our time in the Bay Area. Following closely its historic founding added to the excitement of our stay.

The *Sharon*'s repairs moved forward quickly, and I was pleased to meet the new chief engineer assigned to the ship by the War Shipping Administration. He was wary about taking over the machinery of a ship that had been so badly damaged, and I spent many hours answering his questions about the condition of the engine room equipment. After much time together, I was able to persuade him that each engine component was shipshape. The shipyard crew had faithfully carried out all my recommended repairs, including replacement of the cracked bearing caps. Just before my departure a new second assistant engineer was recruited; I knew that I was leaving the *Sharon* in good condition and in capable hands.

The *Sharon*'s new crew returned the ship to duty in the South Pacific for the rest of the war. After the Japanese surrender she was sold and later sailed under the flags of several countries, avoiding the scrapyard until 1969. I am proud that I helped to return her to the nation's service in its hour of need and to two decades more of useful sea duty.

Like me, large numbers of these workers were refugees from America's Dust Bowl, the economic and environmental disaster of the late 1930s. Many of them enlisted in the armed forces during the war, and others worked to build the hundreds of Liberty ships and bombers that were so critical to the Allies' victory. After the war thousands of these new arrivals settled in California where they and their children helped to create the culture and postwar prosperity of the West Coast.

Chapter 17

Peace and Postwar Reentry

Once in San Francisco, I enrolled in the USMS upgrade school on Geary Street downtown. Crowded with servicemen, San Francisco offered few options for housing, and we finally settled for a room at the Hotel Sutter. The room included kitchen privileges, but these were four floors down from our single bedroom and bath.

I passed my upgrade license examinations easily and the best news of the war for us came during my last week of the school. My request for duty as instructor at the USMS Training Station on Santa Catalina Island was approved. Helen was ecstatic. She feared another dangerous assignment for me in the forthcoming invasion of Japan, which everyone dreaded. On our way to my new assignment, we had a reunion with my family in Santa Ana, California.

Catalina Island lies twenty miles offshore from Los Angeles, and it was said "When a sailor dies, he doesn't go to heaven, he goes to Catalina Island." Our trip over on a sunny July afternoon aboard the SS *Avalon* was Helen's first sea voyage. We rented quarters at 300 Metropole Avenue in the hilly harbor town of Avalon. Our apartment was at the top of a steep three-block climb from the beach.

In addition to the maritime service training site, Catalina was home to schools for the Army and Coast Guard at that time, and there were many servicemen's wives who spent afternoons working on their tans on the beach near Avalon. As I settled down to a pleasant routine of teaching recruits the rudiments of steam engineering aboard ships, Helen loved her time on the beach.

We were on Catalina when the Japanese surrendered on 2 September 1945. The base closed two months later, and I was transferred to the USMS training ship *American Engineer*, formerly the luxury liner *Berkshire*. The ship was based in San Pedro, California, and Helen and I moved to Long Beach where we shared an apartment with another ship's officer and his wife. While we were there Helen discovered that she was pregnant. By the time the holiday season rolled around we were notified that the maritime service was closing most of its training activities, just as a new skipper took command of the *American Engineer*.

I remember the new skipper as being the least competent of those I served under during the war. He had been a gob in the Navy during the last part of World War I and served on merchant ships for many years afterwards. He eventually got his master's license and sailed in intercoastal waterway service. When World War II came he joined the maritime service and was given the rank of lieutenant commander for training-ship duty. He had never served in a war zone and did not understand how to inspire respect from officers under his command. His regular missteps demonstrated how little he had learned about management and human relations.

Shortly after assuming command of the *American Engineer*, the skipper asked if any of the officers and their wives played bridge. I reported that Helen and I played but were strictly amateurs. I would soon regret speaking up. The next day we had a command invitation to join the skipper and his wife in their hotel room in San Pedro for an evening of bridge. The boring evening was made worse by the skipper's wife nagging him. We had no intention of inviting them to come to our apartment in return, but our troubles were just beginning.

By now it was December. I purchased the first Christmas tree of our marriage only to find that no tree lights were available in any stores because of the war. Determined to have my first real Christmas in four years, I fabricated a string of lights in the ship's machine shop, and Helen and I made our own decorations. We arranged to get-together with my family in nearby Santa Ana, but our careful planning came to naught when I learned that our ship was ordered to embark on Christmas Eve for San Francisco and decommissioning. In the biggest morale buster of my service career we sailed on time, dropped anchor at Hunter's Point in the Bay Area, and sat for a month waiting for our turn to be decommissioned.

No sooner had we arrived at our anchorage at Hunter's Point when the ship's audio system made this announcement during the officers' morning coffee break at 1000 hours:

"Mr. Melton: Report to the captain's cabin immediately."

I responded quickly, as any ensign would, and soon was knocking on the captain's door. What followed was one of the more bizarre episodes of my life. After inviting me to sit down he said, "Mr. Melton, I have good news for you. Our wives are by now on their way from San Pedro. You see, I told my wife to pick up Helen, and the two of them are on their way in our car. They will stay in each of our staterooms and have their meals with us. That means we can play bridge night and day since neither of us have pressing duties right now."

I panicked. What the skipper did not know was that Helen was three months pregnant and ill and in no condition for an arduous drive up the California coast. We had not shared our news, planning an announcement after the decommissioning. The skipper asked me to go ashore with him the next morning to a hotel where he had reserved rooms for us so that we could greet our wives. I assumed that we would have lunch in the hotel, but the captain had other plans. When the women arrived we went to his room where he drew from the closet four glasses, an ice bucket, and a bottle of cheap whiskey. He poured a stiff drink for each of us and beamed, "I thought it would be nice to have a drink before we eat, so here's a quick one."

I could tell that Helen had not recovered, and she looked

worse when offered a lunch of saltines and cheap canned sausages. Through it all we were given no chance to express our own wishes. Then the captain herded us all to the dock at Hunter's Point where the ship's boat was waiting. Helen had never spent a night or eaten a meal aboard ship. When we boarded she was exhausted and eager for a nap. But an announcement came from the ship's communication system: "Mr. Melton: Report to the captain's cabin with your wife please."

They were waiting for us with card table, cards, and chairs. The skipper's wife said, "We thought it would be fun to play a few hands before supper." Thus began three days of living hell. Morning, noon, and evenings the regular refrain was: "Mr. Melton: Report to the captain's cabin."

It spoiled Helen's enjoyment of her first time aboard ship, and we soon sensed a coolness in our relations with the other officers. After three days of boredom and embarrassment I was summoned to the skipper's cabin late one afternoon where I found him in a state of agitation. Without offering an explanation he told me that our wives had to leave the ship at the first opportunity on the morrow. We packed and were ready to go immediately after breakfast even though the ship was in the thickest fog I ever witnessed.

I learned that the port authority had issued orders that no ship could leave its moorings and that no boat could enter the anchorage area until the fog lifted. This order did not delay the skipper from ordering Helen and me to join him and his wife aboard the Liberty boat manned by Lieutenant Colajessi, the ship's navigation officer. The perilous fog terrified me for my pregnant wife. Colajessi told me later that it was the worst fog he had ever experienced saying, "To launch a boat out in it was a damn fool act—not to mention that I was defying a bay-wide official ban on marine activity." As we crawled at a speed of two knots through the thick fog we almost rammed the carrier USS *Ticonderoga* at anchor.

I later learned from our chief engineer that other officers of the *American Engineer* had complained about not being allowed to bring their wives aboard. The skipper suddenly realized he had a minor mutiny on his hands and was in a panic to get the women ashore. It seemed that he was trying to end his wife's nagging by bringing her and Helen aboard for bridge. Clearly she ran their marriage. Even more than our impressment for a bridge foursome, what I most resented about my final skipper was how little sympathy he had for his crew during our first Christmas of the new peacetime. It would have been a minor matter to get a day's postponement of our order that sent us from San Pedro on Christmas Eve only to wait in line for decommissioning in San Francisco.

With the arrival of peace, I remember feeling worried about my ability to make a living, and many of my fellow officers felt the same doubts. We joked about the want ad that appeared frequently in the *San Francisco Chronicle* and the *Los Angeles Examiner:* "Retired colonel seeks executive position with growing concern." When the *American Engineer* docked in Suisun Bay to release its officers, crew, and trainees, most aboard were eager to leave the maritime service, yet gloomy about our future prospects. After we went ashore, the *American Engineer* was towed to join the "mothball fleet" of ships in Suisun Bay. It would eventually be scrapped.

On 24 January 1946, I received my USMS discharge in San Francisco. I bought civilian clothes, and it felt strange and foreign to wear them. Helen and I began trying to put the war behind us. We visited my family once more in Santa Ana before departing via chair car on the Atchison, Topeka & Santa Fe Railway for Garden City, Kansas, and my return to civilian life.

Epilogue

Living with Helen's parents in southwest Kansas, we soon realized that transitioning from military service to civilian life would be more difficult for me than for most returning servicemen. Every week thousands of servicemen were returning to a job market that was collapsing along with the wartime production boom. Although there were hiring preferences for those who served in the war, most job applicants were veterans. Besides direct experience, only one factor seemed to be a helpful asset in seeking work: a college degree. This era probably marked the beginning of America's abiding respect for higher education.

The federal government acted to help veterans. Among the last important bills passed by Congress during the presidency of Franklin D. Roosevelt was the Servicemen's Readjustment Act of 1944, known to most as the GI Bill. Few government programs have had so great an impact on the growth of the American economy, and its impact is still felt today. When he signed the bill in June 1944, Roosevelt said, "I trust Congress will soon provide similar opportunities to members of the merchant marine who have risked their lives time and time again during war for the welfare of their country."

When I graduated from Kings Point in February 1944, I was asked to choose between a commission in either the USMS (merchant marine) or the U.S. Navy Reserve. I opted for the merchant marine commission, my way of saying thanks for the educational opportunity Kings Point gave me.

It was an unfortunate choice. Congress neglected to award veteran's status to men of the merchant marine, so I never qualified for GI Bill benefits, including financial assistance to complete my college education. This was a setback because Kings Pointers of my era were rushed through quickly, and the credit hours we earned were far less than those required at any accredited college. I graduated with a mariner's license and some college credits in engineering, but not with a bachelor's degree.

Today Kings Point is still the only one of our five service academies that sends its students into the theaters of war. For that reason, it is the only academy authorized to fly a battle standard, which makes our exclusion from veteran's status for four decades a great disservice. Because fellow Kings Point midshipmen were lost in one of my own convoys, this injustice is not easy to forget.

In addition to the loss of educational assistance, without GI Bill benefits I was ineligible for the job training, hiring preferences, and unemployment payments other veterans received. Neither did I qualify for veterans' small business loans or for a low-interest mortgage to buy a house. In essence, my family was on its own.

In 1988, Congress finally passed a bill that declared all merchant seamen who served in World War II to be veterans of the war, and I soon received a veteran's discharge from the U.S. Coast Guard for my service in the merchant marine. I was grateful for the gesture, but it came far too late for me to benefit from the GI Bill.

When I returned from the Philippines I made another decision that I came to regret. During my service on Catalina Island I received a letter from Kings Point to its graduates requesting information about unusual war-related experiences during their sea training at Kings Point and in service occurring after graduation. I replied with a handwritten one-page letter describing my experiences and the ships I had served on in the Pacific. Kings Point forwarded a copy to the USMS headquarters in San Francisco, and I received a letter from USMS reporting that each of the *Saugrain* volunteers had been nominated for a medal in recognition for bringing home the *William Sharon*. Our work had been selected for honors by the USMS officer in Tacloban, and my services were deserving of a medal. I was asked to send a full account of my experiences to San Francisco with a request that I be awarded the medal. At the time, requesting a medal (the title of which I forgot long ago) made me uncomfortable. Thousands of servicemen were being recognized daily for services rendered. I felt that it would make me a glory hunter, so I let the opportunity pass away.

With the passage of time I have come to regret that I did not follow through on this request. The medal might have held special meaning for me or my family, and it would have been a reminder of the sacrifices I and my fellow Saugrainers made in those trying times. In a meaningful way this book closes that circle. Telling these stories helps to complete the record of a very important period in the history of the Academy and of the merchant marine in defending America and the cause of freedom.

After the war it took several years for Helen and me to get our lives on track. The only real help we received came from family. Helen's father, who had taken a job in the emerging natural gas industry, was able to steer me into a job with his new firm at a station in Liberal, Kansas. This job, with Northern Natural Gas, was my first step in a lifelong career in that field. In 1950 I was hired for a job in Davidson, North Carolina, with Transcontinental Gas Pipeline Corporation (Transco), and I worked in its pipeline operations until my retirement in 1980. During my first six years with Transco I managed to complete enough courses at Davidson College that, when combined with credits from my community college and the Academy, qualified me for Kings Point's B.S. in mechanical engineering.

After retirement from Transco one more job awaited me, training the rising generation of engineers. Helen, who had more than ten years of experience in secondary school administration, placed a small advertisement in the *New York Times*. The experiment led to opportunities for both of us with Stevens Institute of

Technology, staffing agent for the Algerian government. We were hired to work for the Institut Algérien du Pétrole in Oran, Algeria, a junior-college-level technical school, where for two years Helen served as to dean of the faculty and I taught natural gas technology for Algerian and Bangladeshi high school graduates. It was fulfilling to help dozens of young men to develop careers in the industry to which I devoted my own career. Algeria is richly endowed with oil and gas reserves deep in the Sahara Desert, but at the time it lacked the technology and skilled professionals to move those resources to market.

The inspiration for this book came in 1992 when the government of the Russian Federation struck a medal to honor all Allied seamen who participated in the seventy-eight convoys of the Murmansk Run, the Allies' lifeline to the Soviet Union. I was immensely proud to be invited to a ceremony at the Russian Embassy in Washington, D.C., to receive my medal. The Russian admiral presented my medal which reads (in Russian): "Jubilee Medal presented to Herman Melton on the occasion of the 40th anniversary of victory in the Great Patriotic War, 1941–1945."

Medal ceremony, Embassy of the Russian Federation, Washington, D.C., 8 December 1992. *Author's collection*

This gesture from the nation that had been America's greatest postwar adversary highlighted for me the Russians' awareness of the sacrifice and endurance of the American, British, and Canadian merchant mariners who risked their lives to transport food, weapons, ammunition, fuel, and other vital supplies to a nation under siege. Without the hardships and sacrifices of these Allied seamen, the outcome of the war might have been very different.

On my way home from the awards ceremony I reflected on how the United States Merchant Marine Academy became the focal point in my life at a truly crucial time, inspiring me to acquire many of the personal and intellectual skills I would need to build a postwar career and to become a useful citizen. In my heart I always believed that I literally fought for my education. Combat is a tough sacrifice to make for college credits, but my Kings Point degree is an incalculable treasure.

In my life there are three momentous decisions that shaped the man I became: accepting Christ as my savior early in life, marriage to my beloved Helen, and my October 1943 enrollment at Kings Point. This story recounts my months of loyal service aboard four Liberty ships, by far the most memorable times of my life. I am forever proud that, in a small but measurable way, I lived up to the Kings Point motto *Acta Non Verba*—Deeds, not Words.

Appendix 1

Men of the *Cornelius Harnett*, April 1943

Merchant Marine Crew

Name	Nationality	Age	Position
Edgar W. Carver	U.S.A.	61	Master, Commanding
Selwyn Anderson	U.S.A.	43	1st Mate
Joseph Augros	U.S.A.	36	Oiler
Lamri Bensouda	Algerian	22	Asst. Cook
Hardy Brechlin	U.S.A.	24	Able Seaman
Enrique Cervera	Puerto Rican	36	Messman
Luther Craig	U.S.A.	23	Wiper
Willard Davis	U.S.A.	41	1st Asst. Engineer
Robert Drummond	U.S.A.	41	Able Seaman
Thomas Duffy	U.S.A.	30	Fireman
Karl Ebert	U.S.A.	28	Ordinary Seaman
Axel Ekstrand	Swedish	35	Able Seaman
Erwin Erickson	U.S.A.	22	Deck Cadet
Amos Farris	U.S.A.	33	Able Seaman
Charles Fralick	U.S.A.	20	Messman
Wesley Fowler	U.S.A.	22	Radio Officer
Louis Gallop	U.S.A.	25	3rd Mate
Thomas Hardcastle	U.S.A.	25	Clerk
Roughsedge Higginson	U.S.A.	27	2nd Mate
Sigvald Hymann	Danish	20	Able Seaman
Robert Inghram	U.S.A.	21	Deck Cadet
Sanford Kramer	U.S.A.	16	Utility Man
Jack Lamphear	U.S.A.	19	Fireman
Joseph Langer	U.S.A.	21	Deck Cadet
Joseph Laurey	U.S.A.	24	Wiper
Florent Leonard	Belgian	33	Able Seaman
Derwood Mason	U.S.A.	26	3rd Asst. Engineer
Herman Mellema	U.S.A.	48	Chief Engineer
Herman Melton	U.S.A.	22	Engineer Cadet
Joe Mercado	Filipino	42	Boatswain
Ralph Mitchell	British	24	Oiler
William Mizell	U.S.A.	23	Fireman
James Moody	U.S.A.	19	Ordinary Seaman
Francis Morrell	U.S.A.	24	Oiler

Author Peters	U.S.A.	21	Utility Man
George Potson	U.S.A.	25	Messman
Rudolph Serreo	U.S.A.	43	Chief Cook
Carroll Silverthorne	U.S.A.	27	2nd Asst. Engineer
Albert Simpson	U.S.A.	20	Ordinary Seaman
George Smelser	U.S.A.	30	Able Seaman
Nicholas Torres	Puerto Rican	20	Messman
Joseph Walters	U.S.A.	27	2nd Cook
Andrew Watt	British	37	Junior Engineer
Alphonse Wolff	U.S.A.	58	Steward

U.S. Navy Armed Guard

Name	Position
Richard M. Stone	Lieutenant USNR, Commanding
Thomas T. Blasingame Jr.	Radioman, 3rd Class
John W. Bolster	Seaman, 1st Class
Garvie "T" Eldridge	Seaman, 2nd Class
Earl Fralick	Seaman 1st Class
Thomas A. Grattan	Seaman, 1st Class
Palmer F. Hanson	Seaman, 1st Class
Marko Jurasevich	Gunner's Mate, 3rd Class
William E. Kagey	Seaman, 2nd Class
William McAdams	Seaman, 2nd Class
James J. McGill	Seaman, 2nd Class
Sebastian B. Menter	Seaman, 2nd Class
George W. Nelson	Seaman, 1st Class
George A. Newell	Seaman, 1st Class
Joseph A. Novakovich	Seaman, 1st Class
William M. Nugent	Seaman, 1st Class
Thomas E. Nunnally	Seaman, 1st Class
Donald F. Oberg	Seaman, 1st Class
John C. Ogg	Seaman, 1st Class
John A. Owen	Seaman, 1st Class
John Pantaloni	Seaman, 1st Class
Walter Lee Pearce	Seaman, 1st Class
Peter R. Peer	Seaman, 1st Class
James M. Puckett	Seaman, 1st Class
Louis J. Rebaudo	Radioman, 3rd Class
Robert L. Robinson	Seaman, 1st Class
John N. Ryals	Seaman, 2nd Class
Julius J. Tarczali	Gunner's Mate, 2nd Class
James I. Tonkin Jr.	Seaman, 1st Class
John Victor	Seaman, 1st Class
Wilbert J. Warren	Boatswain's Mate, 1st Class
Arnold E. Woolever	Seaman, 1st Class

Appendix 2
Captain A. Van Cromphaut's Report of the Attack on the *Antoine Saugrain*

December 9, 1944
To: War Shipping Administration (Owners)
From: A. Van Cromphaut, Master
Subject: Torpedoing, Bombing and Sinking of S/S Antoine Saugrain

On December 5, 1944, subject vessel was in a six column convoy station 25, escorted by five US Frigates. On board beside the Merchant crew members (43) and the 26 Armed Guard were 373 Army personnel, including officers and enlisted men.

At about 0830 I was in the chart room working up the ship's position when an alarm was sounded for general quarters. Not more than two seconds later I heard an explosion to starboard. Glancing through a porthole, I saw a geyser of water and smoke which seemed to be about fifty feet from the port side amidships of the ship in convoy position 35. Rushing to the upper bridge, I received the report that the medium bomber (Jap) had passed over the convoy from the starboard to the port. No warning signal had been issued from the escort vessels or the Commodore ship. Not a shot was fired from any vessel in the convoy. No damage was done by the bomb.

At about 1218, I was on the upper bridge observing the sun which was supposed to be on the meridian at 1221. The lower atmosphere was clear but there were low hanging clouds in all quarters, except in the south.

A gentle breeze was blowing. There was a moderate northerly swell topped with a light chop. The engines were turning 55 revolutions.

At the time the alarm was sounded for the general quarters a plane was sighted coming in on the port side very low at about deck level. Several ships opened fire but the plane kept coming. At about 1219 I sighted the smoke of a torpedo and ordered full speed ahead. A few seconds later the torpedo struck the stern, blowing off the rudder and breaking off the tail shaft and bending the propeller, also breaking a large hole into the shaft tunnel. The engine room flooded immediately. The ship was then helpless.

I signaled for the lifeboats to be cleared away and ready for lowering.

The plane had altered course slightly and passed ahead of this ship and through the six columns of the convoy at deck level with many of the ships of the convoy firing at it with all guns available until it disappeared into the clouds in the northeast.

At 1234 another plane was sighted coming in on the port beam and I ordered all Merchant crew away from the boats and to their gun positions. Several vessels opened fire on the incoming plane. Then I saw it launch its torpedo. The plane elevated slightly and went over the stern of the subject ship. Then I, with several men who were on the upper bridge, went below into the wheel house just as the second torpedo struck the ship at #2 hold on the port side. The hold flooded immediately. The vessel listed slightly to the starboard and commenced settling by the head. Then I ordered all hands to abandon ship.

The convoy had passed on, but the Frigates, San Pedro and Coronado and the Army tug #454 stood by the stricken vessel and took aboard all the survivors on the lifeboats from the four vessels brought alongside after rescuing the swimmers and the men on the rafts.

The escort vessels and the tug stood by to determine if the ship would still float. Twice during the afternoon I went back to the ship in a motor boat, boarding her for a hurried inspection and to secure the balance of the ship's papers. The ship seemed to be settling more. I returned to tug #454.

The commanding officer then put tug #454 alongside the ship and he and some of his officers and myself made another inspection. #2 hold was flooded to the between deck. We could hear water slushing among the cargo in #1 hold. #3 hold appeared to be dry, but the engine room was flooded to the gratings, and the cylinders were partly under water. Holds 4 and 5 were dry. The vessel was listing badly and was down by the head.

Then the escort vessel reported two more planes coming in. We all boarded the tug and cleared away from the ship, but the planes did not yet come near.

I then asked the Commanding officer of the tug #454 if he was going to put a line on the ship and take her in tow. He replied that the ship was in very bad condition, that he would signal the Commander of the Coronado and suggest sinking the Saugrain by gunfire.

I had made arrangements to stay aboard the #454 if he was going to tow the ship, but at this point he said all survivors were to go aboard the escort vessel. So I being the only survivor aboard, went to the Coronado. Upon boarding that vessel, I asked the Commanding officer if he intended to sink the ship by gunfire.

"Hell, no" he replied, "I wouldn't sink a ship if there was a possibility of towing her in. We'll stand by until sunset and if she is still afloat I'll order the tow boat to put a line on her and tow her stern first."

Before sunset another plane came in for an attack, but before it came within bombing range the two frigates and #454 opened fire and the Coronado was credited with shooting it down. Then the San Pedro, with part of the survivors, left to overtake the convoy.

APPENDIX 2

At dusk, tug # 454 had her hawser on the stern of the Saugrain and proceeded toward the destination at about 5 knots per hour and was escorted through the night by the frigate Coronado.

During the night another towing vessel had been dispatched and at daybreak on December 6, was standing by to assist if necessary. The same morning, December 6, a destroyer #480 came near to relieve the escort.

About 0730, four P-38s hove in sight and while circling overhead, a Jap bomber made a run for the Saugrain, but was shot down by the P-38s before it reached the ship. About 0830, as the P-38's passed into the clouds to the northward, there were three enemy planes sighted from the Coronado. They were in and out of the clouds, and circled from our starboard beam forward at a safe distance. One came out of the clouds on the port beam of the Saugrain which was then about two miles astern of the Coronado. The destroyer #480 and the two tug boats opened fire, four bombs were dropped near the ship and LT #454 but no damage done.

Three more bombs were dropped a long distance to the port of the ship. Then a cloud of black smoke came from the surface of the sea about four miles to the port of the towing vessels and destroyer, unquestionably it was an enemy plane which had been shot down.

The Coronado then under full steam and with a majority of the survivors—including myself—proceeded to its destination where we arrived at 1500 on December 6, 1944.

After checking and rechecking all survivors it was ascertained that all hands had been rescued.

Two enlisted men were injured, one having fallen from the main deck to the tween deck aboard ship when the first alarm was sounded. The other was struck on the back by a life raft floating close by as the man jumped from the deck into the sea. There were a few slight injuries from rope burns and shock.

The report received by me the following day, December 7, 1944, from the officers aboard the tug #454 stated that on December 6 at 1410 another torpedo plane succeeded in launching another torpedo into the stricken ship and the P-38s overhauled the plane and shot it down. About 1500 the ship settled by the bow, upended and sank rapidly, compelling the towing vessel to slip her hawser.

A. Van Cromphaut
Master, SS *Antoine Saugrain*

Appendix 3

Men of the *Antoine Saugrain*, December 1944

Merchant Marine Crew

Name	Birthplace	Age	Position
Anthony Van Cromphaut	Washington	–	Master, Commanding
Aguirre	Honduras	45	Oiler
Frank P. Aello	California	18	Ordinary Seaman
Philip Arcoutte	California	17	Ordinary Seaman
Botwell B. Blanchard	Florida	36	Carpenter
Edward L. Bristo	California	20	Able Seaman
Roy Christen	New Jersey	19	3rd Radio Operator
Glen Davidson	Utah	18	Wiper
Wallace Day	California	18	Able Seaman
Vallerie de Fleron	Alabama	38	Cook
William J. Doriss	California	18	Messman
Philip Dunlop	Utah	23	Wiper
Vasily Falin	Russia	46	1st Asst. Engineer
Fat Man	China	39	Fireman/Water Tender
Frank Fields	Missouri	37	2nd Asst. Engineer
Leon Frackowick	Washington	29	1st Mate
Frank Grady	Iowa	49	Steward
Roy Griffis	Oklahoma	18	Asst. Cook & Utility
Peter Griffiths	Australia	25	Chief Steward
Barney Hafslund	Minnesota	60	Chief Engineer
Norley Hall	Utah	18	Fireman/Water Tender
Earl Hamilton	Illinois	18	Asst. Cook
Paul Jackson	Ohio	24	Jr. Asst. Purser
William James	Maryland	37	Steward
Melvin Johns	Pennsylvania	24	Ordinary Seaman
Salvatore Lomino	New York	29	Able Seaman
Hugh McNeil	New York	18	2nd Radio Operator
John S. McPhee	Michigan	50	Utility
Herman Melton	Texas	23	3rd Asst. Engineer
James Mongan	California	17	Ordinary Seaman
Lee Dick Moy	China	28	Utility
William Naismith	Australia	35	Steward
George Newquist	North Dakota	23	Able Seaman

Daniel O'Neil	Ireland	39	Boatswain
John Parker	Illinois	18	Able Seaman
Joseph Pavlenko	Pennsylvania	21	Messman
Po Seng Ho	China	20	Fireman/Water Tender
Jimmie Proctor	Oklahoma	38	Chief Cook
Benito Racchero	New York	19	Messman
Edwin Ross	Pennsylvania	38	Deck Engineer
Michael Savnik	California	21	3rd Mate
Peter C. Stone	Idaho	24	2nd Mate
Henry Tomlinson	Cayman Islands	33	Oiler
Charles Tyson	Utah	27	1st Radio Operator
William J. Wallace	Scotland	63	Chief Cook
Kenneth Wright	Oklahoma	20	2nd Cook & Baker
Winfred Wright	Arkansas	29	Oiler
Walter Young	Minnesota	29	Ordinary Seaman

U.S. Navy Armed Guard

Name	Position
Dean E. Matthews	(D)L USNR, Commanding
James L. Bell	Gunner's Mate 3rd Class
William J. Brooks	Seaman, 1st Class
Henry "D" Caudill	Seaman, 1st Class
William J. Chesbro	Seaman, 1st Class
George T. Cole	Seaman, 1st Class
Frelen C. Collins	Seaman, 1st Class
Harold C. Compton	Seaman, 1st Class
Cecil R. Currence	Seaman, 1st Class
James B. DeGaetano	Seaman, 1st Class
Robert J. DeVaux	Seaman, 1st Class
William L. Etien Jr.	Seaman, 1st Class
Walter C. Farley	Coxswain
Billie E. Faust	Seaman, 1st Class
Anthony J. Feminis	Seaman, 1st Class
Michael Ferric	Seaman, 1st Class
Lorne J. Finley	Seaman, 1st Class
Ernest Forster	Seaman, 1st Class
LeRoy D. Fowler	Seaman, 1st Class
Grover A. Fries	Seaman, 1st Class
Bert B. Gilley	Boatswain's Mate, 2nd Class
Louis F. Gutfelder	Gunner's Mate, 2nd Class
William J. Marshall Jr.	Signalman, 2nd Class
Robert J. Tocher	Seaman, 1st Class
Douglas E. Whittier	Gunner's Mate, 3rd Class

Notes

6 *The nucleus of the Academy*: Smith, Enscore, and Adams, *Character Defining Features of Contributing Buildings and Structures in the United States Merchant Marine Academy Historic District*, 25–36.

15 *North Carolina Shipbuilding Co.*: Opened at Wilmington, N.C., in 1940 by Newport News Shipbuilding and Drydock Co., the North Carolina Shipbuilding Co. built 243 ships, including 54 Navy vessels, between 1941 and 1946.

15 *Black Diamond Steamship Line*: One of the more than 100 shipping companies that operated some 3,400 American-flag merchant ships on behalf of the War Shipping Administration during World War II.

16 *2,710 Liberty ships*: Sawyer and Mitchell, *The Liberty Ships*, 20.

16 *Liberty ships were based*: Bunker, *Liberty Ships*, 269.

16 *Cornelius Harnett:* (1723–81) was a merchant, miller, farmer, and statesman elected in 1754 to represent Wilmington in the North Carolina General Assembly. As the colonies' conflict with Great Britain escalated, he was named the first president of the North Carolina Council of Safety and became a leader in the resistance to the Stamp Act. When the British later occupied Wilmington, he was captured and jailed, after which his health steadily declined. Although his captors eventually released him on parole, he never recovered and became a beloved martyr to the revolutionary cause. Benson J. Lossing, *Our Countrymen; or, Brief Memoirs of Eminent Americans* (New York: 1855), 83–84.

18 *nearly 145,000 gunners*: "The U.S. Navy Armed Guard."

20 *escorted to Norfolk Navy Yard*: War Diary, Inshore Patrol Section Base, Morehead City, N.C. (1–30 November 1942).

23 *The ship moved out*: Arnold Hague Convoy Database, Convoy HX.220. This invaluable resource is based on the work of Arnold Hague (1930–2006), a retired lieutenant commander of the Royal Navy and a fine naval historian of World War II who, with colleagues John K. Burgess and Don Kindell, painstakingly compiled convoy records that had long been lost or purposely destroyed.

23 *Western Local Escort Force*: Antisubmarine ships that escorted convoys from North American ports to the Western Ocean Meeting Point (WOMP) off Newfoundland, where the Mid-Ocean Escort Force assumed responsibility for the convoys to the British Isles.

23 *Convoy HX-220 consisted of*: Arnold Hague Convoy Database, Convoy HX220.

23 *Lend-Lease*: A program under which the United States supplied Allied countries with food, military equipment, and other supplies. Britain and the Soviet Union were the biggest beneficiaries, receiving 62 and 22 percent, respectively, of the total.

24 *At any time*: Convoy sailing report F-3714, Record Group 38, Box 53, Convoy HX-220 file, National Archives and Records Administration.

27 *Leningrad and Stalingrad*: Soviet-era names for St. Petersburg and Volgograd, respectively. German armies besieged Leningrad from September 1941 to January 1944. The battle of Stalingrad, from August 1942 to February 1943, was the bloodiest single engagement of World War II and resulted in more than 1.5 million casualties.

27 *"is justified if"*: in Woodman, *Arctic Convoys*, 145.

27 *Of the 800 ships*: Bunker, *Liberty Ships*, 62.

28 *The need for*: Kemp, *Convoy! Drama in Arctic Waters*, 237.

30 *Our through-escort*: War Diary of the Commander in Chief, Home Fleet, January 1943.

30 *At least two submarines*: Ibid.

30 *Ships in the convoy*: Arnold Hague Convoy Database, Convoy JW.52.

31 *"The defining horror"*: Felknor, *The Merchant Marine at War, 1775–1945*, 248–49.

33 *Hog Islander*: The name given to ships built to specifications of the Emergency Fleet Corporation in World War I but completed too late for that conflict. A total of 122 ships were launched into the Delaware River from Hog Island, which is now connected to the mainland and the site of Philadelphia International Airport.

33 *20mm Oerlikon cannons*: A widely produced gun used in World War II especially as a shipboard short-range antiaircraft gun.

34 *"opened up with"*: Armed Guard Logs, 1943–45, Record Group 24, Container 190, *Cornelius Harnett* file.

35 *All the planes came*: Armed Guard Logs, 1943–45, Record Group 24, Container 190, *Cornelius Harnett* file, NARA-Md.

37 *GM1*: Gunner's Mate First Class. Gunners' mates are responsible for the operation and maintenance of all gunnery equipment aboard Navy ships.

39 *"We shot one down"*: James Harcus diary aboard the *Ocean Faith*.

39 *Silver Star*: Armed Guard Logs, 1943–45, Record Group 24, Container 190, *Cornelius Harnett* file.

42 *VVS*: Voyenno-Vozdushnye Sily Rossii, literally "military air forces of Russia."

NOTES

45 Stuka, short for Sturzkampfflugzeug, literally "dive-bomber," was a mainstay of the Luftwaffe.

45 *"was continually drunk"*: Felknor, *The Merchant Marine at War, 1775–1945*, 243–44.

45 *Somehow, the El Oriente*: Morison, *The Battle of the Atlantic, 1939–1943*, 369–72.

46 *"Sat 27th"*: James Harcus diary aboard the *Ocean Faith*.

46 *4-F*: A draft classification indicating that the registrant was not acceptable for military service due to physical, mental, or moral defect.

48 *"He dropped bombs"*: James Harcus diary aboard the *Ocean Faith*, Friday, 10 February 1943.

49 *"We are trying"*: Ibid., Thursday, 25 February 1943.

51 *our ocean screen*: War Diary of the Commander in Chief, Home Fleet, March 1943.

52 *Our through-escort included*: Ibid.

52 *ORP*: Okręt Rzeczypospolitej Polskiej, "Vessel of the Republic of Poland," the traditional prefix for Polish navy ships.

52 *RFA*: Royal Fleet Auxiliary, a Royal Navy ship manned by civilians. The tanker RFA *Oligarch* sailed with twenty convoys.

52 *As for distant cover*: War Diary of the Commander in Chief, Home Fleet, March 1943.

52 *Other merchant ships*: Arnold Hague Convoy Database, RA.53.

53 *the only available ballast*: Decoded naval dispatches, Tenth Fleet. Record Group 38, Box 209, Convoy RA-53 file.

53 *Several ships*: Woodman, *Arctic Convoys*, 336.

53 *Those ships with passenger manifests*: Arnold Hague Convoy Database, Convoy RA.53.

56 *The torpedo hitting the Bland: uboat.net, Ships hit by U-boats*. http://uboat.net/allies/merchants/2759.html.

56 *The* Bland *broke in two*: Arnold Hague Convoy Database, RA.53.

56 *The return convoy, RA-53*: Blair, *Hitler's U-Boat War*, 235–36.

57 *Reinhart Reche: uboat.net, The Men — U-boat Commanders*, shttp://uboat.net/men/reche.htm.

59 *stern tube gland*: A fitting that prevents water from coming into the ship via the stern tube, which houses the propeller shaft.

65 *NCO*: A noncommissioned officer, like a petty officer, ranking above seamen but below commissioned officers.

68 *One of them helped write:* Campbell and Macintyre, *The Kola Run: A Record of Arctic Convoys, 1941–1945*. This authentic work describes the passage of JW-52 (pages 164–65) and RA-53 (pages 183–88), and paints an even

more dismal portrait of Murmansk than my own. It remains an indispensable source for the technological and tactical history of the north Russian convoys.

68 *Malcolm Goldsmith*: World War II Unit Histories and Officers (Royal Navy GILB to GOOL).

68 *"I hate my job"*: Burn, *The Fighting Commodores*, 32.

69 *Convoy JW-52 was spotted*: Rohwer and Hümmelchen, *Chronology of the War at Sea 1939–1945*, 189. Rohwer, a German naval historian and veteran of the war, states that convoy JW-52 was spotted by a Blohm + Voss BV 138 flying boat of Kü.Fl.Gr. 706. It is generally believed that the unit was based at that time in the Norwegian towns of Tromsø and Sørreisa.

69 *An He 115:* The downed aircraft were 1864 K6+EH of Kü.Fl.Gr. 1./406, commanded by Hans-Georg Schmidt, piloted by Kurt Riedel with radioman Hans-Joachim Gottlieb aboard and, from the same squadron, 2733 K6+MH, commanded by Arno Gratz with pilot Hans Broy and radioman Kurt Kleißmann on board. See Klackers and Grams, http://www.luftwaffe-zur-see.de/Seeluft/Verlustlisten/Jahr1943.htm.

70 *The aviators' squadron*: Two Norwegian experts were consulted to determine the seaplane station from which the Heinkels attacked convoy JW-52. Many German flight records were destroyed during the war by fire and in bombing raids, but the photo albums preserved by German soldiers of all ranks provide valuable details. Tore Greiner Eggan of Trondheim, a photograph collector whose website features thousands of pictures from the war in Norway, shared pictures and identified the Norwegian locations of 1./406 images. Norwegian military historian Odin Leirvåg wrote, "Between April 1942 and May 1944, Küstenfliegergruppe 1./406 was based in Sørreisa, south of Tromsø. When the unit flew missions against the Murmansk convoys they did not always fly from Sørreisa. If their destination was too far away for their fuel supplies, they would fly from Tromsø or Billefjord after refueling. If there were weather problems as they returned from a mission, they were often diverted to land in Kirkenes, Tromsø or Billefjord."

70 *Kü.Fl.Gr. 1./406 was formed*: Goss and Rauchbach, *Luftwaffe Seaplanes, 1939–1945*, 160.

71 *The Heinkel had*: Dabrowski, *Heinkel He 115*, 146.

73 *Gratz and Schmidt had served together*: Naval flight officers were recruited as a "Crew" or class, mustered on the same day and often tracked together through training and assignment to squadrons. Special bonds were formed, often lasting long after their service. Some veterans published commemorative books for postwar gatherings, much like a college yearbook, with photographs and details of each flier's training and service record. *Crewbuch X/39* shows that Gratz and Schmidt were members of the tenth officers' course of 1939.

74 *"The Russians have been"*: Senior British Naval Officer North Russia Reports (extracts), 17th Monthly Report—1 Dec 1942 to 20 Jan 1943.
75 *P-39* **Kobrushka**: Palov, *From Airacobra to MiG-29*.
75 *"one hit"*: Suhorukov, "Conversations with Nikolay Gerasimovitch Golodnikov, Major-General (Ret)."
75 *In all, more than 4,700 P-39s*: Romanenko, *Airacobras Enter Combat*.
76 *Jagdgeschwader 5*: Luftwaffe Units, Jagdgeschwader 5 "Eismeer."
76 *Sturzkampfgeschwader 5*: Luftwaffe Units, Sturzkampfgeschwader 5.
76 *three Polish destroyers*: Polish navy (Polska Marynarka Wojenna) in Scotland website.
77 *"For your freedom and ours"*: *Polish Scottish Heritage*: The Clydebank Blitz and the Polish navy website.
77 *the Piorun was moored*: Ibid.
77 *Piorun was dispatched*: Zetterlling and Tamelande, *Bismarck*, 251.
78 *struck the Orkan*: Morison, *History of United States Naval Operations in World War II*, 10.147–48.
79 *Operation Weserübung*: Claasen, *Hitler's Northern War*, 7–27.
80 *convoy PQ-17*: Irving, *The Destruction of Convoy PQ-17*, 56.
80 *Reinhart Reche*: uboat.net, The Men of the U-boats, List of All Commanders, s.v. Reinhart Reche.
80 *A total of 560*: The U-Boat Wars, 1939–1945. Commanders of the U-boats, s.v. Reinhart Reche.
81 *only five U-boats*: These were *U-625* (Oberleutnant zur See Hans Benker, commanding), *U-629* (OLt zS Hans Helmuth Bugs), *U-657* (KptLt Heinrich Göllnitz), *U-622* (KptLt Horst-Thilo Queck), and *U-302* (KptLt Herbert Sickel); War Diary, Captain U-Boats, Norway. Captain Peters, 18 January–30 June 1943, 1–29. Commanders in the U-boat service included, from higher to lower, Kapitän zur See (a captain in the U.S. Navy), Fregattenkapitän (commander), Korvettenkapitän (lieutenant commander), Kapitänleutnant (lieutenant), and Oberleutnant zur See (lieutenant junior grade).
81 *one boat every 14.5 days*: Figures based on data from uboat.net.
81 *U-255 torpedoed*: War Diary, Captain U-Boats, Norway. Captain Peters, 18 January–30 June 1943, 31–43.
81 *A patrol line*: The patrol included *U-255*, *U-586* (KptLt Dietrich von der Esch), *U-622* (Queck), *U-629* (Bugs), and *U-657* (Göllnitz).
81 *Reche managed*: Ibid., 118–49.
82 *"thoughtful and quiet man"*: Suhren and Brustat-Naval, *Ace of Aces*, 210.
82 *the gunnery officer's introduction to convoy duty*: Stone, personal log.
83 *Convoy SC-97 was less fortunate*: Arnold Hague Convoy Database, SC.97.

83 *"You fired shots"*: Stone, personal log.

84 *After the war*: *Savannah Morning News*, Richard M. Stone obituary, 5 September 2005.

92 *chair car*: Also known as a parlor car, a chair car is a railroad car fitted with individual seats that face front or back instead of long benches facing each other across a center aisle.

97 *Liberty ship* **Stephen Hopkins***:* Moore, *A Careless Word . . . A Needless Sinking*, 269–73.

98 *engine cadet John Brewster*: "U.S. Merchant Marine Cadets Killed During World War II" website.

99 *"father of shipping containerization"*: *New York Times*, Ray Holubowicz obituary, 11 January 2013.

112 *Antoine Saugrain* was a most worthy namesake for a Liberty ship. Born in France in 1763 and trained as a physician and chemist, Antoine Saugrain was an eminent natural scientist who came to the newly independent United States carrying a letter of introduction to Benjamin Franklin. He was soon invited to join a party exploring the Ohio River Valley where he was wounded in a fight with Indians. Saugrain returned to France to recuperate, but the dangers of the revolution unfolding in his native land drove him back to America, where he married and settled in St. Louis. Saugrain organized the medical supplies for the Lewis and Clark Expedition; and after explorers returned in 1804, Meriwether Lewis enlisted his help in preparing scientific specimens from the trip to send to President Thomas Jefferson. Some of Saugrain's later experiments helped in developing modern phosphorous matches, and he was the first physician west of the Mississippi to inoculate patients with Jenner's vaccine to immunize them against smallpox. He offered this service to all comers, regardless of their social standing or ability to pay. Edmond S. Meany, "Doctor Saugrain Helped Lewis and Clark," *Washington Historical Quarterly 22:4 (1931)*: 295–311.

116 *Norley wrote*: Hall, "The History of Norley Hall."

121 *"floating warehouse"*: Ibid.

121 *Army records of the period:* Casey, *Engineers of the South West Pacific, 1941–1945*, 3.179–90. A remarkable video tour of wartime Finschhafen is available online courtesy of the Australian War Memorial, https://www.awm.gov.au/collection/F07478/. Retrieved 31 March 2016.

126 *a large gunnery unit*: Unit History, 237th AAA Searchlight Battalion (1945).

126 *We were to transport*: Cressman, *The Official Chronology of the U.S. Navy in World War II*, under 5 December 1944.

129 *"six or seven ships wide"*: Kolankiewicz, "The Flag Will Be Our Blanket."

129 *The convoy included thirteen*: Action Report, Task Unit 76.4.7.

NOTES

130 **Mactan** *had been hastily painted:* Philippine Diary Project, "The Great Escape of the S.S. Mactan: December 31, 1941."

130 *Services of Supply:* This was the forerunner of the Army Service Forces, one of three autonomous components of the Army of the United States during World War II, alongside the Army Air Forces and Army Ground Forces, which the SOS existed to support. Its brief included procurement and supply for forces in the United States and abroad, worldwide communications, the construction of ports, roads, ships, and hospitals, "morale and recreational services," publications, administration of military justice, official publications, and so on. Millett, *The Organization and Role of the Army Service Forces.*

130 *LST*: landing ship, tank, a vessel designed for amphibious operations and capable of carrying tanks, vehicles, and infantry.

130 *patrol frigates*: Action Report, Task Unit 76.4.7.

130 *"On this night"*: Hall, "The History of Norley Hall," 28–29.

134 *suddenly the bells*: Ibid.

135 *Roy Griffis also remembers*: Roy Griffis, telephone interview, 29 January 2011.

139 *He vividly remembers*: Hall, "The History of Norley Hall," 28–29.

140 *"popped up like a cork"*: Lenny Scinto interview, 1996.

141 *friendly-fire death*: War Diary, U.S.S. *Coronado* (PF-38).

142 *"large enough to drive"*: Armed Guard Report, SS *Marcus Daly*, 27 December 1944.

142 *The final tally*: Cressman, *The Official Chronology of the U.S. Navy in World War II*, under 5 December 1944. This source also reports that the first torpedo attack upon the *Saugrain* occurred at 09°42'N, 127°05'E.

142 *"one of the fiercest"*: U.S. Naval Administration, *History of the Armed Guard Afloat*, 220.

143 *Six battleships*: Steinberg, *Return to the Philippines*, 65–74.

144 The USS *Halford*'s December 1944 War Diary recorded that the *Saugrain* sank in 10°23'50"N, 125°48'E.

144 *a sneak attack*: Steinberg, *Return to the Philippines*, 85–90. The Tacloban airfield battle was part of the Japanese Operation Wa (also called the Burauen raids), a coordinated assault on all five Leyte airfields. A key Japanese objective of the raids was to regain air superiority over Leyte long enough to land reinforcements and supplies. The all-out attacks on Task Unit 76.4.7 are today considered an integral part of Operation Wa.

145 *our troops were plagued*: Report of Investigation. Alleged Adverse Conditions Existing in 2nd Platoon, Battery B, 237th AAA Searchlight Battalion.

146 *postwar interrogations*: Interview with Commander Moriyoshi Yamaguchi, Operations Officer on the Staff of Vice Admiral Fukudome, CinC First Combined Base Air Force (Luzon), 24 October 1945, U.S. Strategic Bombing Survey, *Interrogations of Japanese Officials*, 178–83.

148 *the Thomas had arrived:* Howard E. Harris, *Augustus Thomas* crew member, letter to Charles A. Jarvis, master of the SS *Adoniram Judson*, first merchant vessel to tie up at the dock in Tacloban after the U.S. Army reoccupied Leyte. http://www.reocities.com/thetropics/1965/harris.htm. Retrieved 2 April 2016.

148 *what some consider:* Rielly, *Kamikaze Attacks of World War II*, 152–53.

148 *The plane crash-dived:* Voyage Report. SS *Augustus Thomas*.

148 *among the first four incidents:* Nimitz, *Operations in the Pacific Ocean Areas during the Month of November 1944*, "Japanese Suicide Tactics in the Philippines Campaign," 70–72.

148 *"special attack" (kamikaze) units:* For many years, the early morning attack on the *Sonoma* and *Augustus Thomas* were accepted as the launch of the "special attack" kamikaze squadrons. More recently, scholars studying the kamikaze phenomenon of World War II have concluded that the Betty bomber crew had not been among those groomed for the "Divine Wind" missions. See Gordon, "47 Ships Sunk by Kamikaze Aircraft."

150 *"Twas in":* Sir William Schwenck Gilbert, "The Yarn of the *Nancy Bell*."

152 *fierce in his hatred:* O'Neil's favorite story was about how his band of guerrillas would hide along a road patrolled by British police on motorcycles. Daniel would tie one end of a long line to a tree on the roadside and lay the rope across the road to the other side. As the motorcycles approached, the guerrillas (lying in wait) would suddenly jerk the rope up to head height, strangling or beheading the unsuspecting riders. The IRA men would then melt away into the countryside.

153 *United Fruit Company:* Boston-based company that operated its own fleet of ships to the Caribbean and Latin America, and one of the leading American merchant ship managers of World War II.

155 *the largest unit aboard:* Operation Report, 237th AAA Searchlight Battalion, King 2 Operation.

155 *The SCR 268 used:* Mindell, "Automation's Finest Hour: Radar and System Integration in World War II," 27–56.

156 *The SCR 584 system:* Conant, *Tuxedo Park*, 270–72.

156 *hush-hush radar equipment:* Searchlight Defence Plan. 237th AAA Searchlight Battalion Less Battery B and One Platoon Battery A.

156 *If the training records:* Unit History. 237th AAA Searchlight Battalion (1945).

157 *"Radar Det[achment] SCR 584":* South West Pacific Area, General Headquarters, *Annex 2 to Operations Instructions No. 73, Troop Movement Directive No. 180.*

157 *The third battalion of the 197th:* Gaines, "Historical Sketches Coast Artillery Regiments, 1917–1950," 197–265.

157 *After September 1943:* Unit History. 237th AAA Searchlight Battalion (1945).

NOTES

157 *the machine guns were repacked*: Operation Report, 237th AAA Searchlight Battalion, King 2 Operation.

158 *"never actively or aggressively"*: Sam Wilks, email message to Michele Ramirez Smith, 31 January 2005.

159 *The 1797th was reactivated*: U.S. Army Center of Military History, Unit Lineage, and Honors http://www.mvd.usace.army.mil/About/Offices/579th-Forward-Engineer-Support-Team-Main-FEST-M/579th-Engineer-Detachment-FEST-M-History/. Retrieved 2 April 2016.

159 *1619th Engineer Map Depot Detachment*: Casey, *Engineers of the South West Pacific, 1941–1945*, 3.207–13.

159 *The* Saugrain *transported*: Ibid., 3.137.

160 *the four map depots*: Ibid., 3.213.

161 *headed for Luzon*: Action Report. USS *LST 1017*.

162 *"Our unit was camped"*: Thomas Holst, telephone conversation with the author, 14 March 2010.

163 *James Foster*: Patrick Tobias, Shorty's grandson, shared details of his life with me in 2011.

164 *"When a job first arrived"*: Leon Kolankiewicz, email exchange with Nancy Scinto Rutkowski, 15 July 2011.

165 *"attached to MacArthur's headquarters"*: Ibid.

168 *"Capt. John Haher"*: Ferguson and Pascalis, *Protect and Avenge*, 298.

170 *"All four Demons"*: Ibid.

171 *the top unit*: Ibid., 349.

175 *Augustus Thomas*: (1857–1934) briefly studied law before becoming a successful journalist, and in 1889 he was named editor of the Kansas City *Mirror*. Later, Thomas organized a touring theater company that included two of the famous Barrymore family of thespians and performed plays written by Thomas. "The Life and Times of Joseph Haworth," http://www.josephhaworth.com/augustus_thomas.htm. Retrieved 2 April 2016.

176 *nearly a month of wasted efforts*: I learned later that the underwater welding of the *Thomas* was eventually completed, after which she was refloated and towed to Hollandia, New Guinea, and then to the nearest full-scale shipbuilding port, in Newcastle, New South Wales (Australia). When war ended, she was towed back to the United States and mothballed in Suisun Bay, in the upper reaches of San Francisco Bay, forty miles northeast of the city. She never again sailed under her own power.

177 *The Mindoro resupply convoy*: Action Report, L-3 U Plus 15 Echelon Resupply Leyte to Mindoro. Cmdr. A. E. Fitzwilliam, aboard *LST 751*, was the convoy commodore.

177 *Hill Airfield*: Ferguson and Pascalis, *Protect and Avenge*, 316.

220   LIBERTY'S WAR

177 *The William Sharon carried*: Armed Guard Logs, 1943–45. Record Group 24, *William Sharon* file.

178 *twenty-nine PT boats*: Action Report, Commander Task Group 77.11. 27, Cmdr. A. Vernon Jannotta, from 1 to 9 January 1945. The PTs comprised motor torpedo boat squadrons 8, 24, and 25; Jannotta commanded LCI(L) Flotilla 24.

178 *Two seaplane tenders*: Action Report. Commander Task Group 77.11, Cmdr. A. Vernon Jannotta, 27 December to 31 December 1944.

178 LCI(L), or landing craft, infantry (large), was designed as a troop carrier.

178 *"loaded to capacity"*: Dwyer, *Seaborne Deception*, 83–89. The 6th and 7th Beach Jumper Units, commanded by Lt. Cdr. L.W. Dunton Jr., were the forerunners of today's U.S. Navy Seals, carefully picked sailors trained in cover and deception tactics at a secret base on Ocracoke Island, N.C.

178 *a formidable deception force*: Mintz and his staff had planned a phony force buildup on Mindoro to set the stage for MacArthur's imaginary invasion south of Manila. The mock installations included fake gun emplacements with large inflated dummy guns designed to fool Japanese air reconnaissance. Dramatized radio transmissions and heavy traffic in bogus coded messages would suggest massive troop and supply movements. The Beach Jumpers were to stage showy loadings of the 21st Infantry on Jannotta's LCI(L)s, timed to coincide with the real landings in northwestern Luzon, which Mintz would abandon as soon as the deception troops were fired upon. The beach jumpers had been trained to guide the PT boats just offshore at night, where the commandos would light smoke pots, Roman candles, and other fireworks for visual effects with taped sounds of an all-out battle blaring from loudspeakers. These and other tactics were intended to convince the Japanese that a full-force invasion was under way on beaches dozens of miles south of the real objective at Lingayen Gulf. Ibid.

178 *"a running battle"*: Deck Logs (excerpts). USS *Bush* (DD 529). The destroyers of the convoy escort screen included the USS *Bush* (flagship), *Edwards*, *Gansevoort*, *Phillips*, *Pringle*, *Sterrett*, *Stevens*, *Wilson*, and *Paul Hamilton*, which had been converted into a fast minesweeper. The convoy and its escort, Task Group 78.3.15, were under the tactical command of Capt. J. B. McLean with his Destroyer Division 48.

179 *"Only those who have seen"*: Report of Operations of U.S.S. *Half Moon*, 1–2.

179 *one of the most astonishing*: Kamikaze Attack, USS *John Burke*: Complete destruction of ship and all on board! www.youtube.com/watch?v=uMs4I-JQVRYM. Retrieved 15 August 2016.

179 *Among those killed*: Deck cadet-midshipman Donald J. Kannitzer of Seattle sailed from Honolulu on 10 October with ammunition bound for the new airbases to be built on Mindoro. See Ryan and McCaffery, *Braving the Wartime Seas*, 241. Ryan and McCaffery's book details the lives of 140 merchant marine cadets and graduates who lost their lives during World War II.

179 *Six members of the* **Sharon's** *crew*: Armed Guard Logs, 1943–45. Summary of Statements of Survivors SS *William Sharon*.
180 *all fires on board*: Destroyer History Foundation, USS *Wilson* (DD 408).
180 *"Normally they circled"*: Action Report. USS *LCI(L) 699*.
182 *The Orestes was beached*: Action Report. USS *Orestes*.
182 *Peter Chung Yin Chue*: Ryan and McCaffrey, *Braving the Wartime Seas*, 447.
182 *unexploded shells*: Morison, *The Liberation of the Philippines*, 48.
183 *reeking from four days adrift*: Report of Salvage Operations of SS *William Sharon*.
183 *William Sharon*: Born in Ohio, Sharon was drawn irresistibly to California's Gold Rush of 1849, where he became a real estate speculator. With the discovery of Nevada's Comstock Lode, America's first important silver discovery, Sharon opened a bank nearby to make loans to miners. He was ruthless in foreclosing whenever he had a chance to gain control of their claims. After becoming one of America's wealthiest men through such schemes, Sharon served ten years as U.S. senator from Nevada, even though he was then living outside the state. He managed to keep mistresses on both coasts, and when one of them claimed that he had married and abandoned her, a scandal erupted that continued for a decade after his death. His spurned lover and her new husband fought for Sharon's vast estate, leading to a knife fight with a U.S. marshal and a fatal hotel gun battle with a judge in the case. See Sharon/Hill Divorce Terry/Field Affair 1883–85 and 1887–90, www.encyclopedia.com/doc/1G2-3498200102.html. Retrieved 15 April 2016.
197 *"I trust Congress"*: American Merchant Marine at War. Merchant Seamen's War Service Act (1945 and 1947).
198 *Because fellow Kings Point midshipmen*: Midshipman Charles Wallace Tamplin of Troy, Ohio, and Midshipman Arthur Jack Gradus of Long Island City, New York, were lost when *U-586* torpedoed the SS *Richard Bland* on 9 March 1943, a hundred miles northeast of Iceland in waters that dipped to nearly 20°F. This ship was the *Harnett*'s sister Liberty ship throughout its passage from New York to Murmansk. See Ryan and McCaffery, *Braving the Wartime Seas*, 302–5 and 394–97.
203 *Merchant Marine Crew of the* **Cornelius Harnett,** *April 1943*: "Passenger and Crew Lists of Passengers Arriving at New York."
204 *U.S. Navy Armed Guard Crew,* **Cornelius Harnett,** *April 1943*: Ibid.
205 *Captain A. Van Cromphaut's Report*: Voyage Report, SS *Antoine Saugrain*.
208 *Crews of the SS* **Antoine Saugrain:** The forty-eight crewmen of the *Saugrain* represented twenty-two American states and seven foreign countries. All spoke English, and each man served the merchant marine well during World War II.

I am grateful to shipmate Joe Dorris, who preserved several *Saugrain* documents including a mimeograph of the ship's crew list.

Joe returned to civilian life and went into police work. In the beginning, he was a motorcycle patrolman with the Fresno, California, Police Department. He advanced through the department's ranks, finally retiring as the chief of detectives. Joe and his wife, Jeanne, raised three daughters, one of whom, Vicky Schuller, helped me gather information about Joe's service on the *Saugrain*. Joe Dorris died in July 2013.

As for the other *Saugrain* shipmates I located during research for this book, Joe's childhood buddy and longtime friend Roy Griffis returned to sea duty after Leyte. His last voyage was to Newport News to pick up a load of coal, which his new ship transported to Italy. After the war, he went into construction, working on California's Friant Kern Canal, which was built to carry water to Fresno. Later he joined U.S. Filter Corporation, making equipment for the production of beet sugar. As his work wound down he moved to Idaho to be near his son, and he spent his last years living with his daughter in Montana near Glacier National Park. He died in 2012.

Norley Hall volunteered to join the repair crew for the *Augustus Thomas*. When some trouble arose over the captain's drinking, he was offered a berth on a troop transport bound for San Francisco. He had one more tour of duty, to Okinawa, before he was discharged. He, too, struggled in a number of jobs before finding a career, finally returning to his beloved Utah and work as a skilled foundryman and, later, service for the Church of Jesus Christ of Latter-day Saints. He and his wife Elaine raised a large family. He wrote of an accident with hot metal that claimed much of Norley's eyesight, but his Mormon faith continues to sustain him.

209 *U.S. Navy Armed Guard Crew List*: Armed Guard Report, 1943–45. SS *Antoine Saugrain*.

Bibliography

Unpublished primary source material

Archival Records

National Archives and Records Administration, College Park, Md.

Record Group 24, Records of the Bureau of Naval Personnel

Armed Guard Logs, 1943–45. Record Group 24, Container 190, *Cornelius Harnett* file.

Armed Guard Logs, 1943–45. Record Group 24, *William Sharon* file.

Armed Guard Logs, 1943–45. Summary of Statements of Survivors SS *William Sharon*. Record Group 24, *William Sharon* file.

Armed Guard Report, 1943–45. SS *Antoine Saugrain*, 12 January 1946, Lt. Matthews. Record Group 24, Container 190, *Antoine Saugrain* file.

Record Group 38, Records of the Office of the Chief of Naval Operations. World War II War Diaries, Other Operational Records and Histories, compiled ca. 01/01/1942–ca. 06/01/1946, documenting the period ca. 09/01/1939–ca. 05/30/1946.

Action Report. Commander Task Group 77.11, 27, Cmdr. A. Vernon Jannotta, 27 December to 31 December 1944; Leyte-Mindoro, P.I., 4 January 1945. page 1. www.fold3.com/image/1/295201664. Retrieved 15 August 2016.

Action Report. Commander Task Group 77.11. 27, Cmdr. A. Vernon Jannotta, from 1 to 9 January 1945; Mindoro, P.I., 14 January 1945. www.fold3.com/image/295206385. Retrieved 15 April 2016.

Action Report. L-3 U Plus 15 Echelon Resupply Leyte to Mindoro. A. E. Fitzwilliam, Commander LST Group Forty-Three. Dated 1 January 1945. www.fold3.com/image/295884795. Retrieved 15 August 2016.

Action Report. Task Unit 76.4.7. Cmdr. H. J. Doebler, USCG, from December 5 to December 6, 1944. Dated 7 December 1944. https://www.fold3.com/image/295219834.

Action Report. USS *LCI(L) 699*, Lt. (jg) P. B. Gates, USNR, 28 December 1944, Enclosure A. Dated 31 December 1944. www.fold3.com/image/295202890. Retrieved 15 August 2016.

Action Report. USS *LST 1017*, B. I. Sobel, commanding. Dated 6 February 1945. https://www.fold3.com/image/295412364. Retrieved 1 April 2016.

Action Report. USS *Orestes*, K. Mueller, commanding. Part 1, 30 December

1944. Dated 5 January 1945. www.fold3.com/image/295201954. Retrieved 15 August 2016.

Convoy sailing report F-3714. Record Group 38, Box 53, Convoy HX-220 file.

Decoded naval dispatches. Tenth Fleet. Record Group 38, Box 209, Convoy RA-53 file.

Report of Operations of USS *Half Moon*, J. I. Bandy, commanding officer, from 27 December 1944 to and including 4 January 1945. 15 February 1945. pages 1–2. www.fold3.com/image/296241576. Retrieved 15 August 2016.

Nimitz, Adm. Chester W. *Operations in the Pacific Ocean Areas during the Month of November 1944*. Annex A, "Japanese Suicide Tactics in the Philippines Campaign." https://www.fold3.com/image/1/296562916. Retrieved 2 April 2016.

Report of Salvage Operations of SS *William Sharon*, Mindanao Sea, Philippine Islands, 28 to 30 December 1944. Lt. R. K. Thurman, USS *Grapple*. Dated 3 January 1945. www.fold3.com/image/293473377. Retrieved 15 April 2016.

United States Pacific Fleet, Headquarters, 1945. https://www.fold3.com/image/1/296562916. Retrieved 2 April 2016.

Voyage Report. SS *Augustus Thomas*, Lt. (j.g.) Charles G. Drake, armed guard commander. 5 May 1945. Record Group 38, Armed Guard Files 1940–1945, Box 46.

War Diary. Inshore Patrol Section Base. Morehead City, N.C., E. J. Estess, commanding officer. 1–30 November 1942. www.fold3.com/image/267917659. Retrieved 30 March 2016.

War Diary. USS *Coronado* (PF-38), N. W. Sprow, from 5 November to 14 December 1944. Dated 14 December 1944. https://www.fold3.com/image/293492776. Retrieved 31 March 2016.

War Diary. USS *Halford* (DD480) for the month of December 1944, R. J. Hardy. The *Saugrain* sank in 10°23'50'N, 125°23'50'E.

Record Group 407: Records of the Adjutant General's Office

Operation Report. 237th AAA Searchlight Battalion, King 2 Operation, Capt. David W. Parkes, commanding Battery A, 28 January 1945. Record Group 407, Entry 13799, CABN 237 0.12–1.13.

Searchlight Defence Plan. 237th AAA Searchlight Battalion Less Battery B and One Platoon Battery A, 15 November 1944, Tacloban, Leyte Island. Record Group 407, Entry 13799, CABN 235-0.1 to CABN 237-0.1.

Unit History. 237th AAA Searchlight Battalion (1945), Maj. James F. Collings, commanding. Record Group 407, Entry 13799, CABN 237 0.12-1.13.

National Archives and Records Administration, Washington, D.C.

Passenger and Crew Lists of Vessels Arriving at New York, New York, 1897–1957, National Archives Microfilm Publication T715, 8892 rolls, Records of the Immigration and Naturalization Service.

Armed Guard Report. SS *Marcus Daly*, 27 December 1944. Author's Collection.

Deck Logs (excerpts). USS *Bush* (DD 529), approved by Cmdr. R. E. Westholm, from December 27 to December 31, 1944, resupply Convoy to Mindoro. www.ussbush.com/mindoro.htm. Retrieved December 16, 2016.

Report of Investigation. Alleged Adverse Conditions Existing in 2nd Platoon, Battery B, 237th AAA Searchlight Battalion, Maj. Dixon Grassman, Assistant Inspector General. June 1945. Book 2, Box 281. Eisenhower Library. Abilene, Kan.

Senior British Naval Officer North Russia Reports (extracts), 17th Monthly Report—1 Dec 1942 to 20 Jan 1943. Halcyon Class Ships—Minesweepers and Survey Ships of World War Two website. http://www.halcyon-class.co.uk/SBNOreports/dec_1942.htm. Retrieved 31 March 2016.

South West Pacific Area, General Headquarters. *Annex 2 to Operations Instructions No. 73, Troop Movement Directive No. 180*. Record Group 3. MacArthur Memorial Archives. Norfolk, Va.

Voyage Report. SS *Antoine Saugrain*. Anthony Van Cromphaut, Master. Author's collection.

War Diary of the Commander in Chief, Home Fleet, January 1943. Transcribed by Don Kindell. Admiralty War Diaries of World War 2 website. http://www.naval-history.net/xDKWD-HF1943a.htm. Retrieved 31 March 2016.

War Diary of the Commander in Chief, Home Fleet, March 1943. Transcribed by Don Kindell. Admiralty War Diaries of World War 2 website. http://www.naval-history.net/xDKWD-HF1943a2.htm. Retrieved 31 March 2016.

War Diary of the USS *Halford* (DD480) for the month of December 1944, R. J. Hardy. www.fold3.com/image/293481510. Retrieved 2 April 2016.

War Diary. Captain U-Boats, Norway. Captain Peters. 18 January–30 June 1943. Translated from German. U.S. Naval War College, Henry E. Eccles Library. https://archive.org/details/wardiaryofcapt194343germ. Retrieved 31 March 2016.

Unpublished memoirs

Hall, Norley. "The History of Norley Hall." Unpublished manuscript, 1983. Saving the Legacy: An Oral History of Utah's World War II Veterans, Box 10, Folder 6. Manuscripts Library, University of Utah.

Kolankiewicz, Leon. "The Flag Will Be Our Blanket." Penn State University Special Collections, HCLA 7469.

Suhorukov, Andrey. "Conversations with Nikolay Gerasimovitch Golodnikov, Major-General (Ret)." Pilot of the 2nd Guards Fighter Regiment (GIAP) of the Northern Fleet Aviation (VVS SF) from March 1942 until the end of the war. Undated. Translated by James F. Gebhardt. http://lend-lease.airforce.ru/english/articles/golodnikov/index.htm. Retrieved 31 March 2016.

Personal Communications

Dorris, Joe. Telephone interview with the author, 25 January 2011.

Foster, James "Shorty." Notes shared with the author by Foster's grandson Patrick Tobias in 2011.

Griffis, Roy. Telephone interview with the author, 29 January 2011.

Harcus, James. Diary kept aboard the SS *Ocean Faith*. Memorials of the Royal British Legion Scotland, Kirkwall Branch Orkney Islands. http://www.rbls-kirkwall.org.uk/memorials/OceanFaithlog.pdf. Retrieved 30 March 2016.

Harris, Howard E. Letter to Charles A. Jarvis. [June 24, 2003]. http://www.reocities.com/thetropics/1965/harris.htm. Retrieved 2 April 2016.

Holst, Thomas. Telephone conversation with the author, 14 March 2010.

Kolankiewicz, Leon. Email exchange with Nancy Scinto Rutkowski, 15 July 2011.

Scinto, Lenny. Interview recorded by his daughter, Gayle Scinto Merritt, 1996. Author's collection.

Stone, Lt. Richard M. Personal log, 5 August–11 October 1944. Courtesy of Marshall Stone, Savannah, Ga.

Wilks, Sam. Email message to Michele Ramirez Smith, 31 January 2005.

Online databases

579th Forward Engineer Support Team-Main (FEST-M). Lineage and Honors. http://www.mvd.usace.army.mil/About/Offices/579th-Forward-Engineer-Support-Team-Main-FEST-M/579th-Engineer-Detachment-FEST-M-History/. Retrieved 2 April 2016.

American Merchant Marine at War. Merchant Seamen's War Service Act (1945 and 1947). http://www.usmm.org/seamanrights.html. Retrieved 15 April 2016.

Arnold Hague Convoy Database, www.convoyweb.org.uk/. Retrieved 30 March 2016).

Destroyer History Foundation, USS *Wilson* (DD 408), www.destroyerhistory.org/goldplater/index.asp?r=40800&pid=40810. Retrieved 15 August 2016.

Klackers, Axel, and Christian Grams, Luftwaffe-zur-See.de, Flugzeugverluste und -unfälle von deutschen Flugbooten und Wasserflugzeugen. http://www.luftwaffe-zur-see.de/Seeluft/Verlustlisten/Jahr1943.htm. Retrieved 31 March 2016.

Luftwaffe Units, Jagdgeschwader 5 "Eismeer." https://www.asisbiz.com/Luftwaffe/jg5.html Retrieved 31 March 2016.

Luftwaffe Units, Sturzkampfgeschwader 5. https://www.asisbiz.com/Luftwaffe/st5.html. Retrieved 31 March 2016.

Philippine Diary Project. "The Great Escape of the S.S. *Mactan*: December 31, 1941." https://philippinediaryproject.wordpress.com/2012/12/31/the-great-escape-of-the-s-s-mactan/. Retrieved 31 March 2016.

Polish navy (Polska Marynarka Wojenna) in Scotland website. http://www.ostrycharz.free-online.co.uk/polish_navy.html. Retrieved 31 March 2016.

Polish Scottish Heritage: The Clydebank Blitz and the Polish Navy. http://polishscottishheritage.co.uk/?heritage_item=the-clydebank-blitz-and-the-polish-navy. Retrieved 31 March 2016.

uboat.net. http://uboat.net/allies/merchants/2759.html. Retrieved 31 March 2016.

uboat.net. The Men of the U-boats. List of All Commanders. http://uboat.net/men/commanders/index.html. Retrieved 31 March 2016.

U.S. Merchant Marine Academy Cadets and Graduates lost during World War II (1941 and 1942). http://www.usmm.org/cadetbio1942.html. Retrieved 1 April 2016.

U.S. Merchant Marine Cadets Killed during World War II. http://www.usmm.org/cckilled.html. Retrieved 20 December 2016.?

The U.S. Navy Armed Guard. http://www.armed-guard.com/about-ag.html. Retrieved December 21, 2016.

World War II Unit Histories and Officers. Royal Navy (RN) Officers, 1939–1945. GILB to GOOL. http://www.unithistories.com/units_index/default.asp?file=../officers/personsx.html. Retrieved 31 March 2016.

Published Secondary Sources

Blair, Clay. *Hitler's U-Boat War*. New York: Random House, 1996.

Bunker, John Gorley. *Liberty Ships: The Ugly Ducklings of World War II*. Annapolis: Naval Institute Press, 1972.

Burn, Alan. *The Fighting Commodores: The Convoy Commanders in the Second World War*. Annapolis: Naval Institute Press, 1999.

Campbell, Ian, and Donald G. F. W. Macintyre. *The Kola Run: A Record of Arctic Convoys, 1941–1945*. London: Muller, 1958.

Casey, Hugh J. *Engineers of the South West Pacific, 1941–1945*. Vol. 3, *Engineer Intelligence*. Washington, D.C.: Government Printing Office, 1950.

Claasen, Adam R. A. *Hitler's Northern War: The Luftwaffe's Ill-Fated Campaign, 1940–1945*. Lawrence: University Press of Kansas, 2001.

Conant, Jennet. *Tuxedo Park: A Wall Street Tycoon and the Secret Palace of Science that Changed the Course of World War II*. New York: Simon & Schuster, 2002.

Cressman, Robert J. *The Official Chronology of the U.S. Navy in World War II*. Annapolis: Naval Institute Press, 1999. https://www.ibiblio.org/hyperwar/USN/USN-Chron/USN-Chron-1944.html. Retrieved 31 March 2016.

Dabrowski, Hans-Peter. *Heinkel He 115: Torpedo/Reconnaissance/Mine Layer, Seaplane of the Luftwaffe.* Atglen: Schiffer, 1994.

Dwyer, John B. *Seaborne Deception: The History of U.S. Navy Beach Jumpers.* New York: Praeger, 1992.

Felknor, Bruce. *The Merchant Marine at War, 1775–1945.* Annapolis: Naval Institute Press, 1998.

Ferguson, S. W., and William K. Pascalis. *Protect and Avenge: The 49th Fighter Group in World War II.* Atglen: Schiffer, 1996.

Gaines, William C. "Historical Sketches Coast Artillery Regiments, 1917–1950. National Guard Army Regiments." http://cdsg.org/wp-content/uploads/pdfs/FORTS/CACunits/CAregNG.pdf. Retrieved 12 December 2016.

Gilbert, Sir William Schwenck. "The Yarn of the *Nancy Bell*." *Fun* 2 (3 March 1866): 238. http://www.victorianweb.org/mt/gilbert/yarn.html. Retrieved 12 December 2016.

Gordon, Bill. "47 Ships Sunk by Kamikaze Aircraft." Kamikaze Images website. http://wgordon.web.wesleyan.edu/kamikaze/background/ships-sunk/. Retrieved 9 December 2016.

Goss, Chris, with Bernd Rauchbach. *Luftwaffe Seaplanes, 1939–1945: An Illustrated History.* Annapolis: Naval Institute Press, 2002.

Irving, David. *The Destruction of Convoy PQ-17.* New York: Simon and Schuster, 1968. http://www.fpp.co.uk/books/PQ17/1968edition.pdf. Retrieved 31 March 2016.

Kemp, Paul. *Convoy! Drama in Arctic Waters.* New York: Sterling, 1993.

Millett, John D. *The Organization and Role of the Army Service Forces.* 1954. Reprint Washington, D.C.: Center of Military History, U.S. Army, 1987.

Mindell, David A. "Automation's Finest Hour: Radar and System Integration in World War II." In *Systems, Experts, and Computers: The Systems Approach in Management and Engineering, World War II and After*, edited by Agatha C. Hughes and Thomas Parke Hughes. Cambridge: MIT Press, 2000. https://mitpress.mit.edu/sites/default/files/titles/content/9780262082853_sch_0001.pdf. Retrieved 2 April 2016.

Moore, Arthur R. *"A Careless Word... a Needless Sinking": A History of the Staggering Losses Suffered by the U.S. Merchant Marine, Both in Ships and Personnel during World War II.* Kings Point, N.Y.: American Merchant Marine Museum, 1983.

Morison, Samuel Eliot. *History of United States Naval Operations in World War II.* Vol. 1, *The Battle of the Atlantic, 1939–1943.* Boston: Little, Brown, 1947.

———. *History of United States Naval Operations in World War II.* Vol. 10, *The Atlantic Battle Won.* Boston: Little, Brown, 1956.

———. *History of United States Naval Operations in World War II.* Vol. 13, *The Liberation of the Philippines: Luzon, Mindoro, the Viscayas, 1944–1945.* Boston: Little, Brown, 1959.

New York Times. Raymond Holubowicz obituary. 11 January 2013. http://www.legacy.com/obituaries/nytimes/obituary.aspx?pid=162269235. Retrieved 1 April 2016.

Palov, Anton. *From Airacobra to MiG-29: The History of the 19th Guards Fighter Aviation Regiment*. 2010. http://www.16va.be/19_gviap_eng_part1.html. Retrieved 31 March 2016.

Rielly. Robin L. *Kamikaze Attacks of World War II: A Complete History of Japanese Suicide Strikes on American Ships, by Aircraft and Other Means*. Jefferson, N.C.: McFarland, 2012.

Rohwer, Jürgen, and Gerhard Hümmelchen. *Chronology of the War at Sea, 1939–1945: The Naval History of World War Two*. Annapolis: Naval Institute Press, 1992.

Romanenko, Valeriy. *Airacobras Enter Combat*. Translated by James F. Gebhardt. Kiev: Aerohobby, 1993. http://lend-lease.airforce.ru/english/articles/romanenko/p-39/. Retrieved 12 December 2016.

Ryan, George J., and Thomas F. McCaffery. *Braving the Wartime Seas: A Tribute to the Cadets and Graduates of the U.S. Merchant Marine Academy and Cadet Corps Who Died during World War II*. The American Maritime History Project. Bloomington: Xlibris, 2014.

Savannah Morning News. Richard M. Stone obituary. 5 September 2005. http://www.legacy.com/obituaries/savannah/obituary.aspx?n=richard-m-stone&pid=15016477. Retrieved 31 March 2016.

Sawyer, L. A., and W. H. Mitchell. *The Liberty Ships: The History of the "Emergency" Type Cargo Ships Constructed in the United States during World War II*. Cambridge, Md.: Cornell Maritime Press, 1985.

Smith, Adam D., Susan I. Enscore, and Sunny E. Adams. *Character Defining Features of Contributing Buildings and Structures in the United States Merchant Marine Academy Historic District*. Champaign: Construction Engineering Research Laboratory, U.S. Army Engineer Research and Development Center, 2014.

Steinberg, Rafael. *Return to the Philippines*. Alexandria, Va.: Time-Life Books, 1979.

Suhren, Teddy, and Fritz Brustat-Naval. *Ace of Aces: Memoirs of a U-Boat Rebel*. Translated by Frank James 2011. Barnsley, South Yorkshire: Pen & Sword, 2011.

U.S. Office of Naval Operations. *History of the Naval Armed Guard Afloat, World War II. U.S. Naval Administration in World War II*, vol. 173. N.p.: n.d. http://www.ibiblio.org/hyperwar/USN/Admin-Hist/173-ArmedGuards/index.html. Accessed 12 December 2016.

U.S. Strategic Bombing Survey. *Interrogations of Japanese Officials*. 2 vols. Washington, D.C.: Government Printing Office, 1946.

Woodman, Richard. *Arctic Convoys, 1941–1945*. London: John Murray, 1994.

Zetterling, Niklas, and Michael Tamelander. *Bismarck: The Final Days of Germany's Greatest Battleship*. Philadelphia: Casemate, 2009.

About the Author

HERMAN E. MELTON

Herman Melton was born in Collingsworth County, Texas, the son of Willie and Myrtle Killingsworth Melton. His parents were pioneers who broke the virgin soil and built a prairie-style home on the rented farm where he was born in 1920. He graduated from Quail Consolidated High School in 1939 and studied briefly at Texas Tech University. In 1941 he enrolled at Garden City Community College in southwest Kansas.

The poverty of his youth shaped his approach to life. His father died when he was ten years old, leaving behind a widow with four children in the face of one of the most severe droughts of modern times. The drought led to massive dust storms that made the region infamous as the Dust Bowl, leading to the near collapse of the United States farm economy, a major cause of the Great Depression.

Herman Melton, July 1943.
Author's collection

In 1942, after the United States entered World War II, Herman received an appointment as cadet-midshipman to the U.S. Merchant Marine Academy at Kings Point, New York. Upon his graduation in 1944, he was commissioned ensign, U.S. Navy Reserve, and ensign, U.S. Maritime Service, and chose to accept the merchant marine's commission. On the day after his graduation, Herman married Helen Louise Dunn, his college sweetheart from Garden City, in a military wedding at the Academy chapel.

During his time as a midshipman aboard the Liberty ship *Cornelius Harnett*, Herman saw enemy action from German U-boats and torpedo bombers on the Murmansk Run convoys of 1943. Later in the war, after surviving the sinking of his Liberty ship *Antoine Saugrain* in the Philippine operation in 1944, he helped to salvage two damaged Libertys before sailing in the *William Sharon* back to San Francisco. In a 1992 ceremony at the Russian embassy in Washington, D.C., he received a memorial medal from the Russian government for his service on the Murmansk Run.

After the war, he joined the natural gas industry and was employed for thirty-six years and across six states by Transcontinental Natural Gas Pipeline Corporation. In his late forties he began work on a graduate degree in his spare time, and he received a master's in education from the University of Virginia in 1976. After retiring from Transcontinental, he taught natural gas technology at the Algerian Petroleum Institute in Arzew, Algeria.

In later life, Herman researched extensively the history of Southside Virginia, an area south of the James River and east of the Blue Ridge Mountains, and published five books about the region. He was interested primarily in industrial and transportation history, as well as criminal justice. Two other books, including *Liberty's War*, were in manuscript at the time of his death in 2013.

The Naval Institute Press is the book-publishing arm of the U.S. Naval Institute, a private, nonprofit, membership society for sea service professionals and others who share an interest in naval and maritime affairs. Established in 1873 at the U.S. Naval Academy in Annapolis, Maryland, where its offices remain today, the Naval Institute has members worldwide.

Members of the Naval Institute support the education programs of the society and receive the influential monthly magazine *Proceedings* or the colorful bimonthly magazine *Naval History* and discounts on fine nautical prints and on ship and aircraft photos. They also have access to the transcripts of the Institute's Oral History Program and get discounted admission to any of the Institute-sponsored seminars offered around the country.

The Naval Institute's book-publishing program, begun in 1898 with basic guides to naval practices, has broadened its scope to include books of more general interest. Now the Naval Institute Press publishes about seventy titles each year, ranging from how-to books on boating and navigation to battle histories, biographies, ship and aircraft guides, and novels. Institute members receive significant discounts on the Press' more than eight hundred books in print.

Full-time students are eligible for special half-price membership rates. Life memberships are also available.

For a free catalog describing Naval Institute Press books currently available, and for further information about joining the U.S. Naval Institute, please write to:

Member Services
U.S. Naval Institute
291 Wood Road
Annapolis, MD 21402-5034
Telephone: (800) 233-8764
Fax: (410) 571-1703
Web address: www.usni.org